D1005635

A CUP OF COMFORT®

Devotional for Women

Daily Inspiration for
Christian Women

Edited by James Stuart Bell
& Carol McLean Wilde

Avon, Massachusetts

Published by
Adams Media, an F+W Publications Company
57 Littlefield Street, Avon, MA 02322. U.S.A.
www.adamsmedia.com

ISBN 10: 1-59869-691-2
ISBN 13: 978-1-59869-691-2
Printed in the United States of America.
J I H G F E D C B A

Library of Congress Cataloging-in-Publication Data
A cup of comfort devotional for women / edited by
James Stuart Bell and Carol McLean Wilde.
        p.   cm.
1. Women--Prayer-books and devotions--English. 2. Devotional calendars.
I. Bell, James S. II. Wilde, Carol.

BV4844.C87 2005
242'.643--dc22
2005011018

*This book is available at quantity discounts for bulk purchases.
For information, please call 1-800-289-0963.*

CONTENTS

This book is dedicated in loving memory to my mother, Edna Graham McLean, and in honor of Joann Allen Wilde Browning, Linda McLean White, Nancy McLean Beauchamp, Barbara Wilde Anderson, Sharron Wilde Scherf, Debbie Sloan Wilde, and Betty Browning Earley.

—CMW

To Judson and Barbara Aulie, great friends of faith and courage who model what it means to walk with Christ in the valleys as well as the mountaintops.

—JSB

ACKNOWLEDGMENTS

Recognition needs to go to all of these women of faith who "testified" to the truth of God actively working in their lives. Kate Epstein, associate editor, should be commended for once again loaning us her wisdom and experience, steering us through all the details of the story acquisition and acceptance process. Finally, to publisher Gary Krebs, who himself has "stepped out in faith" in the business arena by allowing us to continue to contribute Christian titles to the Adams Media line.

INTRODUCTION

Dear Friend,

Flip through this *Cup of Comfort* devotional and you'll see the names of hundreds of women. I'd like to believe that each signature represents someone you'd want as a trustworthy new friend. For each one offers you something truly valuable and beneficial each day as she shares her story. In fact, we all share a significant bond. You're holding a book of devotions *for* women, written *by* women. And each contributor has received—and wants to share with you—a cup of God's extraordinary comfort. As you pause to read these simple affirmations of God's abundant love and provision, we hope that you will open your heart in prayer to receive what God wants to give you that day.

One wonderful benefit of using this book is that you can begin right where you are—at any time of the year—and join this new circle of friends. At the beginning of each day's story, you'll find a portion of Scripture that the writer found helpful as she applied it to her experience. We've also added a brief "word of wisdom" at the end of each piece for your encouragement each day.

You'll also find a longer story at the opening of each monthly section—twelve very personal stories from women who found God's comfort at a significant moment in their lives. Much like women's stories included in the Bible, each of these allows you to appropriate its timeless message, no matter what your stage of life.

I'm especially thankful that so many of you were willing to share your story with other women. So often we forget just how much we need one another—to bear one another's burdens, share each other's joys, and laugh together at our common frustrations. We hope you find refreshing nourishment each time you drink from this special *Cup*.

Some of us may lead a life very different from yours. Perhaps you struggle with a challenge far greater than the ones you'll read about here. But we sincerely hope that you find genuine spiritual encouragement in these encounters with the living God, and sense, dear sister, that you are not alone.

May the peace of the Lord be with you, always.

—Carol McLean Wilde

JANUARY

TIME IS NOT THE ENEMY

"I am the Alpha and the Omega—the beginning and the end," says the Lord God. "I am the one who is, who always was, and who is still to come, the Almighty One."

REVELATION 1:8

$\mathcal{E}$ VERY DAY AT WORK I PLAYED *BEAT THE CLOCK*. While I might beat my ticking torturer occasionally, I often lost my perspective. You see, my job is filled with deadlines. Outgoing mail has to be in the basket by 11 A.M. Incoming requests have to be processed in the morning, and any returns have to go out by 4:30 P.M. Incoming materials have to be processed immediately, with customers contacted within the hour.

I felt deadlined to death, and it showed. Woe to anything or anyone who got in my way! Snapping at my coworkers earned me low marks on my performance review, which came just after New Year's Day.

When my supervisor told me to shape up during the year ahead, I studied time-management self-help books. Most of them seemed aimed at a company's higher echelon of employees, with tips on how to delegate and deal with subordinates. What if you *are* the subordinate? Other suggestions, such as taking a bubble bath, didn't seem practical in the middle of a hectic day at the office!

Then something my pastor said helped me call a time-out. As I rushed into a Sunday study of Revelation, he remarked, "God is in charge of all time."

I felt as if someone had thrown a bucket of cold water on me. God is in charge, not the clock. "We say that every week in our offertory prayer," my pastor went on. "We offer with joy and thanksgiving what you have first given us—our selves, our time, and our possessions, signs of your gracious love." Our *time* is a sign of God's love. My heart pounded. Time is a *gift* from God, not an enemy at all. How often had I rattled off those words without absorbing their meaning? Week after week, God told me to be at peace with the clock, and I hadn't listened.

Then my pastor quoted Revelation 1:8. He continued, "God is the beginning and the end." At home, I searched the Bible and discovered other verses about time. Psalm 90:12 says that we should use our short lives wisely. Psalm 65:8 adds daily joy to the mix. In Luke 12:25, Jesus says that being stressed-out is a waste of time: "Can all your worries add a single moment to your life?" Ecclesiastes 3 reinforces the big picture: "There is a time for everything" (vs. 1a).

To help me remember, I posted Bible verses on my computer. I recited them under my breath when I felt the hands of the clock spinning out of control. The Serenity Prayer found a place next to the verses: "God, grant me the serenity to accept the things I cannot change, courage to change the things I can, and the wisdom to know the difference" (Reinhold Neibuhr).

Julian of Norwich's quote, "All shall be well, and all shall be well, and all manner of things shall be well" gave me calm confidence. When the immediacy of the messages wore off, I removed the words and replaced them with pictures of serene outdoor scenes. "Visiting" them for

3

a moment during the day helps me regain my perspective and remember the greater world.

Visualizing Jesus in my workplace, sitting next to me at my computer, reminds me of God's great presence and power. Comprehending time as a gift changed my thinking and behavior almost overnight. If God is in charge of time, then I can accept it as a gift and use it as God pleases.

Suddenly, I was no longer a *Beat the Clock* contestant. My work deadlines still existed, but with my God-given outlook, I didn't get frazzled so easily. Though customer service is a major part of my job, it's usually indirect. I often viewed drop-in customers as interruptions and fumed inside when they stayed too long or told me more than necessary. But if God is in charge of time, and God loves people, I needed to be better at loving people, too.

Then a funny thing happened. When I took time for people, my job became more interesting. I learned things I'd never know otherwise. One customer collects pop-up books and another is the founder of a local rose society. One surveys avalanche probability for ski resorts. I started appreciating the diversity of human interests. And, wonder of wonders, my work still got done. Deadlines were met. What a gift, indeed, is time.

—JANE HEITMAN

New Year, Clean Slate

"Purify me from my sins, and I will be clean;
wash me, and I will be whiter than snow."
PSALM 51:7

For many people, Christmas is a favorite time of the year. However, I find it refreshing to put away the decorations; remove the drooping, brittle tree; and vacuum up the last needles, icicles, and bits of paper. It's nice to have the house uncluttered again.

Then comes January, my favorite time, a time of new beginnings. No matter what happened the year before, here is a chance to start fresh. Anticipation and hope mingle to propel me forward into the unknown. Just as snow blankets the ground and covers its uneven contours, so the new year stretches before me like a nice, white blank piece of paper. I can choose, in part, the story to be written on it.

God is the God of forgiveness and second chances. By admitting our areas of failure, and committing to turn from past wrongs, we are allowed a fresh start.

Each new day is another chance to start again.

—RUTHANNE N. ARRINGTON

Stay above the Fray

"Don't get involved in foolish, ignorant arguments that only start fights. The Lord's servants must not quarrel but must be kind to everyone. They must be able to teach effectively and be patient with difficult people."

2 TIMOTHY 2:23–24

I once worked in an office where it seemed hardly a day went by without the ladies fighting. The main complaint seemed to be, "Hey, that's not my job, not my problem!" It was a spirit of constant noncooperation that led to constant bickering, especially when negative sparks flew my way. I automatically moved into defense mode, ready to point out my good reason for doing this or that.

What a waste of energy! It took quite a while for me to learn to simply listen, and then decide if I needed to respond to whatever inspired the latest cut-down session.

Of course, adding fuel to the fire only results in burnout—the very thing that Paul wanted Timothy to avoid. Paul gives us his very best advice here. But you know, I think Paul learned his nuggets of wisdom by experience too.

I'll look for ways to help today—whether it's my job or not.

—CMW

God Be Praised!

"Are you called to help others? Do it with all the strength and energy that God supplies. Then God will be given glory in everything through Jesus Christ."

1 PETER 4:11

This was not a simple procedure. Our patient was a four-year-old girl with a cyst in her neck that had been there since birth. The surgery involved the girl's jugular vein, and her carotid arteries were wrapped around and through it.

She was scared.

We were wondering.

Dr. Jim needed a miracle.

We gave the little girl a baby doll just before putting her under, and as Dr. Jim started, many were praying. The surgery lasted two hours. When it was over, and the doctors realized it was successful, Dr. Jim said, "It was done with God's hands and with God's strength."

The words come back to me often, prompting me to self-examination: Where am I serving today? By whose strength will the work be done?

He will be your strength for every helping task.

—FRANCINE DUCKWORTH

He's the Guard

"LORD, you alone are my inheritance,
my cup of blessing. You guard all that is mine."
PSALM 16:5

My adult son met me in the kitchen and hoisted himself onto the counter.

Turning to him, I asked, "What about your wife? And the boys?"

"She's not going with me, Mom. It's her decision." He gripped the countertop, looked down at the floor, and continued, "God help me, the boys have to understand how I feel."

"All right," I said. But it wasn't. The following two weeks were difficult, as if the low limbs of our family tree had been cut off with no way to climb up. My talks with God had no spiritual put-ons: "This is not supposed to happen in *our* family!"

I had to reach a point of realization: I could not guard my son's family from life's inevitable hurts. I had to give them over to the Guardian of all that is mine—until I inherit all that is His.

In our heavenly home, all will be well, all will be peace.

—ANN L. COKER

More Life, Less Worry

"Who of you by worrying can add
a single hour to his life?"
LUKE 12:25

"What if she gets hurt?"

"What if they have a wreck on the way?"

"What if some of the girls ignore her?"

"What if . . ." I had a whole list of "what if" worries to give my husband when our daughter left for her first youth-group retreat.

You see, I'm a worrier. But admit it—it's easy to worry when a child is out of sight, right? I've always worried when others are in charge of her, ever since she fell and cut her lip right before my husband and I went out for our first "date" since adopting her. I called home to check with the babysitter—twice—while we sat at a "relaxing" meal. . . . And the babysitter was my mom!

Okay, I'm a worrier. But I've improved. Really. I've noticed that when I trust God a little bit more, I worry a little bit less. That's better, isn't it? And life is so much sweeter.

Worry unplugs us from God's power source.

—KATHRYN LAY

Mom's Secondhand Wisdom

"The wisdom we speak of is the secret wisdom of God,
which was hidden in former times, though he made
it for our benefit before the world began."
1 CORINTHIANS 2:7

I heard about a little girl who sees and hears birds with deep inner delight. Then her mother comes to her with explanations: "See, this is a robin, and that one over there is a chickadee." Suddenly the girl becomes concerned about keeping it all straight in her mind. She wants to "get it right" and see things the way Mom sees them.

But the apostle Paul tells us the Gospel contains much mystery, or "secret wisdom," and that this is unfolding for us believers. We can't understand it by mere teaching or rote memory. We need to let God's Spirit speak it into our hearts, day by day.

This is how we grow in Him—through our Bible reading, fellowship, and prayer. And by paying attention to our experiences, happy and sad, in order to discern God's wisdom coming through to us.

May you see directly today, not just secondhand!

—CMW

Quiet Waters, Peaceful Heart

"He lets me rest in green meadows;
he leads me beside peaceful streams."
PSALM 23:2

When I was a little girl, my family spent a week each summer in the mountains of New Hampshire. After dinner one evening, my dad set me on his shoulders, took a beach chair in one hand and a small Bible in the other, and went to the river in time for sunset. The setting sun painted the horizon a soft orange and pink. The waters quietly lapped the shoreline.

"The Lord, your Shepherd, wants you to trust Him so your heart can be quiet, just like these waters are quiet and still," he tenderly said to me. I can tell you now that there have been many times when the circumstances of my life seemed more like tempests! Yet each time I look to my Good Shepherd, trust Him and His leading, my heart does feel quieted. Despite swelling seas—and even worsening weather—there is a stillness in my heart that's unshakable. Have you been there beside peaceful streams?

Quiet waters tell me exactly what God desires for my heart.

—RACHEL M. TAMILIO

Certified Mercy

"God is so rich in mercy, and he loved us so very much, that even while we were dead because of our sins, he gave us life when he raised Christ from the dead. (It is only by God's special favor that you have been saved!)"

EPHESIANS 2:4–5

Last January, right after paying off all the Christmas bills, an official-looking certified letter arrived at my home. Shaking in fear that the letter brought bad news, I tore open the envelope.

As a volunteer member of a city committee, I had been given thirty days to submit a certain form to the state's Ethics Committee. The letter stated that I had missed a deadline for filing this form, and now I could expect to be fined up to $1,500!

I remembered dropping that form in the mailbox last July. Surely they would not fine me because someone lost it. I scanned the legal instructions, desperate to avoid paying the fine.

My heart skipped a beat as I found grounds for an appeal. Yes, the state would not apply the fine if I could produce a copy of the form and resend it. I would receive mercy . . . wonderful, checking account–saving mercy. But I had to respond in a certain way in order for the state to apply it to my account.

I could ignore the letter. I could have blamed others for losing my mail. Or I could point to the reason why I could legally receive mercy. Mercy arrived as soon as I followed instructions.

God's mercy is rich—and everlasting. —CMW

Cushioned Sins

"When you were prosperous, I warned you, but you replied, 'Don't bother me.' Since childhood you have been that way—you simply will not listen!"
JEREMIAH 22:21

I spent an hour curling my daughter's hair, helping her slip into a frilly costume and tap shoes, and applying her makeup. Then, like dozens of other parents, I arrived early at the auditorium and left her backstage among a glittery, sequined throng.

As I sank into a cushioned seat and waited for the dance recital to begin, an excited buzz of conversation washed over me. Parents talked about the program, the music, and the flowers they'd brought for their daughters.

Then a fire alarm blared, and a roomful of suddenly uncomfortable adults stared at each other. In each set of eyes, I saw, *I don't smell smoke. And after all the morning hassle, I'm NOT giving up my seat.* And no one moved until ushers forced us to evacuate.

Back at home I have time to consider: Will I give up my well-seated sins and follow Christ tomorrow?

Listen—and let God usher you out of that next temptation.

—LORI Z. SCOTT

On Loan from the Lord

"O LORD our God, even these materials that
we have gathered to build a Temple to honor your
holy name come from you! It all belongs to you!"
1 CHRONICLES 29:16

To see women giving is to see the work of God within their
hearts. In the Scripture above, King David had already offered
his own treasure to build the house of God—his gold, silver,
and precious stones. Then he asked others to contribute, too.

And why shouldn't God's people give? As David said, "it
all belongs to God," and back to Him it will go someday. A life-
changing movement takes place within us when we determine
to give, and it's the spirit of the cheerful giver that brings so
much glory to God. That spirit can spur us to action when we
see any good work that needs doing. Or when we see someone
who needs what only we can supply.

Do you know of any person or need like that in your world
today? How will you respond?

*All things come from God; be generous in
returning them to Him and His people.*

—CMW

"I Not Ready Yet!"

"I am holding you by your right hand—I,
the LORD your God. And I say to you,
'Do not be afraid. I am here to help you.'"
ISAIAH 41:13

Dorothy's little grandson Jake received a bike with training wheels for his birthday present. The gift sparked his interest, but he postponed getting on it until another day. "I try Monday, Mom-Mom," he promised with a grin. When Monday rolled around, he said, "I try *another* Monday. I not ready yet."

I laughed when Dorothy told me the story, but I certainly could relate to his "not ready yet" mind-set. Fear is the biggest hurdle in my reluctance or refusal to tackle "new bike" moments, especially when I'm not sure how they will turn out. Issues that pull me out of my comfort zone and require vulnerability—or a huge step of faith—tend to make me hold back and not do anything at all.

But then I remember how you learn to ride a bike—Daddy holds you till your balance is just perfect.

We have to get on the bike before we can ride.

—MABELLE REAMER

JANUARY 12

Soul Nutrition

"I prayed to the LORD, and he answered me,
freeing me from all my fears."
PSALM 34:4

"Here I am Lord, among all these weeds." This is a good time
to talk to the Lord, in the quiet cool of the morning, sitting
quietly in my garden.

"Lord, you see the anxious and demanding times in my life
right now," I prayed. In all my busyness, my family still needs
me, and so does my garden. It seems the older I get, the slower
I work, and the less I produce.

I feel frenzied working in my garden this morning. I fear
there won't be enough time to complete the weeding, pruning,
and cultivating of a whole garden. Of a whole life.

"Lord, I can see such majesty of your power and assurance
of your love in this place—your garden."

My mind settles into a quiet calmness. Just as I feed my
garden, He will replenish my soul.

Today I will lean toward the sun and bask in His warmth.

—DOROTHY MINEA

Can You Look Past the Looks?

"There was nothing beautiful or majestic about his appearance, nothing to attract us to him."

ISAIAH 53:2

The girl sat alone in church, her long hair wet, her skirt rather skimpy. When our pastor asked us to greet one another, I smiled and shook her hand. But I wondered why she hadn't dried her hair before coming to the service. Her name was Jessica, and I made a point to talk with her each Sunday. Yet I found myself questioning her appearance—especially that wet hair.

One Sunday we were invited to pray with someone sitting near us. Jessica and I joined hands, and after prayer she said, "You've been so friendly to me. In fact, your friendliness is one reason I come to church. You see, my parents don't want me here."

It troubles me to think what would have happened to Jessica if I'd acted on my critical perception of her looks. What if I hadn't accepted her just as she was? And if I'd been alive to see Jesus in person, would I have let His ordinary face obscure His extraordinary message?

Homeliness, too, is only skin deep.

—JEWELL JOHNSON

Condemnation from Whom?

"So now there is no condemnation for
those who belong to Christ Jesus."
ROMANS 8:1

The chants started when she got on the school bus, then followed her into the school and onto the playground. "Fatty, fatty, two-by-four . . ."

I hated that teasing of my best childhood friend. How I wanted to protect her from all harm; I just didn't have the ability.

As I grew older, life tumbled in with all its injustice and injury, now directed at me. I began to insulate myself from the hurts of life, but the pain stayed, even when I shut the door of my heart.

I finally began paying attention to what I was telling myself: "Why didn't you . . . You should have . . . If only you had . . ."

I discovered I was the one causing myself pain. As a child I couldn't stop comments that hurt my friend. But as an adult, I have more power: I can refuse to listen to the voice of self-condemnation.

I can love my neighbor—and I can love myself—with the love Christ gives me.

—JEAN DAVIS

Happiness

"It is a good thing to receive wealth from God and the good health to enjoy it. To enjoy your work and accept your lot in life—that is indeed a gift from God."
ECCLESIASTES 5:19

Suddenly, things are so good! I got the job I wanted, I live in a lovely home, my kids are doing well, and hubby seems happy for the time being.

But do I know how to celebrate? It's almost a crisis situation! It seems I've grown accustomed to expecting the worst, so now, before the next wave of difficulty rolls through the living room of my life, can I just enjoy the moment?

Yes, now that things are so good, I will offer up my gratitude the best I know how. And I will welcome the coming days. For God is already on the path ahead, beckoning me into the destiny He's lovingly planned. I know I won't always be bubbling over with happiness. But He promises me joy, each step of the way, if I choose to depend on Him . . . no matter what.

Show me how to enjoy this happiness!

—CMW

Soft Bread

"Cast thy bread upon the waters:
for thou shalt find it after many days."
ECCLESIASTES 11:1 (KJV)

She was three or four and wanted so much to feed the ducks at the park pond, but rain threatened, and her mother took her to the car. From my bench at lunch the next day, I noticed they were back again. This time, she brought a large bag of bread, but the spring wind carried her tiny handfuls swirling out of sight. The ducks swam after the bread, but the little girl couldn't watch them feed. She cried until her mother saw that the same wind carrying her bread away was now bringing some back from the other side of the small pond. Now she could watch the ducks eating.

We are like that little girl in our expectations.

Whenever we start a new project or attempt a good deed or even hire someone to paint our house trim, we want to see results right away. We have trouble even waiting for the primer to dry, don't we? But let's not become discouraged while doing good. We must keep throwing out the Bread of Life wherever others are hungry to feed. God wants us, like water, to reflect His love, and to feed at His feet daily.

Lord, like bread, keep me soft and pliable, yet strong enough to be nourishment for hungry souls.

—IMOGENE JOHNSON

What Do You Expect?

"You must be ready all the time, for the
Son of Man will come when least expected."
LUKE 12:40

The three men in my family—husband and two sons—sometimes joke about my "ability" to put something on the stove . . . and then forget about it. You see, I'm a multitasker. So I can quickly move from one thing to the next without skipping a beat. But if that "next thing" happens to absorb my interest, the previous thing might get left behind. (Hence, a few memorable burned leftovers.)

There's a kind of spiritual watchfulness that I'd like to take up to a greater extent. For us multitaskers, the challenge is to *focus* on what's truly important. That is why Jesus warned His disciples so solemnly about looking for His return at the end of days. They were to live with watchful expectancy. They couldn't just coast along through their lives with comfortable routines. Deep inside, the eyes of their hearts needed to be wide open.

*When daily distractions arrive, ask God
to help you see things as He does.*

—CMW

Big and Limitless

"He existed before everything else began,
and he holds all creation together."
COLOSSIANS 1:17

At a dark time in our family's life, I was introduced to *The Chronicles of Narnia*, by C. S. Lewis. These seven books have truly hooked me. Their spiritual truths play hide-and-seek with the reader but are great treasures to find. The *Chronicles* are all about four children who take excursions into the enchanted land of Narnia, where they meet Aslan, the golden lion, a symbol of Christ. In Book 2, Lucy makes her second visit to Narnia, where she meets Aslan again:

"Aslan, you're bigger."

"That is because you are older, little one," Aslan answers.

"Not because *you* are?" asks Lucy.

"I am not. But every year you grow, you will find me bigger."

What a wonderful insight! As we grow up in Christ, our God will be bigger to us. Not because we more fully comprehend His true "size"; rather, we more clearly recognize the borderless expanse of His infinite being.

We stand in awe of all God is.

—GWEN RICE CLARK

Working for God's Glory

"Work hard and cheerfully at whatever you do, as though
you were working for the Lord rather than for people."
COLOSSIANS 3:23

A hostess met us at the restaurant door. I recognized her immediately, even though it had been thirty years since I'd last seen her. She didn't recognize me, though, so I reintroduced myself.

She suddenly looked embarrassed. "I'm still trying to figure out what I want to be when I grow up," she laughed. Obviously, she wasn't happy with her occupation. It appeared that she felt bad about being a restaurant hostess in her middle forties.

I felt sad for her, not because of how she made a living, but because of how she viewed her position in life. I prayed for her often after that meeting—not so much that God would move her to another position, but that He'd help her see value in every form of honest work. For when we do our daily tasks to the best of our abilities, God is honored.

Work cheerfully today—it is a privilege to do so.

—NANCY B. GIBBS

Transformation

"Then he breathed on them and said to them,
'Receive the Holy Spirit.'"
JOHN 20:22

When I was a little girl, "magic coloring books" were all the rage. Each page had a picture outlined in black, but instead of coloring the pictures in the usual way, I'd dip a paintbrush in water and brush it lightly across the page. In a flash, a plain, uninteresting black-and-white page would be streaked with red, blue, green, and yellow. The transformation seemed like sheer magic, and this little girl was thrilled.

After Jesus was crucified, the disciples huddled together behind closed doors and barred windows, alone and afraid. Then Jesus appeared in their midst, offering the Holy Spirit to dwell within them.

Immediately their fears left them, and they went out to become bold witnesses for their risen Master. What a transformation! You and I may be plain, ordinary, fearful people. Yet, just a touch from Jesus can transform our lives beyond recognition.

Let the Spirit work unhindered within you this day.

—TANYA FERDINANDUSZ

It Begins with a Thought

"Don't let us yield to temptation, but
deliver us from the evil one."
MATTHEW 6:13

A pop song with the strange title "Oops, I Did It Again!" came out in the year 2000. I don't know if it's about temptation, but it seems to sum up my life experience with dubious enticements. I'm tempted to gossip, to overeat, to feel sorry for myself, to worry, to lash out at women who seem to be competing with me . . . you get the picture. And I'm fairly certain you have your own besetting sins to bemoan.

I pray to be good, Lord!

And often I fail. Yet, through long experience, I've come to see that there is no overcoming temptation by sheer force of will. That is why I need God's grace—His deliverance—every step of the way. And it helps me to recall, it's not only what I do that is important; it's what I'm thinking long before my mouth launches into action.

Pause to consider: How is your thought-life this day?

—CMW

Stepping into the Light

"Your word is a lamp for my feet
and a light for my path."
PSALM 119:105

I stop on the sidewalk and look up into the night. A thin sliver of moon shows through, but no other light. Walking my beagle in the early morning, I use a leash with a flashlight attached to the handle. It throws a splotch of light just in front of me. If my focus drifts, and I let the dog wander off on the scent of a squirrel, she pulls the light after her, and I can no longer see where I'm going. I really need that bit of light cast on the next few steps ahead of me!

Isn't life like that? God doesn't tell me what I will face next year or even tomorrow. I see only the next few steps before me. As long as I keep walking, though, He gives me light enough to continue.

Step within His light, and keep following.

—ELSI DODGE

A Purposeful Pattern

"Breaking the loaves into pieces, [Jesus] kept giving
the bread and fish to the disciples to give to the people.
They all ate as much as they wanted."
MARK 6:41–42

Quilting is popular again. Stores are dedicated to the quilter,
with classes burgeoning and quilting machines ready. It brings
back memories as I look at the multicolored quilts that all
started with just the first two scraps sewn together.

Jesus took five small loaves of bread and two fish. He
handed out the bits and pieces to His disciples, and they fed
5,000 men, besides women and children. The Lord can take a
small scrap and multiply it forever.

When we come to Him with the bits and pieces of our lives,
He arranges frayed edges into something pleasing, a purposeful
pattern we may not discern until we see Him face-to-face. I'm
so thankful He's the one doing the arranging.

A little bit in God's hand goes a long way.

—V. LOUISE CUNNINGHAM

Hunker with Him

> "For where two or three have gathered together
> in My name, I am there in their midst."
> MATTHEW 18:20

As the four hurricanes blew across our town in the fall of 2004, we heard lots of people saying, "We're just going to hunker down and ride it out."

"Hunker down" brings a distinct image to mind, doesn't it? And most everyone was planning to hunker with others—not alone. That's my point: Have you noticed how, in the midst of stormy times, human beings seek one another out and hunker down together? Their troubles tend to drive them into one another's arms, producing a strength that transcends the abilities of any single individual.

When trouble hits, we feel tossed by wind and wave. But the gracious miracle is that we are usually hurled right into someone else! We find comfort in the storm through fellowship with two or three other Christ-believing storm fighters.

And why not? Christ is right there with us.

As we hold hands in a storm,
we share together in Christ's presence.

—CMW

Don't Give Up . . . Endure

"Patient endurance is what you need now. . . ."
HEBREWS 10:36

"If nobody else is going to invent a dishwashing machine, I'll do it myself." Josephine Cochrane was a socialite and had servants to wash her fine china in 1886. The servants were clumsy, though, and broke too many plates and cups. Josephine tried washing dishes herself, but it was a tiresome job, and she knew there had to be a better way. She went out to a shed behind the house and started figuring out how to make a machine do the work.

She handled the transition from socialite to mechanic, but then faced a much harder task. Trying to sell her new machine, she constantly heard, "No." In a 1915 survey, women insisted they'd rather wash dishes by hand in the evening because it relaxed them. Josephine patiently endured for decades before housewives were ready to have dishwashers in their kitchens. Today, dishwashers are a standard fixture in most American homes.

Sticking to it makes it possible.

—LeAnn Campbell

Skin Exchange

"Bear one another's burdens, and thereby
fulfill the law of Christ."
GALATIANS 6:2

We were down on our knees in prayer with the past-due bills spread out in front of us. Hot tears rolled down my cheeks as I begged God to please help my good friend and neighbor. Her husband had died unexpectedly, leaving behind thousands of dollars of debt. She had no insurance, no job, and no way to pay the rent!

Yes, she needed money, but even more, she needed someone to pray for her, and to carry this impossible burden to the Lord. We prayed in faith, believing that God would provide somehow—perhaps through our family. I believe that is the beginning of compassion—to know exactly how your neighbor is experiencing the tough times.

But are you and I ready to help today? Think about the people who cross your path each day. See their faces and feel their hearts. What is it like to have her home life, his work, their friends, problems, and joys? Now . . . take time to reach out.

What burden seems too heavy for a friend today?

—CMW

Kind Eyes

"I am overwhelmed with joy in the LORD my God!
For he has dressed me with the clothing of salvation
and draped me in a robe of righteousness."
ISAIAH 61:10

Springtime on the farm was always muddy. When our young son, Kris, asked, "Can I play outside?" I told him, "Play on the grass and not in the mud." But splashing a big mud puddle with a plastic baseball bat was too much fun. I was striding toward him, ready to scold, when he looked up with a big grin on his face and said, "I just *love* this!"

I went to get the camera.

Later, a muddy, shivering little boy was at my door, asking to come in and wanting clean clothes. And I welcomed him in and cleaned him up.

Our loving Father does the same for us. We might like our "mud puddles" too, until we learn their self-destructive nature and (hopefully) outgrow them. During the whole process of growth, though, we never need doubt God's kind eyes upon us.

Better to bask in God's love than stay in the mud.

—RENEE BOLKEMA

Tying My Shoes

"Commit your work to the LORD,
and then your plans will succeed."
PROVERBS 16:3

Twenty-five years ago, when my daughter, Carrie, was a pre-schooler, she liked listening to recorded stories by Aunt Bertha. Carrie's favorite story involved a conversation between Aunt Bertha and a little girl. "Jesus doesn't answer my prayers," said the girl. "I asked him to tie my shoes, and He didn't do it."

"There are some things God expects us to do for ourselves," Aunt Bertha responded. However, here's the lesson Carrie learned: God won't tie my shoes, so I guess I'll have to find someone else to tie them!

I, like my daughter, often want God to do something for me that He expects me to do for myself. I pray for wisdom in decision making, but then so often refuse to make a decision. I'm convinced God wants me to take initiative more than I do. As my husband says, "You can't steer a parked car."

He will guide my footsteps, but shouldn't I tie my shoes?

—JANE M. AULT

Compassionate Handkerchiefs

"Then they sat on the ground with him for seven
days and nights. And no one said a word, for they
saw that his suffering was too great for words."

JOB 2:13

The incessant ringing of my work phone went nonstop on a day
when several agonizing problems swirled in my mind. Outside,
dark clouds draped the summer sky. Watching Pauline at her
monitor left me even gloomier. The calendar read "Tuesday"; it
still felt like Monday. Worse, *I* felt like Monday. I warned, "I'll
probably burst into tears before this day is over."

Later, a note on my computer offered, "If you need a good
cry, let me know, because I could have a good cry at the drop of
a dime." I sure appreciated that. And I recalled how Job's three
friends wept when they first saw him. Then they sat with him,
wordlessly, for seven days and seven nights.

Suffering comes to each of us. How else could we bear it
without the handkerchief of compassion?

Tears can blind us—or bind us—to God's presence.

—PHILLIS HARRIS-BROOKS

Mother-Heart

"If He causes grief, then He will have compassion according to His abundant lovingkindness. For He does not afflict willingly or grieve the sons of men."
LAMENTATIONS 3:32–33

My son Tim had just gotten his first bicycle, a little red two-wheeler with white tires. What fun! We took it out to the park, and he started learning how to ride, finally making it halfway around a quarter-mile track. Then . . . *crash!*

Off we went to the emergency room, with Tim's chin gashed wide open. At the hospital, my mother-heart ached for the little guy as nurses put him in a straightjacket to hold him still for stitches.

Later, I tried to explain something to Tim about the doctor: Sometimes God uses others to do His work. And sometimes it is painful to do that work . . . and even to receive its benefits.

Can I learn that lesson too? I know this: Today I do want to be ready to carry out God's will—even if it means coming into contact with another's pain.

Obeying God isn't always pleasant; it is always right.

—CMW

Worship!

"The heavens tell of the glory of God. The
skies display his marvelous craftsmanship."
PSALM 19:1

My family lives on a gentle ridge in a house that faces east. Every
night I watch the moon rise like a brilliant balloon that floats
lazily over our roof and comes to rest in the trees out back.

I haven't always noticed. For too many years, life's pressures clouded my panorama. There were no bright constella-
tions, shimmering planets, or trailing spectacles. I looked up
and saw only minivan fumes. Deadlines, gridlocks, and others'
agendas sullied my worldview.

I rediscovered the heavens and renewed my faith through
a household chore familiar to many: the midnight dash to the
grass to housebreak our new puppy. He looked up at the sky,
threw back his head, and howled with joy at the tent of twin-
klings draped over our yard. At that moment, the most common of tasks had become a moment of worship.

Lift up your eyes to appreciate a canopy of miracles.

—DIANE ROSIER MILES

FEBRUARY

VALENTINE'S DAY SURPRISE

"I am trusting you, O LORD, saying,
'You are my God.' My future is in your hands."

PSALM 31:14-15

*I*F YOU'RE ANYTHING LIKE ME, your memory isn't quite what it used to be. It seems as if now that I've hit the big Five-O, I'm lucky to remember my name most days.

But I'll never forget that Valentine's Day. It was February 14, 2001—a busy day of running from one errand to the next. I had taken the day off from work to visit my daughter's sixth-grade class. After I spent a few hours there, I scooted out to my next scheduled meeting in a neighboring town. After that, I drove back to my volunteer duties at church.

The end of that long, hectic day finally arrived, and I found myself happily at home, putting on my comfy nightgown so I could finally crash into my favorite recliner and relax. On the way to that eagerly anticipated spot, I stopped and noticed bright spots of blood dripping to the floor. I couldn't believe my eyes.

I'm not the type to panic, but I felt fear and confusion rising up within me. I walked into the sunroom and asked my husband (who has a degree in nursing) to check it out. He quickly announced, "You need to call the doctor tomorrow."

Over the next few days, I had several medical tests while trying to resume "life as normal." But then my doctor, in a moment of harsh reality, told me frankly, "It's a spreading cancer in your left kidney. Either it will be very good news, and we'll be able to get it all, or . . . it will be very fast."

How do you react to news like that? I remember going through some of the stages of grief—shock, denial, sadness, and finally, acceptance. Then, ultimately, I felt peace. I had always been a person of faith, and it was at this point that God and I became 24/7 best friends. It may sound sacrilegious to say that about God Almighty, Creator of the heavens and the earth, but I had never felt as close to Him as I did during those days. I poured my heart out to Him over and over, finding time in the workday to be alone with my Heavenly Father.

Then I grew quiet and listened. I felt His strength seeping into me from promises in His Word, and I found encouragement in the lyrics of Christian songs. I sensed His power when gazing at His beautiful creation, even by simply looking up into the sky. I felt His love and care warmly shining through the many, many cards, calls, hugs, and promises of prayer for me that came from relatives, friends, neighbors, my church family, and coworkers.

Being an e-mail fan, I heard from dozens of online friends who promised to pray for me. I had people praying for me who didn't even know me. People from everywhere shared their hearts with me, cried with me, and supported me as I waited for the surgery. I felt loved. I felt immensely loved. Here's a sample of the encouragement I received from a friend:

> *My Dear Maralee, there are no words to make it all better (my magic wand broke a couple years ago), but there is one better way—and that is to put you, your family, and your medical team in God's loving hands, and leave the results to Him. So hard to do at a time like this, but the best solution I know. I will do that every day and will be at peace about it because I know how special you are to Him.*
>
> *Love you!*

On April 23, 2001, the doctor removed the malignant tumor along with my left kidney. He was able to get it all—no chemotherapy or radiation therapy, either. God answered our prayers beyond our dreams. We were and are so grateful.

More blessings followed. Eight weeks postsurgery, I walked down the aisle at church as a very proud mother of the groom. My son, Chad, and his bride, Melissa, were married on June 23, 2001. They were entering a new life together—and I was entering new life, too.

Between Valentine's Day and Wedding Day, I experienced the height and depth and breadth of love—in the overwhelming support of those who cared for me, and in the amazing faithfulness of a Heavenly Father who loves us all more than we can imagine.

—MARALEE PARKER

The Adventure of Solitude

"I am convinced that nothing can ever separate us from his love. Death can't, and life can't. The angels can't, and the demons can't. Our fears for today, our worries about tomorrow, and even the powers of hell can't keep God's love away."

ROMANS 8:38

"Sometimes, Carol, I just sit still and let the Lord love me!"

I had asked a friend how she conducted her prayer life, and her answer surprised me. I often think of praying as a task or even a duty to perform.

But then I realized that I've had those times, too, when I sit in stillness and just drink in God's love. At those times I'm convinced that I will be enveloped in His love forever, no matter what happens in my daily life here on earth.

The wonderful thing is that not even our aloneness can separate us from the love of God. Thus, solitude becomes an adventure in spiritual growth, rather than another problem to be solved. Is it that way for you?

Let God's love permeate your heart and mind today.

—CMW

A Love That Shows

"Greet each other in Christian love. Peace
be to all of you who are in Christ."
1 PETER 5:14

Each week I read online newspapers. Imagine my surprise recently when opening a Web page and seeing a photo of my longtime friend Jean posed with a big smile on her face. Waiting in line for a meal at a restaurant, she was unaware that her picture was being taken and was obviously just being friendly with the people around her.

I met Jean thirty-one years ago when she married a childhood friend. Jean's openness endears her to many. Seeing her smiling face in the photo, I couldn't help but think, "Jean is making new friends again."

Jean loves the Lord, and this is evident in her interaction with townspeople. How important that we show the light of Christ in our communities!

And . . . in our faces.

A smile just can't hurt the cause!

—LaRose Karr

Evidence for Existence

"They demonstrate that God's law is written within
them, for their own consciences either accuse them
or tell them they are doing what is right."
ROMANS 2:15

I have a friend who's a police officer. When I asked her about her most effective interrogation techniques, her answer surprised me: "Most people can't wait to unburden themselves from the guilt they feel about their crime. I just give them the space to do it. We talk, I sympathize, and they usually start telling the truth."

Have you noticed the sense of "oughtness" that human beings carry within them from birth? It's a feeling of moral obligation, of duty, bordering on guilt. No doubt it's the reason we find worship of some variety in every culture throughout history.

Suppose we were to ask ourselves, Where does this inner sense of obligation come from?

How would you answer? Scriptures say it's built into creation, because creation has a moral Creator. That built-in law is awesome evidence for the existence of God.

The next time you get ready to take up some duty, pause to offer thanks for your sense of duty—an awesome gift.

—CMW

My Hero!

"Mighty hero, the LORD is with you!"
JUDGES 6:12

He was a fun little fellow, full of charm and energy as he whirled each of us on the dance floor at the annual Father-Daughter Dance. He was always ready with a compliment that made you feel beautiful. He attracted attention by his very presence, and he was my hero. He was my father, and oh, how proud I was of him!

He's still a fun fellow with loads of charm, but his energy wanes. He still attracts attention, but now from the nurses who greet us as I slowly walk with him into the dialysis center. His posture is stooped, but with his hand on my shoulder, we both feel ten feet tall. He's always ready with a joke, despite his pain as a kidney patient, and he makes everyone around him feel better.

His faith sustains him and me, and oh, how proud I am of him. He's still my hero.

No matter our circumstances, through the
grace of God we can still be somebody's hero.

—LISA M. KONZEN

First Steps

"When I was a child, I spoke and thought
and reasoned as a child does. But when
I grew up I put away childish things."
1 CORINTHIANS 13:11

I remember when my son became too big to carry down the stairs. I had always loved the tender moments in the morning when he woke up, all warm and tousled, and wrapped his little legs around my waist for a ride down to our kitchen. But the day came when I couldn't lift him anymore. Years of scrambled eggs and toast had done their work. He was strong enough to take the steps alone, and there I stood, with piggybacks to spare.

How bittersweet, the good job his dad and I had done. All our care equipped our boy to take those first steps toward maturity, toward the day when he'd no longer lean on us as a child. How amazing it will be to relate to him as an adult someday!

*God nurtures us to enter into a mature
relationship with Him.*

—DIANE ROSIER MILES

Always Available

> "Seek the LORD while you can find him.
> Call on him now while he is near."
> ISAIAH 55:6

I kept trying to get through, but the phone kept being busy. I needed to get this work done! Yet, in our busy world, it's not uncommon to come up short when trying to reach busy people. Even women—how many are available during the day? So many of us are tied up with work, volunteering, chauffeuring the kids, or just determined to stay out of touch.

Isaiah calls us to seek the Lord while He is near. It makes me realize how often I take God's presence for granted. After all, He's always near. But do I recognize Him? Do I take time to sink down into His love and enjoy His fellowship?

He is here, yet there is a perfect time to call upon the Lord with all of my pressing needs and important messages—and that time is . . . now.

God is always available, waiting for fellowship
with us—but am I available to Him?

—CMW

Appearances

". . . People judge by outward appearance, but the LORD
looks at a person's thoughts and intentions."
1 SAMUEL 16:7

I remember preparing for our first beach trip following our
daughter's birth. As I hauled playpen, table-mounted high
chair, electric swing, and assorted bags onto our front porch
early that morning, a car slowly kept passing the house. On the
third drive-by, a woman rolled down her window and yelled,
"What time does your yard sale start?"

I was shocked. There I stood in my gown in the predawn
hours, packing for a beach trip—and this woman thought I was
holding a yard sale! Embarrassed, I set her straight.

"But it *looks* like a yard sale," she insisted.

Reality isn't always what it appears at first glance. And
when it comes to human hearts, our perceptions truly differ
from God's. Only with God's help can we catch a vision of the
real, inner picture. Therefore, let's assume the best of all we
meet today, regardless of what first meets our eyes.

When I look, let me truly see.

—RUTHANNE N. ARRINGTON

Just Ask

"Keep on asking and you will be given what you ask for."
LUKE 11:9

"Can I have one of those good-smelling things you've been baking?"

"Yes," I responded, thinking he was rather bold. My banana-walnut muffins did smell good and must have been enticing. He ate the muffin without comment, and then asked, "May I have a glass of water?"

This man who responded to my HOUSE FOR SALE sign didn't follow the customary approach for anything. Instead of asking for an appointment when I opened the door, he said, "Can I come in?" After viewing my house, he asked for a muffin.

When he left, I reflected for a few minutes. I couldn't really feel upset with this fellow. I wasn't afraid of him. He wasn't rude or unfriendly. In a refreshingly straightforward and unpretentious way, he just asked for the things he wanted. He expected to receive them . . . and he did.

Approach God in a simple and direct manner.

—JANE M. AULT

Puppy

*"Whatever is good and perfect
comes to us from God above."*
JAMES 1:17

My daughter, Amanda, kept begging for a puppy. I kept saying, "No! We already have two dogs, and that's enough." Finally, in exasperation, I prayed, "Lord, she wants a dog so much. If You think she should have a puppy, please send us one."

I had in mind a little lap dog for the house, but our neighbors called soon after to say they had found a litter of St. Bernard puppies out in their pasture. Would we like to pick one out?

What a sense of humor God has! Max (short for *Maximus Dogimus*) has been a wonderful addition to our family. Even at 150 pounds, he still likes to climb into my lap to take a nap.

So often we think we know what's best for us and our children. But God's gifts go far beyond our understanding—right into perfection.

*Ask God what He wants for you . . .
and expect something big.*

—RENEE BOLKEMA

Contentment

"Not that I was ever in need, for I have learned how to get along happily whether I have much or little. I know how to live on almost nothing or with everything. . . ."

PHILIPPIANS 4:11–12

Having been reminded that riches can't buy happiness, my husband looked up from our precariously balanced checkbook and said, "I'd like to try being rich and unhappy rather than poor and unhappy."

Most of us long for just a little bit more in the bank. But when will we arrive at the place of "enough"? It seems we never get there.

The apostle Paul had been both rich and poor—and had learned to be content either way. Not that it was wrong to be rich or particularly noble to be poor. It's just that, for him, the key was to have his life's priorities in order and to be spreading the Kingdom values in everything he did.

He knew he could do it when times were good. And he knew that in the tough times, God's love could shine through his life even more brightly.

Learn to recognize when you've arrived at "enough."

—CMW

Never Too Hot

"Give all your worries and cares to God, for he cares
about what happens to you."
1 PETER 5:7

"Hot potato!" I'd yell, throwing the ball quickly to someone else
before it "burned" my hands. I loved that game when I was a
child. Pretending that the ball was a burning hot potato, we
would barely allow it to touch our hands before flailing it wildly to
someone else. Once aloft, the ball was someone else's problem.

Years later, as a busy mother with four young children, I
kissed my husband good-bye as he left on an extended business
trip. Two of my babies were sick, and I was bone tired. *What if
serious problems arise that I can't handle?*

That's when I remembered my childhood game. No matter
what life tosses at me, I can toss the problem—quick as I get
it—to my Heavenly Father. He can handle the heat.

What is it that God can't handle?

—GENA BRADFORD

Mountain Prayers

"[Jesus] went up into the hills by himself to pray.
Night fell while he was there alone."
MATTHEW 14:23

I used to live in the foothills of the Rocky Mountains, with Pike's Peak in plain view from my front door. At the end of a busy day, I'd often trek the quarter mile over to the middle school's oval running track. There I would walk and pray. Sometimes I'd focus on the beautiful mountain peaks before me, or watch the clouds of a thunderstorm gathering above them, or observe the pinkish orange sunset taking shape as night would fall. Most of the time I walked all by myself.

How special to walk with God this way! Yet I know that I can "walk" in the Spirit, and be prayerful, at any time and place. I need not go to the mountains or into a closet. The lifestyle of Jesus tells me that prayer is an attitude to cultivate, day in and day out, no matter where I am.

*I welcome the times of solitude, those precious moments
when I am most receptive to God's fellowship.*

—CMW

Protection

"Just as the mountains surround and protect
Jerusalem, so the LORD surrounds and protects
his people, both now and forever."
PSALM 125:2

I was feeling overwhelmed and restless, so I took a walk in the woods. But even the beauty of nature failed to soothe me. Life's demands and uncertainties would not be quieted. I prayed for peace: "Lord, I need a special word from You today."

A little farther on, the trail forked. I could either follow a stream or climb a mountain. "Which path shall I take, Lord?"

I climbed the mountain, and when I reached the top, I sensed God whisper, "Look all around you." Slowly I explored the view—ranges upon ranges of majestic mountains towering up to a pure blue sky. Tears filled my eyes as my heart held these words: "My love surrounds you like the mountains."

In your times of distress, remember your heavenly protection.

—RENEE BOLKEMA

Martha and Lizzy

"My dear Martha, you are so upset
over all these details! There is really only one thing
worth being concerned about. Mary has
discovered it—and I won't take it away from her."
LUKE 10:41–42 (NIV)

"Lizzy, Lizzy you are worried and upset about many things. . . ."
My heart understood what the Lord meant. Another failed
relationship had me fussing and crying. While I was reading
about Jesus' friend Martha, she reminded me of . . . me.

Martha had a lot of things going on too. She was upset
about dishes and chores—and about Mary's not doing her part
to help.

I think there was more to it though. As a child, did Martha envision her adult life living with her siblings, Lazarus and
Mary? Probably not. Like me, Martha probably thought she
would be married by now.

Whether my speculation is right or not, Jesus knew the
true root of Martha's frustrations. Just like He knows yours and
mine. Question is, will we stop long enough for His teaching
and comfort?

*Sitting at Jesus' feet, can there be a better
place to find peace in our lives?*

—ELIZABETH FABIANI

Not Bad, Just Lost

"If you had one hundred sheep, and one of them strayed away and was lost in the wilderness, wouldn't you leave the ninety-nine others to go and search for the lost one until you found it? And then you would joyfully carry it home on your shoulders."

LUKE 15:4–5

At a women's retreat, the keynote speaker asked all of us to close our eyes and think back to our childhood. I found myself judging the child I used to be: "What a crummy kid, unlovely in every way." I didn't want to remember her or see her.

Then I sensed these words in my heart: "You weren't bad, just lost." Suddenly I could see what Jesus meant when He spoke about the Good Shepherd going to find His lost sheep. He didn't say, "There you are, you bad, dirty sheep!" No, He said, "Great! I've found you! Let Me carry you back home and heal your wounds."

Later at home I took out a childhood snapshot, hung it up on my wall, and blessed the beautiful little girl God had made. How thankful I am that He found me . . . and took me in, just as I am.

See yourself through the Searcher's eyes.

—GENA BRADFORD

When Change Is a Good Thing

"Go and sin no more."
JOHN 8:11

I sat in the church board meeting and couldn't believe I actually heard the words spoken aloud. I knew it was the prevailing attitude in our small congregation, yet someone actually had the temerity to voice it: "But we've always done it that way before!"

I don't agree it's a good reason to keep things going according to the status quo. Yet, if I'm honest, I find myself living by the principle almost daily. I, like some folks, dislike change. And even more daunting than a congregational procedural change is the challenge to let go of some personal habit or secret desire hindering our spiritual growth. What is it for you?

"Go and sin no more" is something we will all hear from the Lord regularly in our lives. But when we truly meet Jesus, change is not only possible, it is virtually guaranteed.

No matter what change is needed,
God promises the strength to make it happen.

—CMW

Welcome

"Anyone who welcomes a little child like this on my behalf welcomes me, and anyone who welcomes me welcomes my Father who sent me."

MARK 9:37

Irena Sendler risked her life to save thousands of children from the gas chambers during World War II. Mrs. Sendler was not Jewish, but it broke her heart to see Jews in Poland sent to concentration camps. She couldn't save everybody, but she smuggled out as many children as possible and placed them with adoptive families.

To hide their identities, she wrote their real names and "new" names on slips of paper, put them in a jar, and buried them in her garden. Sadly, most of the children's families did not survive. The adoptive parents who welcomed them, kept them.

Jesus wants us to welcome children on His behalf. We may not be called to rescue them from murder. But children have simple needs, too—they need hugs, friendly smiles, and people who will listen as they practice their reading skills. Are you one of those people, a Welcomer?

Welcoming a child, you welcome the Lord.

—LEANN CAMPBELL

Learn from Those Critics

"Nazareth!" exclaimed Nathanael.
"Can anything good come from there?"
JOHN 1:46

Someone once said, "The trouble with most of us is that we'd rather be ruined by praise than loved by criticism." Jesus experienced plenty of criticism, even from those who would become His most loyal followers. When Nathanael first heard where Jesus came from, his reaction was negative. He had to see, first-hand, what Jesus was all about before his attitude would do an about-face.

A lady was once asked how many active members were in her Sunday school class. "Forty," she replied. "Twenty for me and twenty against me."

Opposition is common to Kingdom workers, so we must prepare for it and practice standing firm. Yet it helps to remember that we can learn from criticism. Though it's painful having our motives questioned, it can be devastating never to have our actions questioned.

Prepare for criticism by determining to learn from it.

—CMW

More Power in Love

"... Love has no fear because
perfect love expels all fear. ..."
I JOHN 4:18

After receiving the news that my mammogram was abnormal, I scheduled an appointment for a biopsy. I sat in the crowded waiting room and searched the sea of anxious faces. We were all so different, yet we battled the same enemy: fear.

I realized I had a choice. I could continue to meditate on my own worries or focus on the needs of others. Turning to the woman next to me, I asked about her situation. I listened as she poured out her story, then shared with her the security I found in knowing God was with me. When the nurse called her name, I squeezed her hand. "I'll be praying," I reassured her. "God is with you."

She smiled warmly and nodded her head in agreement. Feeling a quiet, inner peace, I returned her smile.

Sharing God's love allays our own fears.

—GINNY CAROLEO

FEBRUARY 20

Attitude of Dependence

"You're going to wear yourself out. . . . This job is too
heavy a burden for you to handle all by yourself."
EXODUS 18:18

My night work as a physician's surgical assistant is quite stressful. It's not uncommon to be called to the operating room and,
during the operation, be paged to an emergency room and at
the same time care for a patient in intensive care who's suddenly
become critical. By the end of most shifts, I'd be exhausted and
near tears.

One night as I was driving to work, I started to pray: "Dear
God, please don't give me more than I can handle tonight." I
repeated those words for several days. As I started to get my feet
under me, my prayer became less panicked, and it seemed that
God knew exactly what I was able to bear.

Since then, I have come to rely on Him throughout the
night. The workload remains the same, but my attitude of
dependence makes all the difference at the dawn of day.

You are always willing to share my burdens.

—CATHERINE M. SCHAFFER

How Much Remains?

"'I assure you,' he said, 'this poor widow has
given more than all the rest of them. For they have
given a tiny part of their surplus, but she, poor
as she is, has given everything she has.'"
LUKE 21:3–4

As Jesus watched people giving their offerings at the Temple, a
poor woman stood out to Him. That's intriguing to me, because
in our culture, it is the rich, the celebrities, the "cool" people
who always stand out. But not so with Jesus.

Why? Because this poor widow gave all she had to the
Lord's work. That made her a bigger person in His eyes than
the smartly dressed, having-it-all-together power people.

What does it mean to you, personally, to give generously
to God's work? Consider your charitable contributions. Or, perhaps a better question would be, What blessings do I miss when
I fail to give?

In numerous Scriptures, God prescribes giving and promises blessing in return. Of course, our motive for giving ought
to have nothing to do with what we expect to get back. What
matters is not how much is given—but how much remains.

When less is left over, isn't there more contentment?

—CMW

Canned Disappointment

"The kingdom of Heaven is like a pearl merchant on the lookout for choice pearls. When he discovered a pearl of great value, he sold everything he owned and bought it!"

MATTHEW 13:45–46

As a child I loved the felt-board stories, snack time, and songs of Vacation Bible School. And all of us kids worked hard to qualify for a special reward to be given on the final day.

Usually our prize was a small toy or a colorful certificate. But one summer we got to choose between two prizes: a New Testament or a can with a real oyster inside. Strange, but true— and most kids wanted the canned oyster, hoping for a valuable pearl inside. After the initial excitement of opening the mysterious cans, those oysters proved a big disappointment. Nobody got rich, and the novelty soon wore off.

We all work hard in hopes of obtaining something of value. And we, too, get to choose between two prizes: treasures on Earth or treasure in Heaven. Which, do you think, will bring lasting joy?

Invest in God's kingdom and avoid disappointment.

—AMY FOGELSTROM CHAI

Comforting Chain Reaction

"When God comforts us, it is so that we, in turn, can
be an encouragement to you. Then you can patiently
endure the same things we suffer."
2 CORINTHIANS 1:6

A movie came out a few years ago with the title *Pay It Forward*.
The idea was that the world would be a better place if we took
our blessings as a call to bless someone else, who, in turn, would
bless someone else. It would set up a chain reaction of giving
that would eventually circle the globe.

When I think of the apostle Paul's words above, I do imagine a chain reaction: God comforts us; therefore, we can comfort others.

Whether physical limitations, financial pressures, or other
tough challenges, our troubles cling to us each day. But think:
Who helps the best when you're hurting? Is it the person who
has all the answers? Or is it the friend who's experienced a
similar affliction, the one who is ready to empathize and gently
encourage? Can you be that kind of comforter today?

Out of our troubles can flow a chain reaction of comfort.

—CMW

Loving Friend

"How precious are your thoughts about me,
O God! They are innumerable."
PSALM 139:17

On a hot summer morning, I was feeling tired and frustrated. My small children had clung to me all morning, and I longed for some time to myself. Then the phone rang . . .

"Hey, girlfriend!" my friend said. "Just wanted to know if you and the kids would like to come over and take a dip in my pool this afternoon."

I accepted. But while packing swimsuits, my enthusiasm waned as I considered chasing my toddlers around the pool. When I arrived at my friend's house, though, she escorted me into the kitchen and pulled out a chair. She had prepared a special lunch on fine china. "Now you just sit here and enjoy lunch while my daughter and I watch the kids."

I sat at the table, eyes filling with tears. How thoughtful of God to shower me with love through a precious friend!

We are always on His mind.

—GINNY CAROLEO

"Will I See Jesus Now?"

"Can a mother forget her nursing child? Can she
feel no love for a child she has borne? But even if
that were possible, I would not forget you!"
ISAIAH 49:15

I was in complete control of my toddler's safety. Our postage-stamp yard was fenced in and picked clean of debris. And a patio door allowed me to watch him as I prepared lunch in our kitchen. Imagine my surprise as I looked up and saw him putting something white into his mouth!

Our lawn was covered with mushrooms that had sprouted overnight. I quickly phoned the doctor, then dosed my son with the recommended ipecac. But the word "poison" must have slipped from my mouth because he made a comment I will never forget: "Will I see Jesus now?"

Sometimes I forget that my kids belong to God and that He loves them even more than I do. My little boy's faith told him that no matter what happens, he doesn't need to be afraid. Jesus is with him—down here or up there.

Circumstances have no effect on God's memory of us.

—AMY FOGELSTROM CHAI

Speaking with Courage

"When they heard Paul speak of the resurrection of a
person who had been dead, some laughed, but others
said, 'We want to hear more about this later.'"
ACTS 17:32

Two thousand years ago, a Jewish carpenter started proclaiming special status with God. But He never wrote a book, never started a political party, never conquered any territory. He hung around with lower-class types and even included women in His circle of friends, until He was executed for treason.

So . . . should we be surprised if many people think our Jesus-worship is a little strange? Some still laugh.

It's our faith in His Resurrection that makes all the difference. If it really happened, then Jesus is the only one worthy of worship. But, of course, some people consider that kind of talk "weird." That's what happened to Paul when he proclaimed Christ's Resurrection to some skeptical Greeks. It wasn't easy, but I'd like to have the kind of courage he had—to proclaim an unlikely object of worship even in hostile territory.

Courageously spread the message: He is risen!

—CMW

Forgetting

"See, I have written your name on my hand. . . ."
ISAIAH 49:16

As children, we'd compare "lifelines" on the palms of our hands to see which of us would live the longest. Where we learned this I don't recall. But I know the little game is of no importance—except when I think of the uniqueness of our position in God.

We actually have no clue as to our life expectancies, but our very beings are nevertheless inscribed on God's hands. He knows not only the length of our days but the quality of our unique personhood, who we are in the depth of our souls.

A friend of mind once quipped that we tend to have "good forgetters." When trouble comes, we forget that we exist in God and our song of joy may take on some sour notes. But we're still there, held in His hand, our lifeline overseen with great care.

Trace the mark of God's love on your life today.

—ANN L. COKER

In a Nutshell

"If Christ has not been raised, then your faith is useless."
1 CORINTHIANS 15:17

The novel *Portofino,* by Frank Schaeffer, shows us a woman who uses a "Gospel Walnut" as a visual aid in presenting the Gospel. As the large plastic nut is broken apart, layer by layer, a new truth is revealed.

Question: If you had to state the Gospel message in a nutshell—in one brief sentence—how would you put it?

Would your statement include reference to the Resurrection? It should, for there is no "Good News" without the best news of all: Jesus is no longer dead after His execution.

Many people try to lump Christianity in with all the other world religions as just one more alternative. But is the Christian faith merely another fine philosophy of life? A laudable system of ethics? It certainly can claim such qualities. But it is so much more. It is a call to live for God today because His Son conquered death forever.

*Offer a prayer of thanks for Christ's
amazing accomplishment.*

—CMW

Stay Safe

"He will shield you with his wings.
He will shelter you with his feathers."
PSALM 91:4

A balmy breeze blowing through the open window beckoned me outside. In the backyard, a mother duck summoned her chicks with a low guttural squawk as I approached. Each duckling kept peeping, and the mother kept calling until each one came near. She then opened her wings and the ducklings scampered underneath as she settled down and covered them. The peeping stopped. Then, when the mother moved forward again, the chicks followed as if trained in choreographic precision.

As I watched this show of caring and being cared for, I smiled. How like the first verses of Psalm 91, where King David describes God's watchfulness over us. But will I choose to stay close, safe underneath sheltering wings? What, today, might tempt me to venture alone into a dangerous world?

Like a protective parent, God invites us to stay close.

—JOY COOLEY

MARCH

GOD IN A JUNGLE GYM

"Don't you realize how kind, tolerant,
and patient God is with you?"

ROMANS 2:4

*H*OW LONG HAS IT BEEN SINCE YOU CLIMBED inside a jungle gym? Because of Joshua, I recently found myself in one.

Working as a substitute teacher in the public schools has taught me to recognize the boys and girls who come from unstable homes. They often can't seem to concentrate on their schoolwork because their private worlds are falling apart. And their tumultuous feelings make it difficult for them to behave well. These children are so fragile that I don't want to do or say anything to cause more pain.

That is why I found myself praying inside of a jungle gym. Joshua, a troubled first grader, gripped the bars and looked into my eyes. He was wondering what I was going to do—and so was I.

All morning long, Joshua had been my challenge. When I greeted the class at the door, he left his backpack on the ground. He was so distracted that it took several reminders before he put it away. He talked loudly, moved constantly, and frequently told me how his *real* teacher did things. He couldn't sit still or follow my directions. One more piece of his world had fallen apart when his regular teacher hadn't been there to greet him at school.

"Joshua, come join us on the carpet."

"Joshua, please be quiet."

"Joshua, what are you supposed to be doing?"

"Joshua, you can't use the computer right now."

"Joshua. Joshua. Joshua." Kindly, but firmly, I redirected him. He made it difficult to accomplish anything with the rest of the class. Frustrated by the constant battle, I longed for the recess break.

But at the end of recess, Joshua was missing.

Leaving the teacher's aide in charge of the class, I searched for him. He was hiding inside the top of the tube slide. I talked him into coming down and we started walking, hand in hand, to the door.

That's when he broke away and ran inside the jungle gym. His tight grip and defiant look showed that he was ready to do battle. I knew I was strong enough to extricate him by force, even if he fought and kicked. But that's not what I wanted. He must come willingly—but how?

I shot a prayer up to God for wisdom. In response, peace and gentleness flooded through me. Without a word, I ducked inside the jungle gym and gently laid my hands on top of Joshua's hands. Keeping eye contact with him, I made sure he could see no anger or impatience in my face, only love and quiet authority. With the slightest pressure possible, I began loosening his fingers from the bars.

He was surprised by my light touch and quickly gave way. The defiant look was replaced by one of wonder. I carefully wrapped my left arm around him in a big hug. He yielded at first but then decided to wrap his legs around the bars.

Gently, I used my right hand to untangle his legs and feet. Again, he responded to my touch. Scooping him up, I ducked out of the jungle gym. Joshua lay limp in my arms as I carried him to the door. All of his resistance was gone. Gentleness had taken him by surprise and broke down his defenses. A little later on, when I looked across the classroom, I saw tears running down Joshua's cheeks.

I wish I could say that the rest of Joshua's day was wonderful, but when a child's life is full of deep hurts, it takes more than one gentle touch to make everything all right. However, with God's help, I now knew what would reach him.

When I got home from school, I sat down to read my devotions. The topic for the day was how God reaches out to us with gentleness, patience, and kindness.

"O Lord," I wept. "You showed me how to reach Joshua in the jungle gym, but that's how You reached me, too, isn't it? At times, I have been like little Joshua—refusing to sit still, and talking instead of listening. Like Joshua, I have tried to hide from You. And when that didn't work, I ran inside my own 'jungle gym' to hang on tightly to the bars of my make-believe world. But You reached out to me with a gentle touch and asked me to come to You."

You see, I have known times when I thought my world was falling apart. I have been filled with tumultuous feelings. I have experienced how fragile I am. I have acted out my fears.

God knew I needed Him, but He wanted me to come willingly. That's why He sent Jesus to my "jungle-gym world" with these words: "Come to me, all of you who are weary and carry heavy burdens, and I will give you rest. Take my yoke upon you. Let me teach you, because I am humble and gentle, and you will find rest for your souls" (Matthew 11:28–29).

Joshua could have chosen to resist my efforts, and I could have resisted God's offer. But it would have been foolish to do so. Romans 2:4 asks, "Don't you realize how kind, tolerant, and patient God is with you? Or don't you care? Can't you see how kind he has been in giving you time to turn from your sin?"

How about you? Is it time to let go, to quit resisting God, and let Him take you up in His arms?

—RENEE BOLKEMA

MARCH 1

Tough Love

"Jesus made a whip from some ropes and chased
them all out of the Temple. He drove out the sheep
and oxen, scattered the money changers' coins over
the floor, and turned over their tables."
JOHN 2:15

Think through your history with Christ so far. When was discipline or judgment clearly a part of your relationship? What
resulted from that difficult time? What things did you learn?

It's wonderful to think of Jesus gazing into our eyes with
love or offering an encouraging word or walking and talking
with us in Heaven. But the verse above reminds me that God
hates sin, and Jesus used a whip to run off crooks in the Temple
who cheated or took advantage of others.

The point is, Jesus is not a "safe" Savior. He comes with
love, but sometimes we require a tough love. For our own good,
judgment may be in order. Can we be thankful that He won't
let us go until we are conformed to His image? Thank God!

Thank Christ for His "severe mercy" in your life.

—CMW

Tamed by Love

"I have loved you, my people, with an everlasting love.
With unfailing love I have drawn you to myself."
JEREMIAH 31:3

Our daughter and family live at a church camp where people
drop off cats to fend for themselves. One granddaughter worked
in the kitchen and fed any cats that came around. Calico had
babies, and our daughter and granddaughter caught the eight-
week-old kittens that had had no human contact. They kept
the kittens in a shed—fed, watered, and loved several times a
day—until they no longer hissed when people came in. They
even learned how to play.

Like someone taking in stray cats and loving them until
they respond, God reaches out to each of us, taking time to
draw us to Himself. When we become His, He feeds us with the
nourishment of His Word. At first we may grumble and com-
plain about all we have left behind. Eventually, though, we see
that anything we ever had was simply on loan from Heaven.

An unfailing love will tame your heart.

—V. LOUISE CUNNINGHAM

Eat, Drink, Remember

"The Lord Jesus took a loaf of bread, and when he had given thanks, he broke it and said, 'This is my body, which is given for you. Do this in remembrance of me.' In the same way, he took the cup of wine . . . 'Do this in remembrance of me as often as you drink it.'"

1 CORINTHIANS 11:23–25

As a little kid, I always enjoyed the times when we had communion at church. Although it meant sitting still a little longer in the pew next to my parents, I carefully watched the trays of tiny cups pass from person to person. But those kinds of Sundays didn't come around often enough for me.

Of course, I now know it's not the frequency of communion, but the meaning, that counts. In Mark 14 and elsewhere, Jesus made it clear that communion is a sacred means of remembering all He has done for our salvation through His self-sacrifice. It is certainly more than a little snack!

Why not take a moment to remember that sacrifice right now? What words of thanks come to mind?

Praise to the perfect Lamb of God, sacrificed for us!

—CMW

A Place for Us

> "There are many rooms in my Father's home,
> and I am going to prepare a place for you. . . ."
> JOHN 14:2

For too long we had lived in church-provided housing. Now, nearing retirement, we needed our own place. As we headed back home after a day of unsuccessful home-searching, we felt like singing the ditty, "Somewhere there's a place for us." Yes, we believe God has prepared a place for us. If not a retirement home here, then most certainly a real place in our Heavenly Father's house.

A sense of place has been important to humans from the beginning. The Garden of Eden, a perfectly prepared place, had everything needed for a good life: food and shelter, beauty and fellowship, spiritual communion with God. Eden also had its restrictions, for it was a place of protection established for the good of God's creatures.

On Earth for a limited time, and in Heaven for eternity, we can rest assured in God's place prepared for our good.

Wherever God is, you can be at home.

—ANN L. COKER

Walk the Talk

"Just say a simple, 'Yes, I will,' or 'No, I won't.'
Your word is enough. To strengthen your promise
with a vow shows that something is wrong."
MATTHEW 5:37

"Just do what you say you're going to do, Mom!" my son Tim said. I'd done it again: made a promise, then couldn't keep it. (Or simply forgot to keep it.)

I've sometimes been caught up short upon suddenly remembering what I said I'd do—and then staring at the half-finished project, along with disappointed others. They trusted my words; I let them down.

A woman of integrity must "walk the talk." In fact, our integrity (or lack of it) reveals the depth of our relationship with Jesus. What words of promise or commitment have you uttered in the last few weeks? And how well are you following through on your pronouncements?

Let your promises be few—and kept.

—CMW

Let Him Touch

"Jesus reached out and touched the man."
LUKE 5:13

One of my cats used to jump on my lap, kiss my chin, and fall back in my arms knowing I would hold her like a baby. I'd softly rub her head and scratch under her chin; she'd lean back in contentment and purr. And with closed eyes, she'd reach her paw up to touch my face for closer contact.

We are cradled in God's arms of love, but most of us find it hard to be completely relaxed. Sometimes we're stiff and resistant to God's warm assurances. Why? Is it because we're used to being rebuffed by human hands? When Jesus touched people, His warmth and healing assured them of His love. Will I let His hand rest on me in this moment of quiet?

Pause for a minute in your busy day:
feel the touch of God.

—V. LOUISE CUNNINGHAM

Renewal

"There must be a spiritual renewal
of your thoughts and attitudes."
EPHESIANS 4:23

What's on your mind today? What kept running through your thoughts last night just before you fell asleep? And what problem or opportunity faces you right now? How you answer these three simple questions can help you know just how to pray today.

As I read this passage from Ephesians, I agreed with the apostle Paul that the culture around me needs transformation, just as it did in first-century Ephesus. Everywhere I turn for news and entertainment, I find all kinds of impurity and violence (see verses 17–19). Like me, the Christians in Ephesus must have wondered how in the world they could live like Christ when a corrupt lifestyle dominated their society.

And how can I escape the pull of my own impure desires? Thankfully, Paul gives me an answer I can live with: I need new thinking, new attitudes. I need the mind of Christ.

*Let the power of the Holy Spirit transform
your attitudes, starting this very moment.*

—CMW

Never Alone

"When I had lost all hope, I turned my thoughts
once more to the LORD. And my earnest prayer
went out to you in your holy Temple."
JONAH 2:7

I recently went through a health crisis involving anxiety
attacks. I would wake up in the middle of the night in a cold
sweat, shaking from head to toe, with an adrenaline rush that
made me believe I was dying of a heart attack. I recall the worst
part being the overwhelming sense of aloneness—and there is
no greater fear than thinking, for even one moment, that you
are completely alone in this world.

I had truly lost all hope before my thoughts turned to the
Lord. I would open the Bible and read aloud the promises of
God until my heart was again at peace. And, true to His Holy
Word, He helped me find healing through some wonderful
therapies. Through it all, I have come to know this: I am never
alone when He is there.

There is always hope in the company of God.

—SARA DAVENPORT

Driving Lessons

"We will stay on the king's road."
NUMBERS 21:22

My family and I once drove down the famous Lombard Street in San Francisco while on vacation. It's the most crooked street in the world. Picture a snake as it slithers down a mountain. That's what Lombard looks like from the top of the road. We accidentally came upon it while exploring, and halfway down we encountered a sign that said, NO THRU TRAFFIC. However, it was too late to turn around.

Over the years I've learned many lessons while driving down the wrong roads. For example, it's not always *which* road we choose that matters; it's *how* we travel the road that determines our destination. The Hebrews of old promised to stay on the king's road without deviation, and we promise to stay on the straight and narrow path throughout our lives. But I wonder what twist or turn will try to throw me off track today or tomorrow.

Let Him guide you around life's sharp curves ahead.

—WENDY LYNN DECKER

Who Are You Going to Please?

"Try to find out what is pleasing to the Lord."
EPHESIANS 5:10

It sure felt good to "wanna be a God-pleaser." I'm referring to the 1980s Christian music group Petra, which encouraged its audiences to "be a God-pleaser, not a man-pleaser." I loved that band!

I already knew how to please people—my parents, teachers, pastors, and friends. I'd learned how to read people quite well, and spent much of my energy trying to win their approval. Thankfully, I also experienced God's unconditional love and acceptance when rejection ultimately came.

I often read this passage in Ephesians, especially focusing on Paul's admonition to avoid foolish talk and empty words. But Paul's greater challenge guides my study now: to find out what pleases the Lord—even if pleasing God brings the rejection of people.

Yes, I wanna be a God-pleaser until the day I die. How about you?

Find out what pleases the Lord, and . . . do it!

—CMW

Like an Eagle

"Those who wait on the Lord will find new strength.
They will fly high on wings like eagles."
ISAIAH 40:31

"Okay, Mom, I know what you're doing—you're like that mother eagle taking those warm feathers out of the nest you've been teaching us about!"

Jeff, in his midteens, needed to make some decisions. In the previous night's family devotions, I contrasted the values of "Eagle Christians" versus the lifestyles of vultures. Eagles prepare their nests and catch food to help their young grow strong and healthy. As the youngsters grow, Mama Eagle prepares the eaglets for life outside the nest.

For years after their dad died, my three sons and I walked alone. I waited upon the Lord each day, and the Bible became a wonderful resource for child-rearing. Through the years, I saw my rambunctious little boys transform into fine young men. Now they're raising little Christian eaglets of their own.

Let us wait on Him for everything we need.

—DEE EAST

Marked Forever

"When you believed in Christ, he identified you
as his own by giving you the Holy Spirit."
EPHESIANS 1:13

As I type at my keyboard, the phone in the kitchen rings. I run past my noticeably naked toddler, down the stairs, and catch it just in time. Returning to my desk, I notice my self-inking rubber stamp is missing.

Creeping up to his bedroom door without a sound, I try to peek in. Unfortunately, the doorknob gives me away with a squeaky *jeeerrrrer*. I hear the familiar *click-slash* sound, and then a soft thud, and then little feet scampering across the linoleum. Finally, I notice the covers on my son's bed wiggling and giggling.

I walk in and gently lift the covers. In black, like poorly organized tattoos, repeatedly, I read my name, address, and phone number on pink skin. With these inklings of information, if he had wondered away from our house, anyone who saw him would know right where he belonged, at home with me!

We're forever marked as God's own possession.

—RHONDA DEYOUNG

Nothing Personal!

"Do as they say," the LORD replied,
"for it is me they are rejecting, not you.
They don't want me to be their king any longer."
1 SAMUEL 8:7

Israel wanted a king—in spite of all that the prophet Samuel had done for Israel—traveling from town to town listening to their problems, settling their differences, and teaching the Law. He deserved their gratitude in his old age. Instead, he got rejection.

Samuel and I have something in common—we don't handle rejection very well. But Samuel, in a sense, walked in God's shoes for a moment. For God Himself was rejected in this controversy. Yes, Israel wanted a king, even though God had faithfully provided for them in the desert, helped them conquer their enemies, and led them to settle in a fertile land. God deserved their praise and undying devotion. Instead, they wanted someone else to rule over them!

Rejection came to Samuel because he represented God. It wasn't personal, Samuel.

Lord, when I feel rejected, show me the bigger picture.

—CMW

Reflect the Son-light

"He is like the light of the morning, like the sunrise
bursting forth in a cloudless sky; like the refreshing
rains that bring tender grass from the earth."
2 SAMUEL 23:4

A good friend of mine is blind. Though he's never seen anything with his eyes, he often baffles me with his amazing ability to describe things in detail. Once I asked him if he could explain colors. He said he pictured yellow as hot, black as cold, red as passionate, and gray . . . that's the color when the sun isn't shining on his face.

Instead of thinking of the sun, I thought of the Son, Jesus Christ. And because I know Him, I'll never have to fear that His light won't shine upon my face.

Jesus calls us, as well, to be a bursting forth of light in a dark world. And why hide behind a cloud? There is nothing like the brilliance of Son-light breaking through after the rains.

Reflect the Light that already fills your soul.

—WENDY LYNN DECKER

Know the Consequences

> "When that day comes, you will cry out for
> relief from the king you have chosen, and
> the Lord will not answer you in that day."
> 1 SAMUEL 8:18

We made up contracts for our teenage boys, outlining the family rules about car, cash, and curfew. Each boy signed his name and agreed to abide by the guidelines—or else forfeit privileges. We loved our boys, but we all held to the agreement: The one who made a bad choice experienced the consequences.

They agreed not to let anyone else drive the car. But after football practice, when another defensive player asked to take their new car for a spin around the school parking lot, they decided that they knew better than us about these things, and handed over the keys. Unfortunately, when their friend shoved the gear into reverse and pressed the gas, he immediately hit another car. The guys had to pay for the other car's repairs, and they lost their driving privileges for quite a while.

In the context of the verse above, we read about a significant turning point for the elders of Israel. They had rejected God's leadership through Samuel and demanded that He appoint a king to rule over them as in nations around them, they said.

So God made an agreement with Israel that spelled out the consequences of their choice. Unfortunately, the people not only rejected God's leadership, but they also lost His listening ear.

Beware what you pray for . . . lest you receive it.

—CMW

Wide-Eyed Learning

"Always be thankful."
COLOSSIANS 3:15

Disrupting the quiet of the diner, my children and I burst through the glass doors, and all eyes turned our way. Soon the cranky voice of my six-year-old daughter erupted: "Hey, they don't have any balloons." Later, she stopped coloring her place mat to whine, "They didn't give me a green crayon!"

I pretend not to hear. But when the food arrives, she tastes the chicken tenders and proceeds to tell anyone who will listen that they are too hot. Finally, Riggs, who is three, starts screaming from across the table, "This isn't chocolate milk! I want *chocolate*!"

Later I came to a sad conclusion: Grumbling is contagious . . . and my kids caught it from me. Determining to reverse the trend, I tried a new tack on a day dedicated to bathroom cleaning. As both kids watched, I said, "Thanks, Lord, for this warm, running water we have for cleaning." You should have seen their wide-eyed stares.

Is there anything you can't be thankful for right now?

—RHONDA DEYOUNG

The Relationship Suffers

"Do not covet your neighbor's house. Do not covet
your neighbor's wife, male or female servant, ox or
donkey, or anything else your neighbor owns."
EXODUS 20:17

Keeping up with the neighbors seems to be a favorite pastime
among some ladies in my town. And I'm not immune. I notice
when Margie gets a new car, or Phyllis has some furniture delivered, or when Helen just seems to keep her flower garden looking like a country club's landscaping.

In fact, it's not hard at all to find something to covet when
we look to our neighbors. The grass is always greener next door
(or at least the car is newer). Sadly, the worst thing about that
kind of jealousy is that it dilutes my heart's praise for all my
daily blessings.

In other words, when I'm trying to keep up with the Jone-
ses, I need to remember what's really at stake: my relationship
with God.

> *Give thanks for all you have—and
> for all your neighbor has too.*

—CMW

Dancing for Glory

"You have turned my mourning into joyful dancing."
PSALM 30:11–12

I recall seeing a primitive painting of bears dancing in the woods. They are standing erect, fat, with skinny legs and paws, smirks on their faces. They're in an old forest, for the trees are almost as wide as they are.

Camped in a national park this summer, I was humming Chris Rice's song "Circle Up": "Grab a hand, twirl a dance . . . and worship Him!" In my imagination I was dancing in honor of the Lord, all by myself in the woods. I looked very much like the bears in that painting—overweight, panting for breath, hands flung in the air as I spun in joy for all He has done.

I twirled between the trees, head up, eyes to the sky, singing in His love. Crunching through bright leaves, wading in toe-numbing water, kneeling to admire tiny tundra plants, I am constantly reminded that God's creation is definitely a place to worship Him.

Have you been anywhere His glory is not apparent?

—ELSI DODGE

Keep Walking!

"I plead with you to give your bodies to God.
Let them be a living and holy sacrifice—
the kind he will accept."
ROMANS 12:1

I find it interesting that, when we think of a "spiritual act of worship," we are to think of offering our . . . *bodies*. What could this possibly mean?

Jane walks into the mall and passes by the bookstore, the dress shop, and the movie theater. Now the Cookie King looms ahead. She is trying to lose weight, but she also loves chocolate chip delicacies. As she gets closer, she sacrifices her taste buds, her stomach, her body.

She keeps walking.

It's one thing to think spiritual thoughts, pray spiritual prayers. It's quite another matter to do spiritual sacrifice. So often it involves our bodies. But what, specifically, will it mean for you in the days ahead?

Commitment to the Lord is not entirely painless.

—CMW

God of the Derby

"Love has no fear because perfect love expels all fear."
1 JOHN 4:18

A colonoscopy! I agonized for a week over the routine test. In fact, my heart started racing the Kentucky Derby. I couldn't sleep. I searched a medical Web site for the symptoms of anxiety and read, "Patient thinks she is having a heart attack." Bingo! My reaction had no physical cause, but my racing heart refused to listen to my brain.

Then I decided to focus on one thing: *I belong to a loving God who wants only the best for me.* I even memorized 1 John 4:18. Although my anxiety didn't disappear like magic, thinking about this verse throughout the week calmed my heart's gallop to a canter.

I did just fine with the test and received a good report. Next time, I won't be so fearful about it (although I'm grateful I don't have to repeat the procedure for another ten years).

His love can soothe storms—and galloping hearts.

—BONNIE DORAN

How Love Looks

"Love is patient and kind. Love is
not jealous or boastful or proud."
1 CORINTHIANS 13:4

"How are things going with you these days?" What a relief it can be to a hurting person to have a teacher, coworker, or neighbor inquire sincerely about our situation. If we gently stick with the question after a few polite responses, we usually find real needs pouring our way.

What does being available to others like that mean to you? It can be a real act of love to ask and listen in this way, because it is a patient, kind way to treat people. As St. Augustine once put it, "What does love look like? It has the hands to help others. It has the feet to hasten to the poor and needy. It has the eyes to see misery and want. It has the ears to hear sighs and sorrows."

*Suppose you were to watch for signs
of people in distress today?*

—CMW

Be There!

"God is our refuge and strength, always
ready to help in times of trouble."
PSALM 46:1

With light steps, Lila strolled into the department-store elevator, swinging her shopping bags. Pushing the button for her floor, she watched the doors close and then turned to gaze at the other passenger in the car.

The man gave her a threatening glare. Lila's breath froze in her throat as goose bumps lined her arms with a chill. Danger lurking in the air, Lila clutched her purse and shopping bags a little tighter. She began to pray. As she silently beckoned God, she felt His presence. As she continued to pray, the hostile atmosphere seemed to evaporate. The elevator doors eased apart, and Lila strode safely away.

At times, any of us can face circumstances that render us weak-kneed and frightened. Like Lila, we are not alone. God is near; it is for us to perk up our awareness and simply be there with Him.

*In a flash of thought, you sense God's loving
presence, and experience His peace.*

—MATA ELLIOTT

97

How Much Love?

"I have loved you even as the Father has loved me.
Remain in my love. . . . And here is how to measure
it—the greatest love is shown when people lay
down their lives for their friends."
JOHN 15:9, 13

"If you love me, then you'll. . ." Have you been there? It seems we
humans want to add conditions to our love, probably because
we know, at some deep level, that the essence of love is self-
sacrifice. The deeper the love, the more complete the quality
of self-giving.

How do we know God loves us completely? Meditate on
John 15:9–13 for some biblical clues. Then consider your own
love-in-return for the Lord.

For me, reading through poet Elizabeth Browning's famous
first line helps me get started:

How do I love Thee [Lord]?
Let me count the ways. . . .

Loving the Lord back is a lifetime endeavor.

—CMW

Forgiven and Not Forgotten

"He calls His own sheep by name and leads them."
JOHN 10:3

After the service, I saw her coming toward me. She was so friendly, even though she'd suffered significant brain damage. I frantically tried to remember her name so I could greet her, but it wouldn't come. I thought, "It's okay, I'm sure she doesn't remember who I am."

As I opened my mouth to say hello, she said, "Hi, Merry." She not only knew my face but also my name. I was humbled. This was one of God's precious children, whom He dearly loved. Her brain may have been diminished but not her heart. My brain was fine but it seemed I had a heart of stone.

That day God allowed me to see the importance of a name. It is the very essence of a person. That's why Jesus knows her name and now, by His grace, so do I.

I will never forget it. Her name is Peggy.

To know her name is to demonstrate her value.

—MERCEDES EVANS

Faith Overcomes

"I can't help myself, because it is sin inside
me that makes me do these evil things."
ROMANS 7:17

If you had to list a few of your addictions, what would they be? Counselors tell us that an addiction is any mood-altering substance, experience, or person that we rely on for nurturing, that keeps us from knowing and feeling a deeper, unresolved hunger.

Have you realized yet that you can't fight and defeat it on your own? The apostle Paul, too, clearly struggled against sinful influences in his life. So we need not give in to despair. You see, our addictions can move us into a new, less grasping approach to life. It's an approach that allows us to extend our hands for help, in faith.

A certain church father once said, "God is always trying to give good things to us, but our hands are too full."

*Today, consider loosening your grip a bit on
things that bring only temporary satisfaction.*

—CMW

God the Romance Writer

"God is love, and all who live in love
live in God, and God lives in them."
1 JOHN 4:16

Antonio and I met while on vacation. On our last date together, we walked on the beach at sunset, built a drippy sandcastle, and pretended to find artifacts from the Roman Empire on that Caribbean beach. I was surrounded by tropical beauty, well rested from a grueling job, and completely smitten.

Too bad Antonio lives in Italy. But for a single girl like me, innocent romantic encounters are treasures.

I felt I'd caught a fresh glimpse of God, as well. I hope it doesn't sound too strange, but during my Caribbean holiday, I fell in love with my Lord all over again. I recognized He is the author of every true love story. He ignites, rekindles, and stokes the flames of love between a man and a woman and between a woman and her God. As He loves me in spirit, He will bring me human love as well, at just the right time.

God writes beautiful love stories. Is He writing yours?

—ELIZABETH FABIANI

Abandoned

"Don't abandon me, for you made me."
PSALM 138:8

Facing a tight deadline, I rushed to our private school and began printing my manuscript. An hour later, fifty pages had been completed. I stared at the printer in disbelief. At this rate, it would be hours before my cyber-words hit paper.

Abandoned to a machine's excruciatingly slow performance!

Accepting there was nothing I could do but wait for the sluggish printer to finish, I strolled through the school. I stopped at the prekindergarten classroom, and the teacher, busy with a student, asked if I would help a little boy tie his shoe. I helped that child and others and was greeted by large smiles and happy voices, everybody eager to talk.

As I left the classroom, I realized I was right where I was supposed to be: left helpless by technology, hardly abandoned by the Lord.

God's plans for you are always perfect.

—MATA ELLIOTT

Useless Trust?

"If Christ was not raised, then all our preaching
is useless, and your trust in God is useless."
1 CORINTHIANS 15:14

To think that Jesus remained in the tomb like any other religious leader in history—what a picture of "useless trust"!

But what would a living hope look like? We might simply look to the Cross, where an eternal battle has already been won on our behalf. Now we hopefully await that victory's full manifestation at Christ's return. Many Christians weekly recite that hope in these words from the *Book of Common Prayer*:

Christ has died.
Christ has risen.
Christ will come again.

Memorize this powerful declaration; it's everything you need in order to have trust and hope—a *useful* trust and a *living* hope—right now.

How futile living without hope can be!

—CMW

Weighty Prayers

"Share each other's troubles and problems,
and in this way obey the law of Christ."
GALATIANS 6:2

Back and forth on the Internet my friend Kelly and I lamented our singleness—until Kelly posed a striking question: "Should we try focusing on praying for each other's needs rather than beating our own to death?"

"Yes, absolutely!" I said. We set a specific time to pray for each other, promising to report back. The result: How I view my singleness was changed forever.

Before, I was wrapped up in what I want or don't have. Now I think, *Who better to pray for my single friends than me?* I know what they are going through. I am not the only one beating on Heaven's door, crying, "God, where is Mr. Right?"

You've struggled? You may be wrestling with something now. Chances are, you're not alone. But remember: When you take your eyes off your own struggles, you can see clearly how to help someone else.

*When your worries weigh you down, try praying
for those who carry the same weight.*

—ELIZABETH FABIANI

Read Back

"You both precede and follow me.
You place your hand of blessing on my head."
PSALM 139:5

Do you realize that you are a "God-carrier" on earth? If you doubt it, look back through your history with Him to this point. Do you see the events, the special moments along the way, when the Lord was clearly there in you?

God's genius is woven into the fabric of our life's events. Have you taken a look at His handiwork lately? Consider: When have you sensed that God's unique purpose was at work in your ordinary circumstances?

I've found I can discern God by reading back through my life story, tracing the gracious hand that reached out to guide me here, warn me there. And in each instance gave one more drop of saving grace.

*We are unique, chosen to be indwelt by
the almighty Creator of all that exists.*

—CMW

Way Out There

"No eye has seen, no ear has heard,
and no mind has imagined what God
has prepared for those who love him."
1 CORINTHIANS 2:9

How do you explain to a blind man the beautiful sunset shades of red and orange, or the rainbow's delicate bows of color? How do you describe to a deaf man the delightful sound of a baby's first bubbly coo or belly laugh? All comparisons, all explanations, all descriptions are inadequate; all parallels fall far short of the reality we are trying to portray.

So how can we, so earthbound, expect to understand Heaven? All descriptions fall far short of the glorious reality that awaits us across death's threshold.

I do sometimes wonder what Heaven will be like, though, and at times I even worry about it being so different from my present reality. Yet, just as the blind know that sight is something wonderful, and the deaf are sure that hearing is something precious, we can be sure that Heaven will be just out of this world!

Heaven is different—but better.

—TANYA FERDINANDUSZ

APRIL

NO MORE SLITHERING FEARS

"I can do everything with the help of
Christ who gives me the strength I need."

*L*AST NIGHT MY DAUGHTER, MOLLY, AND I HAD A close encounter with a snake. I'll spare you the details. Let's just say he was huge and only inches from my arm when I saw him, sang opera, kicked myself in the back of the head trying to get away, then spent half an hour hyperventilating. For the next several months, I'll imagine snakes everywhere I look.

People who aren't afraid of snakes can't understand. They may tell me all they want that he's harmless, "the good kind of snake to have around." That does not compute. He's a snake and I don't care how many rodents he kills or that he means me no harm.

The only thing that helped me calm down last night was Molly. She was clearly more upset, and it seemed like the motherly thing to do to forget myself and comfort her.

We called a neighbor who, instead of killing the thing, chased it right into my flower bed and told me what a good thing it was to have there. Thanks for nothing. An hour later Molly and I drove to meet my husband and son at the ballpark. I was calculating how closely we'd have to walk to the overgrown backfield (which looks like snake paradise) when Molly asked, "Mom, how can I stop feeling so scared?"

I suggested we say a prayer and ask God to help us. We talked first about how God made snakes, and just because we can't appreciate their beauty and usefulness doesn't take away from the fact that they're God's creation—like we are. Then I remembered that "I can do all things through Christ who strengthens me." I asked Molly if she really believed that. (In my heart I asked myself.) Then we asked Him to take away our fear.

Next thing we knew, we were caught up in a Little League game, and the snake was all but forgotten. That is until this morning. You see, when Molly and I saw the snake, we were looking into my flower bed, where I'd carefully arranged everything for planting. I'd spent a long time at the nursery selecting the plants, giving great thought to where each one would grow best. Then I'd set out those plants, the bags of top soil and mulch, the special time-release plant food, my gardening tools—even my CD player so I could listen to worship music while I played in the dirt.

Now I stood there frozen, knowing good and well I wasn't going anywhere near that flower bed where a snake had been just fourteen hours before. Where was he now? Those plants could die in their pots for all I cared.

Then I thought of Molly, coming home from school. She would see the plants still in their pots and know that I'd been too scared to plant them. What would that say to her about the power of prayer—about the ability and desire of God to help us? And what about her mother's faith?

I walked over to my porch rocker (after checking all around and underneath for you-know-who). I remembered how my heart had gone out to Molly last night when she was so scared and sitting there, and it occurred to me that my Heavenly Father cared as much—even more—about how I was feeling right now. After all, He was the one who'd sent those verses to comfort me.

Do you know what I did next? I pulled on my gardening gloves and planted those plants. I was a little tense at first, but by the sixth or seventh one, I was singing. I knew I wasn't alone. I dug my holes, added my topsoil, set everything just where I wanted it. I fed and mulched and watered. As I planted each plant, I studied the little picture card included in the pot—the "best case scenario" picture. With the right amount of sun and rain, and with my tender care, this is what my plant might look like someday.

Later I showed Molly the pictures and pointed out which plant was which. "You see that scraggly little plant? It could look like this one day."

I couldn't help but wonder whether God has a picture like that of me—my "best case scenario" picture. The seeds have been sown. The Word of God is the time-released food that I need. With the Father's tender care, and with just the right amount of Son, how far will this scraggly little plant go? Even my slithering fears can't stop His plans.

—Mimi Greenwood Knight

Only Happy

"Here on earth you will have many trials and sorrows.
But take heart, because I have overcome the world."
JOHN 16:33

"Things are going okay, I guess," my girlfriend said. "But sometimes I wonder, *what's the point?*"

It made me do some hard thinking about what it means to
be happy in life, and how that goes along with our call to be
joyful. How would you describe the difference between happiness and joy?

No doubt joy has a more long-term quality to it—a looking
beyond the present circumstances for what endures, whether in
good times or in hard times.

Certainly, everyone wants to be happy in the moment.
And we can be grateful for the variety of happiness poured
into our lives. But joy, whether we are suffering or content, can
spring only from a foundation deeper than life's events. Our joy
is anchored in our relationship to the Eternal One.

He promised us tribulation in life.

—CMW

A Peace Like No Other

"I am leaving you with a gift—peace of mind
and heart. And the peace I give isn't like the peace
the world gives. So don't be troubled or afraid."
JOHN 14:27

Lately my dreams are of my grandmothers. These dreams are so real they are like visits from those lovely old ladies. So real I can smell the dusting powder Grandma Walker always wore; so real I can sense Grandma Stokes's sturdy arms around me and feel her fingers guiding mine in an intricate crochet pattern.

I awake with joy that I have been with the women I loved most in my childhood. I awake in the sure knowledge that my grandmothers are in Heaven, waiting for me to join them. What peace of mind and heart this gives me!

I feel no fear, either, that I might be joining them sooner than expected. I feel only the peace that they are waiting, just beyond my day vision.

Let your mind be cradled in the peace of God.

—NITA WALKER FRAZIER

Accountable

"If another believer sins against you, go privately and
point out the fault. If the other person listens and
confesses it, you have won that person back."
MATTHEW 18:15

When someone has hurt you, do you go to her in a spirit of rec-
onciliation and forgiveness? Forgiving is harder than excusing,
because to forgive we must summon up our courage and hold
the other person accountable. That's why Jesus told us to lovingly confront the one who's done us wrong.

This kind of forgiving means entering into a relationship,
determining to treat the other as a worthy human being—worthy of our full respect and involvement. To excuse, on the other
hand, minimizes the other as being not quite valuable enough
to take up our energies. We simply choose to ignore her and go
on our way.

Think: *Who do I need to forgive today?* Could your risky
decision to approach this person possibly become the start of a
new, enduring friendship?

Today, pray for the grace to honor the personhood
even of those who cause you pain.

—CMW

Showing Up

"Let everyone see that you are considerate in all that
you do. Remember, the Lord is coming soon."
PHILIPPIANS 4:5

The cell phone rang just about the time we pulled into our
driveway after a busy, exhausting day. One of our church members
had fallen. She was in good hands, however, and was in
the emergency room at a hospital in the next town.

"Should I go?" I asked my husband, Roy.

"She has several people with her," he answered. "But do
whatever you feel you should do. . . ."

I decided to go to the hospital. I prayed with my friend
before the doctor came in to see her, and it seemed my presence
had calmed her spirits.

A few weeks later, she called me. "I just wanted to thank
you for coming to the hospital on the day I fell," she said. "I
wasn't nearly as afraid when I saw your face."

It made me think: Sometimes all it takes to be considerate
is . . . showing up.

In the midst of busyness, take time to care.

—NANCY B. GIBBS

A Place Prepared

"There are many rooms in my Father's home, and I am going to prepare a place for you. If this were not so, I would tell you plainly. When everything is ready, I will come and get you, so that you will always be with me where I am."

JOHN 14:2–3

All my life I've dreaded one question more than any other when meeting new people: "So, where are you from?" Probably not an intimidating inquiry for most people, but for those of us who grew up as "Army brats," it's a different story. Do I explain that I lived in eight different places during the first ten years of my life? Do I comment that "hometown" is a foreign word to me? Or do I just name the city of my birth and leave it at that?

I struggled with that question for a long, long time.

But I also take comfort in the Scripture above, which speaks directly to every human's longing for complete and lasting settledness. None of us have that . . . yet. But it's promised. And for those of us who've moved more times than we can count, that promise of an everlasting home holds very special meaning and hope.

Heaven is waiting for God's children.

—ANNE GOLDSMITH

APRIL 6

What's on Your Mind?

"For the Word of God is living and active.
Sharper than any double-edged sword, it penetrates
even to dividing soul and spirit, joints and marrow;
it judges the thoughts and attitudes of the heart."
HEBREWS 4:12

For a moment, try to recall the myriad thoughts you've had in just the last ten minutes. Jot a few of those thought-themes in your journal for a moment.

Do the things you think help you grow spiritually?

One of the great truths of our lives is this: We can choose our attitude, each day, each moment. We can fill our minds with the pure, the lovely, the admirable, as we seek to grow in Christian character.

Our lives can be filled with noble assumptions—beget by a mind-set that sees the good, that approaches each human encounter expecting the best. So, as you move into each day, realize that a quality of attitude will flow out of your life and touch others for the good—even before you utter a single word.

As the seedbed of character, attitude makes all the difference.

—CMW

Excellent Soil

"I pray that Christ will be more and more at home in
your hearts as you trust in him. May your roots go down
deep into the soil of God's marvelous love."
EPHESIANS 3:17

As a Mother's Day present, my children gave me a lovely hibiscus plant with peach-colored flowers that matched our living room drapes. We enjoyed the plant immensely when it was new to our home but soon noticed the leaves turning yellow. I watered it faithfully and moved it to a sunnier area. Nothing I did seemed to help.

Then one day I noticed tiny white bugs flying around the leaves. I purchased insecticide and have been fumigating ever since. How could such a lovely plant go downhill so quickly? And what work it is to keep it barely alive!

Not so with us. Yes, we too need to grow and blossom and produce fruit. But we draw from a special soil assuring us of continued health. Nothing is required—but to grow and be thankful.

God's love fills us with every form of nourishment and light.

—CAROL GUTHMILLER

Beware Smooth Talkers

"Watch out for people who cause divisions and upset people's faith by teaching things that are contrary to what you have been taught. Stay away from them. . . . By smooth talk and glowing words they deceive innocent people."

ROMANS 16:17–18

The young lady at the airport seemed amazingly sincere and intelligent. She was talking about reincarnation and making some powerful points. Was I being drawn in?

I walked away and thought, "No, that just isn't right." I took out my Bible to prove it to myself.

Can you tell a false teacher from a true one? Take a moment to think about that and name some distinguishing characteristics that you'd apply to a false teacher. What kinds of teachings would you look for? What kinds of questionable motives?

Christians have always had to stay on the lookout for false teachers. They are not easy to detect. In your prayer time today, ask the Lord to keep you alert to the ever-so-clever "deadening" of what is real, living, and powerful: God's eternal Word.

May we stay alert to smooth talkers
with questionable teachings.

—CMW

Cover Your Mouth

"Take control of what I say, O LORD,
and keep my lips sealed."
PSALM 141:3

With my friend crying on my shoulder over the serious results of repeating a bit of gossip she believed was true, I thought of some first-grade advice: "Cover your mouth!"

This rule for my young students is printed on the chalkboard and read aloud at least once every day. *You don't want to be coughed on, Suzie? Then don't cough on someone else, for coughs and sneezes spread diseases.*

Does God ever tell us to cover our mouths? Yes. Because words spoken too lightly, sent out on the air like moisture droplets from sneezes, can never be retracted. Even a sincere apology won't undo the damage.

I remember when doctors used to judge our health by how our tongues looked. It seems that God, our Great Physician, measures spiritual health by how our tongue . . . *speaks.*

*When the mouth is closed,
the tongue can't do much damage.*

—GWEN RICE CLARK

119

Why Hurt Yourself?

"Get rid of all bitterness, rage, harsh words. . . .
Instead be kind to each other . . . forgiving . . .
just as God through Christ has forgiven us."
EPHESIANS 4:31–32

My friend Carolyn told me about seeing some beautiful paintings of tropical birds. Having spent her childhood in Brazil with missionary parents, Carolyn was delighted with the lovely works of art. She was appalled, however, to meet the artist—a woman who had hoped to be a missionary, but under parental pressure got married instead.

"Never in my life have I seen such sadness," Carolyn said as she described the deep, angry frown lines cutting into the woman's face. She'd felt wronged and was determined to "wear" the hurt all her life.

How tragic! No doubt God calls us away from bitterness because He knows how much it damages us. In fact, isn't that why God is so saddened by our wrongdoings, seeing how much we're hurting ourselves?

Today, choose what to make of your circumstances.

—FRANA HAMILTON

Work with the Worker

"...Put into action God's saving work in your lives, obeying God with deep reverence and fear. For God is working in you, giving you the desire to obey him and the power to do what pleases him."

PHILIPPIANS 2:12–13

It's about this time of year that I see how well my New Year's weight loss and exercise plans are going. Either I've faithfully counted calories and worked out and can see the results or I haven't. Just one look in the mirror of me wearing last season's shorts and T-shirts says it all.

Sometimes I need to recommit to the program, especially when I can't see much improvement.

When we're disturbed about the fact that our faithful service seems to produce few tangible results, we can stop to consider: What long-term effects may come of this that will be a greater blessing than the satisfaction of meeting a short-term quota?

After all, many "jobs" may not show immediate results—like child-rearing, teaching a Sunday school class, or working with your husband on a stronger marriage. And a time of boredom or dissatisfaction can be good for us. How else could we develop patience, perseverance, and hopefulness, the true building blocks of Christian faith?

Christ is the real Worker behind every Christian work.

—CMW

All Things New

"The one sitting on the throne said,
'Look, I am making all things new!'"
REVELATION 21:5

Inspecting my face in the mirror, I noticed the crow's feet looking more pronounced, and the wrinkles around my mouth were deeper. I applied night cream, which I hoped would work wonders on my face as I slept.

According to the Bible, God does much more than even the most expensive beauty-cream "magic." He can make us completely new, inside and out. In fact, the verse above shows that God is making us new, even as our bodies age.

How does He do it? He stirs our hearts to read the Bible and pray. He gives us role models to show us how to live in joy and health. He gives us family and friends who love us. And He gives us opportunities to share all of His love and kindness with others. What rejuvenating effects it all works on our spirit! A few wrinkles hardly seem to matter.

Let God renew you from the inside out.

—JANE HEITMAN

No Place Better

"The Lord continued, 'Stand here
on this rock beside me.'"
EXODUS 33:21

For fourteen years I took my first graders to the Cincinnati Zoo.
One of the great attractions was the Nocturnal House, home to
after-dark creatures. As we entered the shadowy corridor, some
little one would always ask, "Teacher, can I stand by you?" Soon
a small hand would clasp mine tightly as we moved on.

Moses had just come from a mountaintop experience
where he received the Ten Commandments. But what a letdown for him when he reached the valley below! There his
people frolicked before a golden idol. At that point God began
to encourage Moses, giving him a special place to stand.

Have you experienced that closeness to God, that solid
Rock beneath your feet when all your world seems quite
unsteady? I'm simply amazed that the King of the Universe
beckons a mere human, "Come and stand by me."

But where else would I rather be?

When God calls, run to His side.

—GWEN RICE CLARK

There's Still Time for Her

"He does not want anyone to perish,
so he is giving more time for everyone to repent."
1 PETER 3:9

Someone once said of an acquaintance, "She's no failure; she's not dead yet." In other words, while there is still breath, there is always opportunity for a radical turnaround in life's direction.

Some people view their lives as a whole, single experience that can be summed up now and then as either a failure or a success. But others view life as a multitude of different, single experiences. The only need is to enter into each experience as it comes, and to live it to the fullest for God's glory. What kind of person are you?

Would Jesus recommend the one-thing-at-a-time view? In this view, of course, no one could ever be labeled "a failure" while still alive. Repentance, renewed faith, astounding success—they're all possible. Starting now.

*Remember that, while there is still life,
every life is redeemable.*

—CMW

/Making /Music

"Then you will sing psalms and hymns and
spiritual songs among yourselves, making music
to the Lord in your hearts."
EPHESIANS 5:19

I can identify only a few birds by their calls. The meadowlark
and canyon wren provide melody to my footsteps when I'm out
for a walk, so I know those. At home, robins call, "Cheer up,"
and mourning doves sigh. I recognize these feathery friends
instantly.

But one day a bird I'd never heard visited my feeder. It
perched on the post singing a brilliant aria. A birder friend
identified it as a yellow warbler. I thanked God for the bird's
beautiful song and the lift it gave my heart.

When we sing psalms, hymns, and spiritual songs, God
draws us closer to Himself and to one another. We are reminded
how great God is. We sing about His majesty, love, mercy, forgiveness, peace, power, and comfort. These songs lift our spirits
above our earthly concerns and focus them on our Creator—
and our fellow creatures who know Him too.

Sharing music with others shares God's greatness with them.

—JANE HEITMAN

The Right Answer

"All is meaningless,"
says the Teacher, "utterly meaningless."
ECCLESIASTES 12:1

In Ecclesiastes, the Teacher was making a case for life's apparent meaninglessness. It's easy to do: Just focus on one achievement or acquisition at a time, as he did, and try to make it ultimately satisfying.

It never works. There is always a letdown.

And there are two possible responses to the problem. One is to say, "There is no meaning to be found, anywhere; for I have tried everything."

The other response is, "This desire for meaning, combined with its absence among the things of earth, means it must be found somewhere else." This seems to be the Teacher's ultimate conclusion (if you read to the end of his book).

So think it over: If you were to rank the good "things" of your life according to how much you look to them for fulfillment, how would your list look?

Ultimate meaning in life can come only from above.

—CMW

Enjoy–and Give

"This is the day the Lord has made.
We will rejoice and be glad in it."
PSALM 118:24

I searched for tomatoes in our vegetable garden this morning, planning to make soup. Humming the praise song "God Is So Good," I stooped down to gather the ruby red globes whose stalks bent low to the ground.

I sensed the Lord smiling down on me as I filled my basket and headed toward the house. The late summer sun caressed my neck, and if I had been a little younger, I would have skipped along the path to the kitchen door.

I paused as I reached the threshold: *Can I rightly be joyful in a world wrestled to its knees by war, disease, and poverty?*

It's true that I'm undeserving of God's blessings, loved by pure grace alone. But surely it would be wrong not to accept His gifts with a glad heart. And surely it would only be right to help salve the ills around me, starting with my neighbor this very day.

Be thankful for what you have, and willing to give it away.

—BETTY JANE HEWITT

Oh, for a Cleaning!

"No matter how deep the stain of your sins,
I can remove it. I can make you as clean as
freshly fallen snow. Even if you are stained as
red as crimson, I can make you as white as wool."
ISAIAH 1:18

"You're getting warmer," I told my oldest daughter as she crawled out from behind a wing chair and paused in front of the fireplace. It was Easter morning, and Kate was the only one of our girls still hunting for her basket. I always tried to come up with new hiding places each year, and I was pleased with the unique spot I'd found for hers.

"I see it," said Kate, reaching into the fireplace. Her face fell, and I cringed as we looked at her basket of soggy candy. It was covered with black spots and droplets of moisture. Even the yellow bow was stained and droopy. I hugged Kate, apologizing. It had rained overnight, and the flue had been left open. Over breakfast our family talked about Mommy's mistake.

"My candy's ruined," said Kate. "Too bad Jesus can't wash it clean like He did to us when He died on the cross."

Out of the mouths of babes come wise words.

—BETTY RAY HUNTER

Suffering

"The LORD asked Satan, 'Have you noticed my servant Job? He is the finest man in all the earth—a man of complete integrity. He fears God and will have nothing to do with evil. And he has maintained his integrity, even though you persuaded me to harm him without cause.'"

JOB 2:3

Ouch! When we're hurting we usually try to discover the reason for our pain. That's a wise move when mysterious agonies wrack our bodies. At those times, we need to see the doctor.

But the question of suffering goes deeper: Why does it exist at all, especially in a world God loves? Job wrangled with God and his friends about this but never received a straightforward answer. Consider God's amazing statement regarding Job's suffering in the verse above. What is said there about *the reason?*

Actually, the reason remained a mystery to Job. Yet he learned of God's greatness and wisdom—a lesson more valuable than anything else. We could say that his pain had some good effects—it grew his own soul, and it called onlookers to be compassionate people.

Will your sufferings this year have redemptive results that go beyond the question "why"?

—CMW

Soothing the Anger

"If your enemies are hungry, give them food to eat.
If they are thirsty, give them water to drink.
You will heap burning coals on their heads,
and the LORD will reward you."
PROVERBS 25:21–22

My brand-new neighbor proceeded to vent a profane rage at me for trying to clobber her cat with my broom (well, the ornery thing *had* bitten and scratched me when I tried to pet him). For sure, stroking a strange cat was not a brilliant idea. But he was, after all, squirming belly-up on my porch. In pain, I wanted to blast back at the hollering woman, but a sudden sense of calm stopped my angry words.

I turned away to doctor my wounds, and when morning came, I baked a prune cake. While it was still warm, I took it next door and rang my neighbor's bell.

Her expression said, "You want more, huh?" Until she saw the cake. "Why would you do this for me?" she asked through tears.

But wasn't I doing it for myself as well?

When anger simmers, try cooking!

—IMOGENE JOHNSON

Feel His Caring

"Then Bildad the Shuhite replied to Job:
'How long will you go on like this?
Your words are a blustering wind.'"
JOB 8:1–2

"Oh, don't feel that way!"

That's how Susan's mother always responded whenever Susan shared a little bit of emotion. If Susan spoke of anger, sadness, or fear in her life, it was always a similar reply from Mom.

Isn't this the way Job's "comforters" treated their suffering friend? Clearly Bildad (in the verse above) wanted Job to stop emoting.

But it doesn't work that way. We can't just turn our feelings on and off. And especially with others we care about, we need to listen to how it is with them, the real story. Then we can respond in ways that draw them out.

For example, suppose someone close to you says, "Whenever you get that preachy tone, it makes me angry."

How would you reply?

God works within our emotions as well as in our minds.

—CMW

While You Have Me

"Believe in the light while there is still time;
then you will become children of the light."
JOHN 12:36

I have retinitis pigmentosa, a degenerative disease of the retina. As my vision slips into darkness, I am becoming fascinated with light. All the bulbs in my house must be at least 75 watts, the better for me to read. My kitchen appliances, even the floor, is white.

The floor, though, must be mopped daily to wash away the stains my family tracks on it. You see, white reflects the light but catches the dirt.

Each night before falling asleep, I recite the Scriptures I have committed to memory. I follow Ephesians 5:8 with today's verse. My Bible references the Ephesians verse back to John 12:36. Rightly so, as both verses talk about the light of Jesus. It is this light that fascinates me the most. Thankfully, I do not have to see in order to luxuriate in its brightness.

May you bring light to a darkening world today.

—NITA WALKER FRAZIER

My So-Called Dinner

"Laughter can conceal a heavy heart."
PROVERBS 14:13

I put my best foot forward and fell right over it. We'd moved to a small rural town where we had neither relatives nor friends, but the church members there were friendly, and some quickly invited us for dinner.

I felt obliged to return the favor, so I mailed an invitation and went shopping. At the market, I asked the meat-counter attendant how to prepare the brisket I'd selected. Then I clipped a recipe for a luscious-looking cake from the local paper.

Reckoning day came, however—the day of brisket tougher than jerky, and a cake recipe that had apparently omitted the crucial word "self-rising."

After my so-called dinner, I wanted to cry. But my new friend told of her own dinner fiasco—which somehow managed to top mine.

Isn't friendship wonderful? And isn't laughter an excellent cushion if you must fall on your face?

To maintain your sanity, maintain a sense of the ridiculous.

—IMOGENE JOHNSON

Awesome Appreciation

"He must become greater and greater,
and I must become less and less."
JOHN 3:30

Have you ever begun a casual conversation with another woman, and after a few minutes you suddenly realized, this lady is *important?* Perhaps you thought, "I wish I'd known she was an Olympic gold medalist." Or, "So she was once a state senator!"

You quickly felt a bit humbled, right?

In our desire to make humility a virtue in our lives, one thing works quite well: getting a clearer picture of who God is, day after day. The truer our picture of Him, the larger He becomes and the smaller we see ourselves. That's how it was for John the Baptist in our verse above.

True humility comes from recognizing who God is. Not that we shrink in self-esteem. Rather, we are humbled by His love for us—and grow in confidence as His Spirit leads us through life.

*To grow in humility, grow in your
appreciation of God's awesomeness.*

—CMW

Good Reasons for Life's Delays

"God has made everything
beautiful for its own time."
ECCLESIASTES 3:11

Nine men were trapped underground for days in a flooded
Pennsylvania mine. The rescue crew quickly started using a
1,500-pound drill, but the bit broke, and rescue efforts were
stalled for an additional eighteen hours. The men underground,
now in the deafening silence, could only wait.

What seemed tragic at the time turned out to be a blessing. Experts later revealed that the huge drill bit would have
poked into the small airhole the men were using to breathe;
water would have cascaded in and drowned them. The
eighteen-hour delay gave the water time to subside, allowing all
the men—eventually—to be saved!

Our waiting times are excruciating—and usually for a
reason. We cannot possibly know what God is up to when all
seems silent. We can know, however, that He wills our best—
and stays ever so close.

God's timing has a perfection that's beautiful.

—JACKIE M. JOHNSON

Personal Reply Required

"Jesus and his disciples left Galilee and
went up to the villages of Caesarea Philippi.
As they were walking along, he asked them,
'Who do people say I am?'"
MARK 8:27

Have you noticed the incredible diversity in the church today? Just a glance through the religion section of your local newspaper will convince you of our differences. What a variety of services, ministry styles, and forms of discipleship!

But in the midst of all this variety, the foundation of unity remains. It has to do with how we all answer the ancient question once directed to the apostle Peter: "Who do you say I am?" We can differ on worship styles, administrative procedures, and evangelism methods. But we must be clear about the person of Jesus. He is "the Christ, the Son of the living God." For his response, Peter was blessed by the Lord Himself.

Do you want that blessing too? Then consider: Who is Jesus, for you, right now?

Let God reveal the truth in faith,
and know Jesus personally.

—CMW

True Reflection

"If you keep looking steadily into God's
perfect law—the law that sets you free—and if
you do what it says and don't forget what you heard,
then God will bless you for doing it."

JAMES 1:25

As I stood outside the dressing room waiting for my grand-daughter to try on school clothes, I glimpsed my image in the mirror at the end of the hallway. How slim I looked!

It's true, I've lost a few pounds recently. But in that mirror, I appeared positively svelte.

Then I looked again . . . and began to suspect the dreadful presence of "reflection deception." Was this amazing body-slimming piece of glass purposefully placed simply to increase sales? (After all, if I'd been the one trying on clothes, and had seen myself in an outfit that made me look twenty pounds lighter, I'd probably buy it.)

Thankfully, the Word of God doesn't distort my image. The Bible "tells it like it is" so I can become my best self, the self God created me to be. All I have to do is keep looking, steadily looking, day by day.

*Look into the Word today with
open eyes and attentive heart.*

—JEAN DAVIS

Be Where You Are

"I am nothing—how could I ever find the answers?
I will put my hand over my mouth in silence."
JOB 40:4

Ever stood perfectly still in a place of light, silence, and openness? I stood on a Colorado mountain ridge overlooking a vast plain—and felt I could stay there forever.

I listened to the birds, and that was all.

What does it take not to just listen to the sounds of the birds but to *be there* with them? What does it mean to be where you are?

I have a friend who tells me, "Where you is, is where you is." She's trying to make the point that if I'm always on my cell phone, I'm somewhere else. If I'm videotaping my experience, I'm not truly *having* the experience. As strange as it sounds, we should practice this: Be where you are!

If I can, I'll break out of this room sometime today and take a walk. I'll look for light and space and open my soul for a morsel of peace.

God is present to you; be present to Him.

—CMW

Lucky

"He orders his angels to protect you wherever you go."
PSALM 91:11

I liked everything about my new job working evenings—everything but the thirteen-mile drive home on a deserted road. "Don't drive that road without a gun," a policeman advised me. But I didn't own a gun, nor would I know how to use one. And . . . Couldn't I rely on God's angels for protection?

One night as I sped through the darkness, I heard a flapping sound—a flat tire. I pulled over and noticed I'd parked beside an automobile proving field. As I pondered what to do, headlights began to weave across the field toward me. At the gate, a lone figure got out of his car. "Lucky I just finished my shift," the security guard said as he began changing my tire.

Luck? I prefer, "Heavenly blessing." Or perhaps, "Angelic protection."

Call on the angels. They're everywhere,
but they don't always wear white robes.

—JEWELL JOHNSON

Shy Is Okay

"'Who am I to appear before Pharaoh?'
Moses asked God. 'How can you expect me
to lead the Israelites out of Egypt?'"
EXODUS 3:11

Moses was shy. But is that so bad?

A few years ago, I was looking for a church to attend. I had heard about certain "dynamic" preachers in the area and thought I might listen to a sermon or two.

No matter how many well-crafted and inspiring messages I heard, though, I kept going back to the other preachers. They were the ones whose typically less-than-polished presentations still gave me the impression that they had traveled down paths of life that I, too, had journeyed. I sensed that they still had a bit of shyness left inside.

It's not the dynamic person who speaks to my heart. It is the person in touch with the rhythms of her own heart, in touch with an inner life that makes contact with my own. How delightful!

Introvert or extrovert, affirm your approach to life.

—CMW

MAY

A MOTHER'S DAY GIFT

"He gives the barren woman a home, so that
she becomes a happy mother. Praise the Lord."

PSALM 113:9

*S*HE WAS JUST SIXTEEN, A JUNIOR IN A FLORIDA high school, not really ready for marriage but destined for motherhood just the same. A new law permitted her to legally end her pregnancy, but she said no. Her doctor suggested adoption.

Four thousand miles away in Hawaii, my husband and I sat weighing our options. Many painful, invasive tests revealed that adoption was our only hope to be parents. But waiting lists were long and limited to in-state residents. The nature of my husband's work required frequent moves. Another transfer came through—one that brought us to the town of the young girl.

A small redbrick church just down the road from our temporary apartment beckoned us to worship that first Sunday morning. Later, when the minister came to call, we surprised ourselves by confiding our deep desire to adopt. We'd never lived in one place long enough to qualify, but we still had hope. The pastor and the people seemed warm and friendly. We felt right at home—and they became our family away from home.

After the Mother's Day service that spring, the minister pulled us aside to meet with him in his office.

"Sorry to keep you waiting," he said a few moments later. His large brown eyes radiated kindness and warmth, seasoned with a touch of childlike excitement. Under his thick red moustache, I thought I saw a piece of a grin. "Now tell me," he began, as the grin accelerated to a smile, "do you still want to adopt?"

Jim and I were amazed by a string of divine coincidence. The minister knew a nurse. The nurse knew the young girl's doctor. One of our neighbors knew a lawyer who had just adopted and would be willing to help.

Like the final stages of birth, once everything is ready, events tend to happen rapidly. Late one Friday afternoon, the telephone rang. All the years of waiting telescoped into one golden moment when the speaker said, "Mr. and Mrs. Swearingen, you are now the parents of a healthy baby girl." On Monday, we could take her home.

Two grateful hearts bursting with praise entered our little church that Sunday morning. A red rose on the altar caught my eye—the traditional symbol of new life in a church family. I wondered who might be sharing a birthday with "our" baby.

I wasn't to know. The sunlight streamed through the stained-glass windows. As the organist finished the prelude, our pastor stood, and the room fell silent. For a brief moment he studied that rose on the altar. At last he spoke: "Friends, this little rose is a mystery. No one here knows where it came from or whom it represents. However, we give thanks for its beauty." We stood to tell our story.

—MARCIA SWEARINGEN

Following the Call

"They wept together, and Orpah kissed her
mother-in-law good-bye. But Ruth insisted on
staying with Naomi. . . . 'Your people will be
my people, and your God will be my God.'"
RUTH 1:14, 16

"Mom, I just love college!" Our younger daughter, Rhea, bounced through the front door on her second trip home from school.

Only two weeks earlier, her older sister and I drove out of state to move items into the dorm room. The first day, without warning, Rhea lay down on the bed in front of us and began to cry.

When offered a hug, she said, "No, don't hug me, I'll cry more!"

The very next day she was back to her old self, introducing herself to students and making friends wherever she went. These would be "her people" from now on.

While it is hard to leave home, our daughter knows she was called to this particular college. As she walks close to the Lord, I hope she will thrive there and even find ways to serve Him.

*When answering God's call, we may need to leave behind
the familiar and go into the unknown.*

—LaRose Karr

An Accomplished, Heartless Woman

"'Are you the king of Israel or not?' Jezebel asked. 'Get up and eat and don't worry about it. I'll get you Naboth's vineyard!' So she wrote letters in Ahab's name, sealed them with his seal, and sent them to the elders and other leaders of the city where Naboth lived."

1 KINGS 21:7, 8

Why can't I accomplish more? The question haunts me often. It's usually attached to some form of guilty "should." Do you feel it too? In your career, or in your family life, you have nagging feelings that you should be doing something else, definitely something *more*. If not something great, if not something world-changing, well . . . something . . . at least mildly significant?

Would it be all right to declare a moratorium on "doing" for a while, until we get heavily into "becoming" as the prelude to doing? My friend Elizabeth, who is a counselor, once said to me, "We forget the miracle of who we are; we're stuck in a culture that rewards getting ahead, but offers no incentive for getting a heart."

Beware becoming an accomplished, heartless woman. Jezebel had absolutely no boundaries on her ambition. Sadly, her name became synonymous with everything you don't want to be.

Stop for a moment this day to ask,
How is my heart becoming?

—CMW

Bright Treasures of Darkness

"[God] reveals deep and mysterious things
and knows what lies hidden in darkness."
DANIEL 2:22

When my fourth-grade teacher distributed the fat black crayons, instructing us to completely blacken out our artwork, I balked. Paisley rainbows filled my paper—alongside flower petals, feathers, and stars. I loved my picture just as it was, so why blot it out?

I didn't know we'd be scratching through the greasy, opaque layer with popsicle sticks, and that I'd see my beautiful colors wondrously reappearing with each stroke.

Discouragement often extinguishes what we love. It snuffs out mystery and wonder. Maybe a parent dismisses our passions, a teacher criticizes our creativity, even our friends misunderstand our dreams. Such events seem to deface our original, God-given palette still glowing beneath. Let's peel them all away! Like colored scarves pulled from a clown's sleeve, if we're willing, God will draw out our pain as well as our buried yearnings.

If gloom has overlaid your hopes,
wait upon God to reveal what's underneath.

—LAURIE KLEIN

You're in It Too

"Since we are surrounded by such a huge crowd of witnesses
to the life of faith, let us strip off every weight that slows us
down, especially the sin that so easily hinders our progress.
And let us run with endurance the race that God has set
before us."

HEBREWS 12:1

Our family loves its photo albums. Those myriad pictures of the
past remind us of what's important in life and teach us how to
live in the future.

How do they do it? The albums tell the stories of parental
pride as we walked down graduation aisles. They show us learning teamwork as we scored the winning soccer goal—or didn't.
They record the images of generations of ancestors who sacrificed everything to give their children the best they could.

Our Bible, too, is much like a family album, isn't it? It surrounds us with the history of our faith-ancestors, just as if they
were looking on to see how we will run forth with the message. So next time you find yourself paging through your own
family's photo album, why not also reach for the album of God's
family? I'm confident you'll see yourself on every page.

You are not alone in the race of faithful endurance.

—LISA M. KONZEN

Blessings in Grief

"Jesus wept."
JOHN 11:35

My father was so sick, ailing with several life-threatening diseases in his last days. I cried about him during those days.

Was Jesus there with me? Yes, He knows grief and even weeps. And I am sure that somehow, even in grief, the Lord is working within me for spiritual growth. At the very least, painful events in my life produce in me pity and compassion. And the world could do with a few more ounces of those holy virtues. I can't help but feel for, and love, my fellow sufferers.

If God is at work in our sufferings, then it is the work of love-production. Yes, perhaps God is always at work for a bit more compassion in the world—starting with me.

God is at work in all the circumstances
of our lives—even the painful ones.

—CMW

Striving for Truth

"I cling to your decrees.
Lord, don't let me be put to shame!"
PSALM 119:31

My Mary was a good student who worked hard for every good grade. Once when she was in fourth grade, she took a math test and quickly jotted all the right answers. The teacher graded her paper just as quickly and, shoving it under Mary's nose, snarled, "You cheated." The bell rang, and Mary raced home to tell me what had happened.

I was furious. Though she was only nine, I knew Mary's young character was as beautiful as her innocent, tear-stained face. "Come on, honey," I said, "let's go see Mrs. Jones."

My children aren't perfect, but I was convinced Mary just didn't have it in her to cheat or lie. I didn't have to talk very long before Mrs. Jones was convinced too.

Years later, Mary laughingly recounted the episode. Then, hugging me, she added quietly, "Mom, even to this day, I've tried to live up to your faith in me. Thank you."

God and mothers know their children's hearts.

—MARILYN KREYER

Healing Touch

"He touched her, and instantly she could stand straight.
How she praised and thanked God!"
LUKE 13:3

What works best when you need help or consoling? A few choice words of pithy advice? A well-stated admonition? A systematic review of the reasons why you might feel downhearted?

It's likely that none of these methods will reach in and soothe your aching heart the way a wordless touch can. Warm contact helps heal the part of us that does not respond to mere reason. Words certainly have their place in our relationships. But there is a time and place, too, for the wordless touch.

We won't be able to demand that kind of touch from anyone today. However, the great thing about touching is that when we are open to giving it, we often find it coming our way, too, usually just when we need it.

Be alert to a friend or a child who
needs your gentle touch today.

—CMW

Women Who Fluff Too Much

"Now let your unfailing love comfort me,
just as you promised me, your servant."
PSALM 119:76

Okay, I'll admit it; I have a thing about pillows. Sofas, beds, chairs—at my house, pillows abound there in different sizes, textures, and patterns. I've even arranged as many as nine against our headboard. But who's counting when it comes to comfort?

Inevitably, guests adjust them, kids toss them, my husband crams them beneath bad knees. Fido nips a cushion's corner, trailing stuffing. But I like to keep them just right. Not that I begrudge anyone comfort, but I also want order restored. My order. (I wonder, is there a Decorators Anonymous?)

Isn't it so often the minor irritations that leave our emotions threadbare? And sometimes it's much easier to focus on things than on people. That's when our priorities, like my scattered pillows, can use a gentle rearranging.

*Our Comforter, the Spirit, invites us to lie back,
breathe deep, rest awhile.*

—LAURIE KLEIN

When There Are No Words

"We don't even know what we should pray for, nor how
we should pray. But the Holy Spirit prays for us with
groanings that cannot be expressed in words."
ROMANS 8:26

I sit in my favorite chair this morning with hands lifted in
praise. What is going through my mind? I'm not quite sure.

This is a moment to remind myself: Many prayers need
no words. My life with the Great Listener goes far beyond my
ability to formulate grammatically correct sentences. Or to dig
deep into my soul to describe with verbs and adjectives, as best
I can, what I know and want and feel.

God's Spirit is a hearer of our souls. And when we choose
to unveil them, our souls are always revealed before the All-
Knowing in a pristine purity of truth. Our job is simply to
recognize that we are engaged in a remarkable celestial conversation every moment of every day. Even now.

Let your prayers of the heart
never stop engaging God's mind.

—CMW

Can You Hear Me Now?

"The LORD hears his people when they call to him
for help. He rescues them from all their troubles."
PSALM 34:17

My friend told her young son it was time for his nap. "Papaw,"
he called, as he started to cry. "Papaw!" Trevor's grandfather
was hundreds of miles away, but he knew if anyone could keep
him from his mother's proposed nap, it was his beloved Papaw.

Throughout the Scriptures, we read of many who called
out to the Heavenly Father when needing help. The Hebrews
called when Pharaoh and his army were chasing them, King
David called when the guilt of adultery and murder slammed
into his soul, and the ten lepers called when they needed a
touch on their physical bodies.

Unlike Trevor's Papaw, God is always within hearing distance when we call. Problem is, will we pick up the phone
and dial?

God promises to hear whenever we call out to Him.

—PAMELA J. KUHN

Geographically Incompatible!

"The kingdom of God is within you."
LUKE 17:21 (NIV)

My husband and I have lived in three different states over the years: Florida, Illinois, and Colorado. Each has its unique benefits and attractions, along with its own specific drawbacks. I love the tropics, but my husband Gary says he "hates to sweat." He loves the mountains and deserts. We've joked that we're "geographically incompatible."

It seems to be human nature to seek the just-right place to settle down. But where is "just right"—that magical place of satisfaction we're looking for?

It's always around the next corner, over the next hill, tied to the next promotion, waiting to be revealed during the next vacation, sure to blossom out of the next relationship. It's "out there," and we're headed toward it, surely!

Yet Jesus said, "The kingdom of God is within you." "Just right" isn't out there somewhere; it is deep within.

Seek to live from the inside out.

—CMW

A Special Place

"It is right that I should feel as I do about all of you,
for you have a very special place in my heart."
PHILIPPIANS 1:7

My friend Kim stopped by my office one Monday morning and
asked whether I'd like to go out for lunch. Talking it over, we
agreed to meet at a local restaurant.

"Kim, you will appreciate this story," I said as I took a seat
in the booth with her. While we began digging into icy shrimp
cocktail, I told her what had happened over the weekend with my
teenage son. Kim laughed and shared a few stories of her own.

That simple meal brightened my day, and the afternoon
went much smoother, our lunch being a refreshing break from
an overly busy morning.

I am once again reminded how pleasant it is to sit with a
friend and share family stories. The more we share with any
other person, the deeper our bonds of relationship will grow.
Then some very special heart-places form within us both.

*Our friendships act as anchors—not only
for storms but in life's calm waters too.*

—LaRose Karr

Chasing Contentment

"No matter how much we see, we are never satisfied.
No matter how much we hear, we are not content."
ECCLESIASTES 1:8

I don't know who said it, but it makes a lot of sense to me: Happiness isn't something you *experience*; it's something you *remember*. That is, it comes after the fact, always. It is a result rather than a goal. Paradoxically, usually it is the result of striving for a goal that focuses attention away from ourselves.

To become totally involved in pursuing our passions, rather than our happiness, brings us to the point, later, in which we realize that we have—surprise!—reached a state of peace and contentment. The poster on my office wall, with words by Nathaniel Hawthorne, puts it so well: "Happiness is like a butterfly; the more you pursue it, the more it eludes you. But when you turn your attention to other things, it comes, and sits gently on your shoulder."

Let happiness land where it will,
in its own time and place.

—CMW

When Is It a Touch?

"I will comfort you as a child is
comforted by his mother."
ISAIAH 66:13

My grandson, Ethan, is cutting teeth, and his mommy has sought out every pain-relieving remedy. We've joked that she could write a *Teething for Dummies* book. She just wants to do everything possible to ease the little guy's pain. She'll use icy teething rings, gum-numbing gel, or a distracting bright toy. When those don't bring relief, all Melanie can do is hold Ethan tightly and gently rock him.

God is spirit, so we can't feel a physical touch from Him. Yet He still comforts us as a mother does. He uses the kind words of our friends, the encouraging biblical stories of others who endured pain and emerged stronger. He even uses the distraction of beautiful displays in nature.

But when our hearts are still aching, God may well use our emotions, our imaginations, our sense of presence. In fact, are such forms of comfort so very different from a physical touch after all?

*Jesus did touch us humans—even
physically—and He will soon return.*

—PAMELA J. KUHN

Guilt: True or False?

"Jesus stood up again and said to her, 'Where are your accusers? Didn't even one of them condemn you?'

"'No, Lord,' she said. And Jesus said, 'Neither do I. Go and sin no more.'"
JOHN 8:10–11

My friend Sherry is saying things like this: "I worry that everybody is down on me, ready to exact their punishment for . . . I don't know what. I just feel guilty all the time, like I have to keep justifying my right to even exist."

Danger here! A woman in the throes of false guilt is not just aware of wrong-*doing,* but of wrong-*being.* That kind of feeling can get so bad that it becomes a prime motivation for truly self-destructive behaviors. I must stay close to my friend today.

With true guilt, when we have admitted our wrongs and experienced forgiveness, the guilt is resolved. But it takes great courage to go on and confront the feeling of wrong-being, of worthlessness at the core of our character. But believe me, it's worth the work.

*For just a few moments, let yourself
feel the freedom of being guilt-free.*

—CMW

Look Up!

"She had been bent double for eighteen years
and was unable to stand up straight. . . . Then [Jesus]
touched her, and instantly she could stand straight.
How she praised and thanked God!"
LUKE 13:11, 13

I felt like a rusted hinge. So I tried a low-impact exercise class. Crouched on all fours, our instructor said, "It's good for your heart if you spend time on your hands and knees." Apparently, our hearts pump better when hanging free in the rib cage; with more oxygen, energy and endurance increases. I smiled, reminded that kneeling in prayer fortifies hearts, too. Although our bodies may not bow that far, our spirits can. Scrubbing floors or picking up toys—when coupled with prayer—doubly benefits us.

That day I walked home a little taller before reading about the bent-over woman in Luke 13. I like to imagine her name was Hope. Looking down for so many years, did she sense that one day she'd look up into a brand-new life? That is how I want to live each day, even when my faith seems firmly enmeshed in the dust.

No matter the view ahead,
God invites us to exercise hope.

—LAURIE KLEIN

Those Helpful "Don'ts"

"Do not commit adultery."
EXODUS 20:14

I once saw a cartoon showing Moses just returned from Mount Sinai with the stone Ten Commandments in his hands. He's reporting his encounter with God on the mountaintop: "It was hard bargaining—we get the milk and honey, but the anti-adultery clause stays in."

But must a life of faith be a series of hard-bargaining rounds? It's true that some things are clearly wrong and a number of "anti-" clauses must stay put. Yet some people think God sighs with disappointment when His creatures have a little fun.

That's a contrast to my sense of who God is. I've been surprised at how much joy flows from the pages of Scripture—pure fun: singing, dancing, shouting, playing, making music. Surely God smiles at our joy. The "don'ts" are all about keeping us from ruining our own party!

*Can you see God's commands as an
invitation to live a happier life?*

—CMW

Heavenly Reminders

"He lifted me out of the pit of despair, out
of the mud and the mire. He set my feet on solid
ground and steadied me as I walked along."
PSALM 40:2

It is mid-October, and the petunias outside our front door are now robust bushes of beautiful blossoms. Previously, due to the summer's record-breaking rainfall, their spindly stalks and limp buds seemed to defy any future life. Now, in the middle of fall, with the welcome arrival of the sun, they are bursting with vitality.

I've felt a kinship with these scrawny plants because this past summer had brought an excess of "rain" into my life, as well. The resilience of the petunias encouraged me as I doggedly fought simply to exist in the midst of the storm. Now looking down at my personal rainbow of purple, soft yellow, and dusty pink, I have renewed hope. I can sense God's comforting presence, and I know my time to blossom will surely come.

God always creates a path through the difficult places.

—CAROL ANN LANDIS

Foretaste of Heaven

"From Mount Zion, the perfection of beauty,
God shines in glorious radiance."
PSALM 50:2

"Yes!" Another moment of perfection. Working as a radio DJ, I really got a charge out of engineering the perfect segue between one song's end and the beginning of the next song. When everything came together in perfect, split-second timing, wow! It was heavenly.

When have you experienced a moment of perfection? Maybe you rang the high notes in a choir competition. Perhaps you nailed a difficult gymnastic landing and felt "in the zone" of athletic perfection. Perhaps you'd just cut a perfect camellia from your garden and set the single bloom in your best crystal vase. Yes! Perfection.

At that very moment, God's radiant glory cuts through life's everyday fog, and our hearts ache for more.

*Cherish those moments when something
heavenly graces your daily routine.*

—CMW

Where Will He Reside?

"You must love the Lord your God with all
your heart, all your soul, and all your mind."
MATTHEW 22:37

I was putting up my Nativity set when one of the figures fell to
the floor. I knelt sadly beside the broken pieces; it was the baby
Jesus who lay broken.

What meaning does my manger have if my Savior isn't
there? What meaning does my existence have without His
presence at the center of it?

He is so much more than a figure in a Nativity set. He
dwells here within me, right now, to lead me, to be a real and
personal friend.

My grandsons, Jordan and Jared, held the pieces together
in their fingers, and I glued. They seemed intent on rescuing
the glass figure and putting it back into the manger. Will these
boys grow in eagerness over the years to keep the Savior at the
center of their lives?

In the deepest part of our being—there He is!

—JOYCE ROBERTS LOTT

Collecting Treasures

"Mary quietly treasured these things in her
heart and thought about them often."
LUKE 2:19

When my husband and I got married, we moved far away from
our parents but visited when we could. One summer when we
were back home with our three children, we decided to play
baseball in my parents' backyard. While we were laughing, having fun, being silly, I looked over to see my mother sitting on
the porch.

I recognized the longing on her face. And I knew what she
was doing—recording the moment so she could have a clear
memory to sustain her until our next visit.

My children are now grown, and when they come home to
see us, I find myself collecting memories of precious moments
with them. Sometimes I stand back from the activity and simply watch, taking it all in. Then, on those days when I miss
them most, I can pull out a happy event from the treasure I've
stored.

Let us treasure each moment with our loved ones.

—JEAN DAVIS

Reframe

"I don't mean to say that I have already achieved these things or that I have already reached perfection! But I keep working toward that day when I will finally be all that Christ Jesus saved me for and wants me to be."

PHILIPPIANS 3:12

"You have the right to make mistakes," said my friend, "and to make them your teachers." What a great way to put it!

Rather than wallow in guilt, probably the best thing we can do now is to reframe our mistakes. Guilt keeps our minds focused on the original error and so compounds that error, over and over again, perhaps for an entire lifetime. What a waste of precious energy!

Reframing mistakes means determining to think about them in ways that dissolve their devastating qualities. Instead of seeing them as terrible disasters, we begin to view them as normal and natural results of the courage to make decisions and take risks.

I realize that I can and will make mistakes. But I'm learning to refuse to allow them to call into judgment my personal self-worth.

Your value to God always exceeds the sum of your mistakes.

—CMW

Eyes Turned to Me

"Thus hath the Lord dealt with me in the days wherein he looked on me, to take away my reproach among men."

LUKE 1:25 (KJV)

I was deeply distressed, wounded by the words of my brother. They were not meant to injure me; his words simply reflected his heartfelt understanding . . . and he was being faithful to what he believed. Nonetheless, it hurt.

A week after our painful conversation, as I entered the same building, I noticed an older woman seated at a small table across the large open room. She'd been there then and heard the wounding words; she would know what was going on now, the background, the details. While she would not agree with me, she would know I was aching inside.

From across the wide space our eyes met, and she smiled at me, warming the innermost recesses of my heart. It was a smiling, healing look, a gaze that today, years later, brings tears as I remember it. In her smile was the compassion of the Lord.

Look at one another with compassion
to see the grace of God.

—DEBBIE LOWE

Just Accept

"Take delight in the LORD, and he
will give you your heart's desires."
PSALM 37:4

I recently received one of those chain letters in the mail, the kind that promise tons of money if you only send your name on to the next person in line (along with a five-dollar bill). I know those letters are silly. But sometimes I sit and daydream about five-dollar bills overflowing my inbox. I'd be rich in no time! But phony schemes always hurt someone else in order for you to profit, and that's no way to satisfy my heart's desires.

A better approach calls me to a more trusting openness to life's way of gifting me beyond my shabby expectations. It is the releasing of the clamped teeth, the clenched fists, the hunkering down against a world I perceive as demanding and critical.

Really, can we ever do this: create a world of satisfaction for ourselves rather than receive our happiness as a gift from God?

*We are not the best qualified to
engineer our own happiness.*

—CMW

Wandering

"We have this hope as an anchor
for the soul, firm and secure."
HEBREWS 6:19A

We were waiting in a cafeteria line at one of the Smithsonian museums in Washington, D.C. My two-year-old son was holding on to my hand when he suddenly turned around and let go to get closer to his grandpa. But as he turned away from his daddy and me, he panicked. He couldn't see us anymore. Though Grandpa and Grandma were right there, he thought his parents had deserted him. The funny thing was, we were anchored to the spot; we never moved.

Sometimes we forget God's settled presence with us, this anchor for our souls. We turn away and panic because we think we've been left on our own. Has God indeed moved away when our need is the greatest?

No, God never moves away. In hindsight we may well see that we did some ill-advised wandering.

What is more enduring than the love of God for you?

—SUSAN LYTTEK

Crystallized Crisis

"Forgive the person who offends you. Remember, the
Lord forgave you, so you must forgive others."
COLOSSIANS 3:13

I mindlessly assembled the ingredients for my cup of tea, antici-
pating its sweet and soothing taste. Instead of forming a blissful
smile, my face contorted in a sour frown. Shaking the glass
sugar container again, I noticed a large, crystallized lump
blocking the opening.

As I reached for a knife to break up the crystals, the lump
reminded me of something else. I saw a lump of hurt and angry
feelings buried deep within my own heart. Sure, I had reasons
for my feelings, but as they gathered and clung together, they
created a hard-heartedness within me that I could no longer
ignore.

Slowly sipping my unsweetened tea, I pondered how a lump
of unconfessed sin could hinder the refreshing nourishment of
God's love in and through me. For the first time, I truly wanted
freedom from this pain. I asked Him, if need be, to break my
crystallized heart.

Broken by Love, you will be stronger than before.

—CAROL ANN LANDIS

On the Adventure

"May he grant your heart's desire
and fulfill all your plans."
PSALM 20:4

Suppose I choose to live a life of faith (which will involve plenty of risky decisions along the way), and I thereby miss out on all kinds of fun, fulfilling, satisfying things and experiences? At times, when I compare my life to a successful friend's life, I've wondered what I did wrong here. She's a star in the business spotlight; I'm working backstage. She's driving an expensive luxury vehicle, while my '91 Hyundai sits at the local Wal-Mart with a dead battery. Did I really sign up for this character-building adventure? That thought has crossed my mind occasionally. Are God's plans for us always in our very best interest? Couldn't we devise a more self-fulfilling life on our own? Yet, to be convinced of God's goodwill toward me is the only way I can be moved to live a life of holy risk, of faith in Him.

And where did I ever get the idea that God's will and mine must always be separate and necessarily at odds? Would it be possible to come to the blessed place in which I finally see that "what God gives" is exactly the same as "what is the very best for me"?

Celebrate God's involvement in the unfolding drama of your life's adventure.

—CMW

Rewriting

> "How can I curse those whom
> God has not cursed? How can I condemn those
> whom the LORD has not condemned?"
> NUMBERS 23:8

I was out of work. That, I could deal with. But I'd been fired without notice, and in spite of a good performance history, the company refused to pay my unemployment compensation.

Did I want to lash out? Yes. I had never been fired before; I was hurt and disillusioned. But shortly thereafter, I attended a Christian writers conference and heard a speaker make this point: "Good writers don't write, they rewrite." That hit home, and I could apply it to almost anything.

For instance, "Good Christians don't live the Christian example, they relive it." Or, "Good workers don't just find employment, they get re-employed." And by rethinking, we begin to see new possibilities.

I chose not to curse the injustice. I sought another position, and God used the difficulty to steer me into a job where my skills were put to better use. That, I could deal with!

Others may be at fault; we choose how to respond.

—SUSAN LYTTEK

Essential Advice

"There is a special rest still waiting for the people of God.
For all who enter into God's rest will find rest from their
labors, just as God rested after creating the world."
HEBREWS 4:9–10

"Take your base!" My son Dan, the Little League pitcher, had
loaded the bases—again. As his coach strolled out to the
mound, I imagined the advice: "Don't try to aim the ball, Dan.
Just let it go."

As every athlete knows, trying to force a shot or a throw
tightens the muscles, tenses the mind, raises the panic factor
("Suppose I miss!"), resulting in the classic "choke"—a wild
blunder. "Just relax" is much more than a polite word of advice;
it's an essential part of the game.

Maybe it's an essential part of life, overall. For example, my
role does not include forcing everything to work out okay for
me all the time. Ultimately, I'm not in control of the Constant
Happiness Department. Becoming more competent, clever, or
diligent has never guaranteed a steady peace of mind. Usually,
the biggest blessings have come by surprise.

What hard task might become easier
today with a little relaxation?

—CMW

The Power of Words

"The words of the wicked are like a murderous
ambush, but the words of the godly save lives."
PROVERBS 12:6

Beverly was ten years old and in the fifth grade. Her family was
in the lower income bracket in those days, so she wore skirts
fashioned from feed sacks.

One day, a girl sitting close to her in school told the teacher
that Beverly had taken ten cents from her desk. Instead of taking Beverly aside, the teacher accused her in front of the other
students with heart-stinging words.

Beverly was poor, but she wasn't a thief.

This verbal ambush happened fifty-five years ago, but it
created a hurt that has lasted through the years. Beverly long
ago forgave the teacher, but when she thinks of the fifth grade,
that painful memory blows through her mind like a chill
north wind.

God will help us to choose our words wisely.

—NORMA C. MEZOE

Danger to Come

"In the future you will see me, the Son of Man,
sitting at God's right hand in the place of power
and coming back on the clouds of heaven."
MATTHEW 26:64

In one of C. S. Lewis's fiction books for children, *The Lion, the Witch and the Wardrobe*, Aslan the Lion is a God figure. Little Lucy contemplates what it will be like to meet him, asking, "Is he . . . quite safe?"

The answer comes: "'Course he isn't safe. But he's good. He's the King, I tell you."

In another part of the book, we read, "At the name of Aslan, each one of the children felt something jump in his inside. Edmund felt a sensation of mysterious horror."

It makes me think: What is it about God, or the life God has given me—so risky and unsafe—that I need to face squarely today? Isn't it better to stay in direct contact with hard truth than to slide through life clinging to sentimental self-deceptions?

Jesus will return as Savior . . . and Judge.

—CMW

JUNE

THE BONUS CHILD

"Children are a gift from the Lord;
they are a reward from him."

PSALM 127:3

*A*H, JUNE—THE MONTH OF ORANGE BLOSSOMS and brides. When our daughter became a June bride, I sat in the front row of the chapel—crying. I was happy for the couple, but I had mixed emotions; our bonus child had grown up and was leaving home.

Three decades ago, when I had become pregnant at age forty-three, I hesitated to tell my friends. I could almost hear them thinking, *Don't they have enough kids to support? Now they're having their sixth one!* I was four months pregnant when I finally got up the nerve to tell a friend about the baby.

"Great," Mary said. "In a big family there's always enough for one more. Relax. This will be just fine."

Lee, my husband, also had a positive response. "This child will be our bonus baby. Just wait and see," he said with a twinkle in his eye.

"Does he have insights I don't know about?" I mumbled.

But when I told Bryan, our seventeen-year-old son, he said, "Man, will I look stupid to my friends. I'm in high school and my mom is having a baby. That's dumb."

I had my own worries. When I did the math, I came up with some uncomfortable scenarios. I'll be forty-eight when this child starts kindergarten. That's nearly a half-century old. When she graduates from high school, I'll be sixty-one. And on our child's college graduation day, I'll be nearing seventy—if I live that long. What if Lee or I dies before she graduates or is married? What about the child? How will it feel to have parents as old as a grandparent pick you up after school? Will she ask us to park a block away so her friends won't see us?

In spite of the nagging worries, I was happy to be pregnant. I loved children and couldn't wait to hold this new life in my arms. We named her Ann Marie. Her siblings, with the exception of Bryan, were thrilled to welcome her home. But that problem soon took care of itself. When Ann Marie was a few weeks old, Bryan came home from school one day for lunch and found me in a frenzy.

"There's no lunch," I said. "I haven't had time because the baby's been fussy."

"Give her to me," he said, taking Ann Marie from me. Bryan was instantly smitten. From then on, we heard no more about being embarrassed by a new baby sister.

When Ann Marie potty-trained herself at an early age, Lee reminded me, "See, I told you. She's our bonus baby."

By the time Ann Marie started kindergarten, I was relieved to see that my concern about being the oldest parent of a kindergarten child was unfounded. Several of the mothers looked older than me. But who had time to worry about age?

In the next years, Lee and I kept busy driving Ann Marie to softball practice, flute and voice lessons, school activities, and her friends' homes for sleepovers. During those years, I began to see the advantages of being an older parent. When Ann Marie, at five, asked to carry two purses to church—hers plus my large, old bag—I didn't protest. And I raised no objections when, as a fifth grader, she wanted to wear my clothes to school. We had a free spirit on our hands and allowed her to be her own person, something younger parents may not have tolerated.

The miracle of it all was that Ann Marie didn't view us as older parents. Never once did she mention our ages, and neither did we. Occasionally I wondered why I'd believed the myth that older moms and dads can't cope with the rigors of parenting. We were doing just fine.

Lee and I were there when Ann Marie graduated from high school and college, but on that June day when her dad walked her down the church aisle, I felt a twinge of sadness. Now our mother-daughter relationship would change.

With a twinkle in his eye, Lee again reassured me: "We've had her for twent-eight years—a gift we didn't deserve. Just the Lord being generous, I guess."

I knew he was right.

—JEWELL JOHNSON

Little Hearts, Big Loves

"Whatever is good and perfect comes to us from
God above, who created all heaven's lights."
JAMES 1:17

The letters sent by my daughter's second- and third-grade classes are priceless to me. They are thank-you notes for the little items I've sent for their classroom store (the money being used for field trips). My daughter gives the children some background about me, and then they send such wonderful notes:

> "My teacher is lucky to have such a cool Mom."
>
> "I wish you were my mom."
>
> "How old are you?"
>
> "I love you."
>
> "Bless your heart."
>
> "You are an incredabel Mom."
>
> "We all apresheatge all the matereles you sent us."
>
> "You are really awsome."
>
> "I bet my teacher loves you from here to the sky."

How beautiful it is when hearts can express love so freely. These children have never met me, and many of them come from unloving homes. Yet they are filled with thanks.

Can we express such free-flowing thanks for all the little treasures God gives us each day?

"Thank you" is the best prayer of all.

—DOROTHY MINEA

Back to the Savior

"O death, where is your victory?
O death, where is your sting?"
1 CORINTHIANS 15:55

I could hear Mom's labored breathing as I walked down the hallway to her room in the nursing home. Soon nurses gave her oxygen, and she breathed silently. Mom had been ill for twelve years, and I had watched helplessly as her health deteriorated.

She couldn't remember my name, but she always had a smile for me when I visited. And she seemed to listen intently as I read to her from a little New Testament and Psalms. I touched her arm and prayed for her.

Throughout the day, it seemed death was hovering in the corners of Mom's room. Then a nurse came in to check on her, and as we looked at her face, we realized she wasn't breathing. While I had sat beside her, holding her hand, Mom's soul had slipped from her worn-out body and gone home to be with the Savior she loved.

For the Christian, death is a homecoming.

—NORMA C. MEZOE

Supplies

"This same God who takes care of me will
supply all your needs from his glorious riches,
which have been given to us in Christ Jesus."
PHILIPPIANS 4:19

Many years have passed since the brisk spring morning when I stood beside my father and watched him plant seeds in well-cultivated soil. When the seeds were covered with rich earth, my father then pounded stakes into the ground, marking head and foot of each row. Next, he ran cotton string from stake to stake, leaving about two to three inches of string dangling from the stake.

"Why don't you cut the string at the top?" I asked.

"The ends are left for the birds to build their nests," my father replied.

On cue from nature, those strings Dad had supplied became frayed from the beaks of little nest-builders.

This memory brings to mind our Heavenly Father's supplies for us—the things we need to build our lives in Him: the Holy Spirit, the Scriptures, the fellowship of believers, the privilege of prayer. What glorious riches held out to us!

*Use God's supplies today for
yourself—and for others in need.*

—DOROTHY MINEA

Why Worry?

"Don't worry about tomorrow, for
tomorrow will bring its own worries."
MATTHEW 6:34

There's an old joke about a worrywart old woman who proudly
stated, "I've worried about things all my life, and not one of
them came to pass!" That's the amazing thing: If we can pre-
dict a future that never happens, we can choose to bypass a
future that isn't necessary. Certainly all the fake futures I've
made up in my mind so far have mostly proven unnecessary.

If you're a worrier like me, you do tend to rehearse the
future quite regularly. That's why most of us need a supernatu-
ral kind of peace to fill our days. It's the kind of peace that can
quell my worry habit; it's got to help me reach the point where
I can calmly say, *I refuse to get bent out of shape about a future
that may never show up.*

*When tempted to worry, use this memory test:
What were you worrying about this time last year?*

—CMW

Footprints

"Christ, who suffered for you, is your
example. Follow in his steps."
1 PETER 2:21

My goal was to reach the high point of the Great Sand Dunes,
but climbing 750 vertical feet of sand wasn't easy. Often my feet
would slip or bog down. The task became more manageable
when my husband made a trail for me to follow. He reached for
my hand and, as I carefully stepped into his footprints, I moved
upward without faltering.

I thought of other footprints I'd followed in my life. Some
of them gave me a solid foundation, like the faith of my parents. Others led me astray. As I placed another foot into my
husband's tracks, I decided there was only one set of prints
completely reliable: the footsteps of Christ. He holds my hand
and reveals my life's course, step by step.

Following the footprints of Jesus,
we can be sure of our path.

—PAULA MOLDENHAUER

Awe

"When the people heard the thunder
and the loud blast of the horn, and
when they saw the lightning and the smoke
billowing from the mountain, they stood
at a distance, trembling with fear."
EXODUS 20:18

I listen to the rain pounding down on the roof on a summer afternoon. Feeling the rumble of thunder deep within my chest, I remember my childhood mind-picture: The angels are bowling. I can imagine the huge pins careening around in the heavens, smashing and bashing against one another with tremendous force.

Today I can draw an even more powerful picture of hot and cold air masses clashing as they produce desk-shaking thunder and computer-blowing lightning strikes. And I'm still a bit afraid of that heavenly display of God's power.

I do feel small, overawed, and also I feel blessed. Suppose I, and human creatures like me, were the most powerful and the most intelligent of all beings in the universe? How sad it would be. There is awe in the cosmos because the cosmic Creator is awesome.

*If it rains today, be sure to sit
by the window for a moment.*

—CMW

Words of Love

"[David] sang this song to the LORD
on the day the LORD rescued him
from all his enemies and from Saul.
I love you, LORD; you are my strength."
PSALM 18:1

I admit it. I was playing a video game when my teenagers came home from school. My daughter, Carey, came in and laughed when she saw me. She sat down, and we talked a little, but mostly we focused on the game. I wasn't very good at it, which Carey found quite amusing. I caught her humor and soon began laughing at myself.

Eventually Carey rose to leave but paused at the door. She turned and said quickly, "Mom, I sure do love you." Then she darted from the room.

I sat, astonished into silence, as a warm feeling overwhelmed my heart. How good it was to hear those words of love!

I pray regularly, asking for God's help. And sometimes I even remember to thank and praise Him. But how long has it been since I've blurted unashamedly, "God, I sure do love you"?

Even the Lord loves to hear of our love.

—CORA LEE PLESS

Take the Time

"Come, let us worship and bow down.
Let us kneel before the LORD our maker."
PSALM 95:6

The servant enters and walks down the marble-columned hall to the steps of the throne. She stops in front of the august personage and slowly bends at the waist, letting her body display the state of her heart. She bows low and stays that way for many moments.

Here is complete servanthood, loving respect, and even a healthy fear.

The "good life" surely must include a recognition that my many blessings have not come to me merely as a result of my innate brilliance or ingenious planning! Life does not work that way. In fact, perhaps the whole of our life is simply an invitation to perfect the art of worship. Both our blessings and our crises summon us to bow before the sovereign Lord.

How good, then, to take time for worship in my day!

Bow your body to the honor of the only
Being who deserves your reverent adoration.

—CMW

Abba

> "'Abba, Father,' [Jesus] said,
> 'everything is possible for you. . . .'"
> MARK 14:36

"Dad, come quick! Sam is frozen with fear, and we can't get him down!"

We'd spent the morning convincing our five-year-old that no matter how high he climbed, he couldn't fall off a sand dune. When he later begged to hike with his siblings, we let him go. But now he was at the top, we were at the bottom—and our baby stared down, petrified.

My husband rushed up the dunes. I knew running vertically in sand had to make his muscles scream, but his face showed only determination to reach his scared little boy. Soon they came down together, my son clinging to Daddy's hand.

Later, it made me think: *What would it be like to cling to Abba's hand today?* First, though, I will climb up in His lap for a moment of peace and rest.

> *Let God be Abba—Daddy—for you,*
> *this day and every day.*

—PAULA MOLDENHAUER

Exhausted

"Everyone will run until exhausted,
rushing back to their own lands like hunted deer,
wandering like sheep without a shepherd."

ISAIAH 13:14

Rushing . . . wandering . . . exhausted. This verse was me! I came to a point in my life when I recognized that my personal needs and desires were strangers to me. This was new and scary. My goals and plans had always come from the outside, from the others I sought to please. Now, no one was telling me what to do with my life. I was goal-less, depressed—busy with living, but not engaged with life.

Strangely enough, in the midst of busyness, we may discover that we have nothing very important to be busy *about*. At those times, we may need to explore where we are headed, and why. We've become like a ship without a port of call. We keep bumping off various relational islands, shouting, "Tell me, everybody—is *this* it? Or *this*? What do I really want?"

*The worst form of busyness is the kind that
keeps our destination unfocused.*

—CMW

Spic and Span

"Pay all your debts, except the debt of love
for others. You can never finish paying that!
If you love your neighbor, you will fulfill
all the requirements of God's law."
ROMANS 13:8

We have lived in the same house for almost twenty years. So I can't understand why, when it comes to cleaning the house and mowing the lawn, everything suddenly seems larger. It takes me longer to perform even routine tasks. Could it be that I'm getting older and slowing down?

Perhaps I must refine my priorities more closely. Do I continue to teach Sunday school, even though dust clings to the living room furniture? Do I talk with a friend in need, even though the carpet begs to be vacuumed? Do I drive a relative to the hospital for tests, though the bathroom needs painting?

I would love to live in a picture-perfect house—spic and span—with a beautifully manicured lawn. But then, how many people in my world are too distressed to even notice? What can I do for them instead?

May you wisely use the time and energy you're given.

—CORA LEE PLESS

Comfort in Presence

"How quickly I would escape—
far away from this wild storm."
PSALMS 91:4

A crack of thunder jolted me awake as it rattled through the walls. A quick flash followed, as did a muffled scurrying of feet that stopped by my bedroom door. "Mommy," a quivering voice whispered. "I'm scared. Can I sleep in here with you and Daddy?"

"Sure, honey, come on in," I whispered back. A pillow and favorite blanket plopped on the floor next to me. One down, two to go.

The next resounding boom brought my other two rushing into the room with their pillows and blankets. Within a few minutes their restlessness gave way to peaceful sleep.

We couldn't stop the storm, but my children felt a sense of safety and comfort in just *knowing we were there*. Likewise, in the frightening, dark moments of our lives, in a world so filled with violence and hatred, God's presence wraps us up and holds us tight so we can rest, safe and content in Him.

God's presence covers you like a soft,
warm blanket on a cold, stormy night.

—MABELLE REAMER

Just As It Is

"True religion with contentment is great wealth."
1 TIMOTHY 6:6

For some people, achieving peace and contentment means to dull the awareness, to relax into a state of unconcern, or to take up a simple, mind-numbing chore. But suppose we regularly tried increasing our *attentiveness* to reality, rather than trying to escape from it?

Rather than diverting our minds with the latest fashion in entertainment, instead of daydreaming or taking a nap, suppose we held our gaze steady for a few moments each day, simply focusing on what . . . *is?*

Imagine: No judgment about the things that are and can't be changed. No clinging to the things that are lost and can't be found. No longing for what has been but will never be again. Content with the actual reality of the only life we have.

In gratitude for what is—all of it a gift—could we not find a peaceful contentment?

Take a moment to survey the
goodness of your life, just as it is.

—CMW

A Veil of Tears

"I will be your God throughout your lifetime—
until your hair is white with age. I made you, and I
will care for you. I will carry you along and save you."

ISAIAH 46:4

Sometime after my mother-in-law's hip surgery, I asked, "How are you doing?" With a somber look, she put aside her walking cane and sat down.

"I'm fine now. But the surgery was one of the most difficult journeys of my life. Fear was my companion more times than I care to count. And what pain! Its intensity shocked me." Nodding, I swallowed. She hid her emotions well; I never suspected she'd endured such agony.

"I cried a veil of tears so thick, it threatened to block out my Savior's dear face," she said. "But I learned something precious too. When we're alone with our pain, God speaks to us in tones we can only hear if we are set apart and quiet."

She smiled, and I knew that in surviving her pain, she'd let God renew not only the strength of her hip, but the strength of her spirit as well.

*No matter our age, God will carry
us through this veil of tears.*

—LORI Z. SCOTT

God's Protective Hand

"I give them eternal life, and they will never perish.
No one will snatch them away from me."
JOHN 10:28

It was nearly a year before I could drive past the place on the road where my husband had died. A shiny section of metal fixed the guardrail where the accident had happened, but nothing could fix my broken heart. The thought of my husband dying alone on this road was too much! Why didn't God protect him?

Twelve years have passed, and God has brought help and healing in many ways. But that one question still plagued me: Why did God remove His protective hand?

Then one morning I discovered something special while reading my Bible. God, our Father, *never stops* protecting His children, especially when they die. He never let my twenty-eight-year-old husband go. God held him in His protective hand and carried him to his heavenly home.

Our human bodies won't last forever, but when we trust what Jesus did for us on the cross, our souls are eternally secure.

God never lets His children go.

—SUSAN KELLY SKITT

Now What?

"Dear brothers and sisters, whenever trouble comes your way, let it be an opportunity for joy. For when your faith is tested, your endurance has a chance to grow."

JAMES 1:2–3

I remember learning in grade school about the lowly oyster. I was amazed at its ability to do the miraculous. Irritations get into the oyster's shell. Unable to expel them, it slowly uses them to make something precious and beautiful.

Can we do the same with the irritations and grievances that keep rubbing into us each day? According to James, we can. All it takes is a particular attitude. Normally, when we see trouble coming we begin moaning and complaining. Suppose we thought, "I don't like it, but it is, at least, a chance to grow"?

Not easy! But endurance, like a pearl, isn't cheap. So let us ask God to show us how to let every event of our lives be a means of growth—even if it's simply the progress of patience and perseverance within us.

Pearls are valuable because it costs much to make them.

—CMW

Just Practicing

"The LORD is my light and my
salvation—so why should I be afraid?"
PSALM 27:1

Has your imagination ever run wild?

I got goose bumps when I heard the tapping noise behind me. I was driving to church on a dismal, foggy night, down a lonely mountain road. *You never lock the car,* I thought, *and you didn't check the backseat. Someone could be there and you'd never know it.*

Nervously, I glanced in the rearview mirror. A veil of darkness. *Tap, tap, tap.* By this time, my heart pounded and the hair on my neck stood at attention.

I spoke into the darkness, "Lord, You are my light and my salvation, and I refuse to fear. If anyone else is in this car, I will not be harmed." *Tap, tap, tap.*

Finally, I reached an intersection. When I turned to peer into the backseat, my coat constricted my movements. The belt was caught in the door, its buckle *tap-tap-tap*-ing in the breeze.

Calling upon the Lord will always give you strength.

—PENNY SMITH

Prayer Beyond Words

"In the same way, the Spirit helps us in
our weakness. We do not know what
we ought to pray for, but the Spirit himself
intercedes for us with groans that
words cannot express."
ROMANS 8:26

For years, I've struggled with a painful disease called fibromyalgia. Especially during times of stress, the pain in my shoulders and lower-back spasms bring tears to my eyes. I try to exercise, as the doctor recommends, but often the effort seems hardly worth the pain.

Of course, I've prayed often for the Lord to deliver me from this affliction—trusting the Holy Spirit to say what I cannot express.

But I also know that God wants me to trust like my fellow-sufferer, Paul. When he was the most dependent upon God, then the ministry of God's love flowed through him to the greatest extent. With that in mind, I bring my requests, and let the Spirit do the asking. Then I'm confident that I can live with God's answer.

When we feel weak, it can be a sign of blessings to come.

—CMW

Mismatched Socks

"At the right time he will bring
everything together . . . creating in
himself one new person from the two."
EPHESIANS 1:10, 2:15

I grabbed a pair of socks on my way down the stairs and hurriedly pulled them apart. They didn't match! My youngsters had been helping with the wash and had tried to pair all the socks, but a few got away from them. The extras were the leftovers my washing machine had spit out over the past few months. And while I'd hoped their partners would miraculously turn up, I knew they were destined for my rag basket.

Ever feel like a leftover, mismatched sock? Some of us are worn down, have stretch marks and lots of pulls and tears! We don't seem to fit and would love to belong to someone, somewhere, who would make us feel complete.

Suppose you took a moment to gather yourself around this truth: God created you for Himself—*on* purpose, and *for* a purpose. You and Him rolled up together . . . a perfect match.

In the fellowship of God's family, there are no leftovers.

—MABELLE REAMER

Make the Best Choice!

"Come to me, all of you who are weary and
carry heavy burdens, and I will give you rest."
MATTHEW 11:28

I recently came across a little prayer that went something like this: "Lord, do not let us do more, if in doing less we might do it better." Do you agree that we need to choose wisely what we should be busy with in our days?

To choose well means preparing our minds, in advance, for the toughest of decisions. We often must decide between mere quantity and quality in our Kingdom work.

Ultimately, our prayers, like this one, can focus on our need for rest in the world. When we spread ourselves too thin, we seem to miss everything of real importance. The call to us then is to take time out to confess our occasional blindness. As we worship with one another, we can lean on one another, too. We can ask for the help we need to see clearly, among all the options, the best choices.

*We need to know when to work
and when to rest from work.*

—CMW

The Cloud That Follows

"I don't want you to forget, dear brothers and sisters, what happened to our ancestors in the wilderness long ago. God guided all of them by sending a cloud that moved along ahead of them, and he brought them all safely through the waters of the sea on dry ground."

1 CORINTHIANS 10:1

A close friend says I have a little cloud over my head, like a cartoon character bound for tough times. Another claims, "God gives you such marvelous things to write about!" The things to which they both refer are hardly "marvelous" to me. For example, my first trip abroad found me wailing in the middle of the Cairo Airport with a lost ticket. And this happened after the hotel misplaced my luggage.

And the trip to my first writer's conference? From the moment the train did the chow-chow-chow at the railroad station, until the limousine's flat tire, the cloud followed me.

But it is that same cloud that follows me, and that gives me such wonderful stories to tell, that has also led me into a marvelous relationship with God!

The presence of the Lord is our rear guard.

—PENNY SMITH

Come As You Are

"I will obey your principles.
Please don't give up on me!"
PSALM 119:8

As David begins his longest psalm, we find this heartbreaking plea, "Don't give up on me!" David clearly understands the nature of his relationship with God. In one breath, he confidently determines to obey God's decrees; in the next, he shows how desperately dependent he is upon God.

David, the teen who single-handedly killed a bear, a lion, and a giant, reveals what he fears most—separation from the Lord. "Don't leave me," he touchingly cries. That's what a little child says to a parent when physical or emotional strength fails. "Don't leave me . . . I won't make it without you. . . ."

David testifies to human weakness, unashamed. But aren't we supposed to be stoic, independent, self-sufficient, help-yourself-ers in this life? Or does David have it right after all?

*We can come before the Lord with all our
imperfections, fears, and weaknesses.*

—CMW

All Dressed Up

"Since God chose you to be the holy people whom he loves, you must clothe yourselves with tenderhearted mercy, kindness, humility, gentleness, and patience."

COLOSSIANS 3:12

If you're a typical mom, probably at least once you've been dressed in pajamas and slippers when you dropped off your children for school. Or, if you're like me, it's a regular habit. Sure, for church or a PTA meeting we might primp a little. But on the days when we face cooking, cleaning, and a host of other sweaty chores, jeans with holes in the knees suffice. Or pajamas for the school run.

On one such scruffy morning, it occurred to me that sometimes we do the same thing with our hearts: make do with a grungy attitude. When we're running late for soccer practice, when our children forget their homework (again), when we face loads of laundry, we neglect to "dress up." Instead, we grump at our husbands or get impatient with our children. If we would make the effort to put on our best clothing—mercy, kindness, patience—how much more attractive would we be?

Dress your heart in its best clothing.

—LORI Z. SCOTT

From Head to Heart

"I have hidden your word in my heart
that I might not sin against you."
PSALM 119:11

How I wanted to earn the prize—a whole week at junior-high summer camp! The challenge? Just memorize and repeat 200 Bible verses. I locked onto the task like a bulldog. Over and over, I read each verse aloud until it stuck in my mind. Then each Sunday, I recited the verses word by word while my patient Sunday school teacher checked for accuracy. Yes, I went to camp that summer, paid for by some dear soul who understood the life-changing value of Bible memorization.

I agree with young David, the psalmist, who declared that God's Word alone had the power to keep his way pure. So many times one of those hundreds of verses has popped into my head just when I needed help, comfort, or guidance.

Now as a much older believer (who can't remember where I parked my car at the mall), I really appreciate the wisdom of Psalm 119.

*Meditate on His Word, and delight in
His ways—you're sure to find His path for your life,
no matter how young or old you are.*

—CMW

Tender Loving Care

". . . We are his people and the sheep of his pasture."
PSALM 100:3

"Sammy is hurt, Mom," my teen son cried. The black wool on the sheep's belly was covered with blood. He had gotten too frisky at the barbed-wire fence surrounding the pasture. Watching my son tenderly stroking the injured animal reminded me of the picture of Jesus as the Good Shepherd who carries the sheep on His shoulders.

We carried Sammy to the vehicle and transported him to a veterinarian for treatment. After a bit of surgery, he was as good as new.

Sometimes we, as God's people, need TLC to restore a wounded spirit, a broken heart, or a painful loss. The Good Shepherd enters the pasture of our experience in various ways to bear us up. It may be through another of His sheep, His people, to encourage and comfort in our time of need. Such occasions will teach us how to do likewise for others when the need arises.

*Follow him from the pastures of care
into the places of ministry.*

—PENNY SMITH

Ready to Respond?

"He refuted all the Jews with powerful arguments in
public debate. Using the Scriptures, he explained to
them, 'The Messiah you are looking for is Jesus.'"
ACTS 18:28

"Show me the facts," says my friend, a lady who seems to need
absolute proof before she will believe. Together, we search the
Scriptures, much like Apollos did with Priscilla and Aquila
almost 2,000 years ago.

I'm thankful for the example of this young man who passionately preached what he knew. I'm even more thankful for
Paul's discerning friends who took Apollos aside and explained
the way of God so clearly. Because he faithfully proclaimed
what he knew (John's baptism), God led him to mentors who
could complete his biblical education. Then, armed with all of
the facts, Apollos took on all scholarly doubters, whether Jew
or Greek.

Can you identify with Apollos? Meet regularly with
informed believers who can graciously field all questions and
find answers with you in the Word. Then you, too, can confidently proclaim that Jesus is the Messiah.

Be ready to respond to sincere questions about the Christ.

—CMW

The Smallest of Gifts

"Who despises the day of small things?"
ZECHARIAH 4:10A

My children love to give me gifts. I have whole collections of stickers, dried dandelions, rocks, and artwork adorning various windowsills and shelves in my home. My youngest is now one and a half and has begun to shower me with her own wonderful child-gifts.

Today, as we sat together on the beach, she gave me . . . sand. Handfuls and handfuls of it. The first handfuls were wet, and I used them to build a small castle tower beside my beach chair. But the gifts became increasingly more and more dry, and I found I could no longer even save them long enough to pile them.

I see my children's childhood slipping through my fingers just like that sand. In a distant future day that will seem like only hours from this minute, my daughter may well be accepting precious child-gifts from her own daughter. Today's Scripture reminds me to enjoy the gift of each day—and all the precious little things that inhabit it.

Every day, every brief second is a precious gift.

—ANGIE MURCHISON TALLY

Broken, for God's Use

"He has broken my strength in midcourse;
he has shortened my days."
PSALM 102:23 (NRSV)

My son Dan was just goofing around in the living room, running around and turning somersaults when, suddenly, an errant foot struck the coffee table. I watched as several pieces of beloved pottery flew through the air before shattering upon impact into jagged shards

He felt terrible. I felt worse. I loved those handmade works of art, and now they were broken. The teapot, sugar bowl and creamer had no future use, except as a bittersweet reminder of our own fragility.

Have you noticed, though, how God uses broken things? A broken flower blossom gives off sweet perfume. Only broken soil can accept seeds to produce a ripe crop of wheat. And the bread must be broken if it is to sustain our lives.

So . . . What about a broken person?
What about you?

*Ask God to take up the broken pieces in
your life and make a thing of beauty.*

—CMW

The Gift of a True Friend

"There are 'friends' who destroy each other,
but a real friend sticks closer than a brother."
PROVERBS 18:24

I was fighting the blues, and they were winning. I was unemployed, broke, frustrated. *God, where are you?* My heart ached and I wondered, "How long can this last?"

Resuming my online job search, I first fired off a quick e-mail to my girlfriend. I briefly touched on how I felt. Two minutes later my phone rang, and I recognized my dear friend's voice right away. As I choked back tears, she insisted, "I want you to let it all out; dump it all out on me."

I did, and she listened. When I was out of words, she encouraged me as only a real friend can. While nothing had changed, I was already feeling better.

A true friend provides a safe haven for our hurts as well as our joys. If you are hurting today, know that God, too, sees your pain and loves you as the best of all friends.

Could you let the Lord be your best friend?

—RACHEL M. TAMILIO

Airborne Promises

"If I go up to heaven, you are there."
PSALM 139:8

Cruising airborne at 30,000 feet fills me with awe as I peer at the miniature landscape from a celestial perspective. Up here, some clouds appear dense and billowy. Others seem transparent and streaky. Several rest high and others hover low as we fly by in whisper-quiet comfort. Then I catch a glimpse of rainbow hues chasing each set of clouds as the aircraft forges through the sky.

Like clouds, difficulties may transform themselves, but they will always fade in and out of our lives. Misty haze occasionally veils our skies, but the promise of God's love and ever-present companionship stays close by us. No matter how or where life's challenges manifest themselves, God autographs the clouds of our lives with a rainbow of promise.

God is with us in the depths—and in the highest altitudes.

—ANGELIQUE C. THOMAS

JULY

GOD HEARS

"The earnest prayer of a righteous person
has great power and wonderful results."

JAMES 5:16

*W*E CALLED OURSELVES "PRAYER-WALKERS," AND if you are new to the idea, I'll explain in the simplest terms: We walk; we pray.

Our little group started out with the best of intentions, but no one knew what the evening would hold, or if there would be any measurable results. But we stepped out in faith.

The cool breeze on that wondrous evening in July refreshed my small team of prayer-walkers as we made our way up the steep country road. This was the first time our group had ventured into my tiny town, which consisted of one main street and one traffic light.

My team had been assigned to pray over the homes and the church from the top of a steep, winding hill. I fixed my eyes on the road ahead, familiar with the narrow curve and the fact that not even a sidewalk separated us from the traffic. Cars came dangerously close as we hugged the guardrail and carefully stepped through the tall grass.

Though this was a small town of about 1,200 residents, the road served as a thoroughfare to other, larger towns. Even though Sunday evening traffic was typically lighter than weekday traffic, it was still a busy road. We approached the curve with trepidation due to the lack of visibility for drivers on both sides of the road. Nervously, we glanced behind us and ahead of us to dodge oncoming traffic. I prayed for God's protection as we walked, so exposed to potential harm.

As a car approached from behind, we picked up our walking pace to round the curve as quickly as possible, passing the home of one of my daughter's classmates. Knowing this family had fallen on hard times, I said to the team, "Wait. We need to pray over this home and over this family."

Apart from a miracle, it was likely the family would lose their home to the bank. We stood shoulder to shoulder along the guardrail, held hands, and prayed audibly. We prayed for God's provision for them. We prayed for salvation of each soul in the home and asked the Lord to keep His hand upon the children and protect them from the hazardous traffic that ran past their modest house.

As we closed the prayer and said "Amen" in unison, my daughter turned to me and asked, "Mom, do you think God really hears our prayers?"

We had barely taken two steps when a car driving by caught my eye. It had no license plate on the front but I felt compelled to look at the license plate on the back bumper. I followed the car with my eyes as it deliberately slowed down. The license plate read, "G-O-D - H-R-Z." My eyes grew wide. Unable to speak, I pointed to the passing car, and the rest of the team cheered "Hallelujah" and "Glory to God" as they, too, read the license plate.

"Well, there's our confirmation," said Brenda, one of the other prayer-walkers. "If there was any doubt about God's hearing the prayers of His people, let this be a message to us all."

As of this writing, the family for whom we prayed remains in their home. Though we've seen few changes in the natural realm, we believe God is at work in the spiritual realm. As it says in James, our prayers have "great power and wonderful results."

What would have become of that nice family if we had failed to stop and pray? Yet with danger all around us, we received the confirmation we needed to keep going. I cannot explain why God chose to use a license plate to communicate to us that night, and perhaps this side of Heaven I'll never know. That's okay. I'll continue to ask Him about everything and listen for His answers.

After all, I have it on good authority: God hears.

—ELISA YAGER-VILLAS

Moving Metaphors

"As Christ's soldier, do not let yourself
become tied up in the affairs of this life. . . . just as
an athlete either follows the rules or is disqualified
and wins no prize. Hardworking farmers are the
first to enjoy the fruit of their labor."
2 TIMOTHY 2:4–6

What can a soldier, an athlete, and a farmer have in common?
How about a mother of two-year-old twins, a concert pianist,
and a master gardener? Hey, these examples work for me! I'm
willing to watchfully endure and play by the rules if I can take
a bite of the fresh-picked, juicy prize at the end of the season.
Yes, these metaphors are a bit mixed up, but the point is, Paul's
words motivate.

What gets you going? For me, it's knowing that the days
ahead will be challenging at almost every level—personal, and
even national, as terrorist threats continue around the world. I
understand clearly what lies ahead—plenty of sweaty perseverance, discipline, patience, and focus.

Thanks, Paul, and thanks, Timothy—message received.
Get set and go, because it's time to move out.

Let the Word motivate you to faithful living each day.

—CMW

213

Faithful

"Fear not . . . for your Creator will be your husband. The LORD Almighty is his name! He is your Redeemer, the Holy One of Israel, the God of all the earth."

ISAIAH 54:4–5

After a twelve-hour flight from Japan with two small children, I was exhausted. Lugging a stroller and two large bags, I stumbled wearily to Baggage Claim. My heart was heavy with grief, and I realized I couldn't lift the four huge boxes off the conveyor belt. They were all my earthly possessions. *Lord, please be my husband now. I need You.*

A harsh voice cut through my reverie. "What is all this stuff?" a customs official asked as he squinted suspiciously at the boxes.

"I am moving from Japan."

"Oh *really*," he said sarcastically. "What for?"

Tears welled up in my eyes. "Because my husband has left me."

The man looked abashed and muttered, "Oh, sorry." Then, turning to another guy who was passing by, he said, "Larry, this woman needs help." Weak with relief, I followed three burly men who pushed through the crowds. God had provided men who did the job my husband used to do.

Are you alone or in need?
Lean on the Husband who never leaves.

—COLLEEN YANG

Bandages for the Broken

"The LORD is close to the brokenhearted;
he rescues those who are crushed in spirit."
PSALM 34:18

"I have nothing left," sobbed Diana on the other end of the phone. "I've lost my health, my friends, and my dreams. I'm barely hanging on. Why has God allowed this?"

I had no answer for her.

But I knew what it was like to be bruised and broken. I had battled chronic illness, depression, and marital stress for years. Gently, I offered to Diana the one thing that had helped me—the truth about our life with God.

"Some things in life we will never understand," I began. "We still live in a fallen world and often experience suffering. But in the midst of it, we can turn to God for comfort. When life is painful, He's there to wrap His arms of love around us."

Before hanging up, we prayed together. I asked God to comfort Diana and reveal His love to her. As we prayed, I sensed her turmoil give way to God's peace.

This is not the best of all possible worlds—not yet.

—MARY J. YERKES

Balance

"Do not merely listen to the word, and so deceive yourselves.
Do what it says. Anyone who listens to the word but does
not do what it says is like a man who looks at his face
in a mirror and, after looking at himself, goes away and
immediately forgets what he looks like."

JAMES 1:22–24

In the years when my husband and I studied in Bible college,
we spent many evenings with other students discussing the
Scriptures. Did I say "discussing"? I should have said "arguing."
While passionately quoting our school verse, 2 Timothy 2:15,
we pointed and exclaimed while fervently splitting hairs over
theology and doctrine.

If only we had read the verse that comes before: "Command them in God's name to stop fighting over words." Fortunately, we resolved most of those discussions in a friendly
manner and can still laugh about it all today.

How about you? How do you balance your zeal for truth
with the call to kind treatment of those who disagree?

*Your manner of life will often speak
louder than your arguments for truth.*

—CMW

Risky

> "[Nebuchadnezzar] ordered some of the strongest
> men of his army to bind Shadrach, Meshach, and
> Abednego and throw them into the blazing furnace."
> DANIEL 3:20

"Oh, you're one of those born again-ers," said the lady at the cash register. I had mentioned that I'd just come from my women's Bible study group. The frown on her face told me she disapproved. "People should keep their religion private," she continued. And then she said nothing more—and refused to make eye contact with me during the rest of the checkout process. Apparently, I had made an enemy.

No doubt you, too, have endured times of discomfort or embarrassment because of your faith. But who of us has had to risk instant death for our faith? The three young men who snubbed King Nebuchadnezzar knew what it meant to stand for the right, regardless of the consequences. Facing a fiery furnace is no fun!

So here's the question on my mind at the moment: How "risky" is my faith?

Why not prepare to take some heat for the Lord?

—CMW

Feed the Good

> "There is another law at work within me that is at
> war with my mind. This law wins the fight and
> makes me a slave to the sin that is still within me."
> ROMANS 7:23

According to a Native American legend, a grandfather was telling his grandson about his struggle with good and evil. "It's like there are two wolves in me. One is a good wolf and the other a bad wolf. One wants to do what is right and the other what it knows is wrong."

Troubled and anxious, the little boy asks, "Which one is going to win?"

Grandfather pauses to look deeply into the youngster's eyes before replying: "The one I feed."

Like the apostle Paul, all of us have a civil war raging within us. We will supply one side or the other with what it loves to feed upon. And each day we make up our menu. Every moment we choose the special diet for our souls.

Feed upon the Word of God to
strengthen your will to do good.

—RACHEL M. TAMILIO

Savory Fellowship

"Beloved, let us love one another, for love is from God;
and everyone who loves is born of God and knows God."
1 JOHN 4:7

It was the end of the day just before the start of another annual
Christian bookseller's convention, this one held in New Orleans
in July. Since early that morning, I had worked hard alongside
Mike, Adam, and Daphne, setting up our publisher's huge booth
and placing books on their designated shelves. Trouble was, the
convention hall wouldn't turn on the air-conditioning until
the next day when buyers arrived! As security officers locked
the exit doors, we gathered by the loading docks, each one of us
drenched in sweat, hungry, and thoroughly exhausted.

But then Adam announced great news: he had made reservations for us that evening—at NOLA, Emeril Lagasse's famous
restaurant. Fantastic!

Just a few hours later, our previously smelly, grimy work
crew shared a rare evening of joy as we ate together, all clean,
comfy, and satisfied. As I finished the best steak I've ever had,
I truly felt the love and mutual appreciation that sparked our
hysterical laughter.

Yes, fellowship like this must be a foretaste of heaven.

*No matter what the task, our fellowship—our working
together in Christ—is something to savor deeply.*

—CMW

Motherhood and Mother Nature

> "There the child grew up healthy and strong.
> He was filled with wisdom beyond his years,
> and God placed his special favor upon him."
>
> LUKE 2:40

"Mom, I have to do a science project," said Ricky, my fifth grader, as he slid his backpack onto the kitchen table. "I want to see if one environment is better than others for plants," he explained.

His plan was simple. Choose three healthy plants, place each in a different environment, record their health and growth. He placed the first plant in front of a bay window where it received the morning light. He kept the soil moist. The second, he set in a room with no light, just water. And the third, he put in a closet with no light or water. You can guess which plant thrived.

Jesus grew up "there"—in a family environment of love and caring. He grew healthy and strong, just as we wish our own children to grow. But will you determine to satisfy a child's thirst for love and affirmation today?

> *Strong and healthy children are daily*
> *nourished by love and truth.*

—MARY J. YERKES

"No"

> "The LORD is my shepherd; I have everything
> I need. . . . he leads me beside peaceful streams."
> PSALM 23:1–2

A few years ago, I interviewed for a job back in Orlando, my hometown. If I accepted the position, we would have to sell our newly built dream home in Colorado and move our teenaged sons to a new high school. But we could live close to our aging parents who needed help, so the decision loomed large in my life. In fact, it all kept me up at night as my mind refused to let go and stop wrestling with my potential future.

This wasn't my idea of walking beside a peaceful stream with the Shepherd! However, I learned something crucial: God will use even our *lack* of peace to guide us. And in those times, the dreaded "no" will be the means of that peace. Have you also found it so?

Lord Byron once said, "When we think we lead, we are most led." How can that be? For one thing, when we're so focused on making up our mind about future actions, we lose sight of where those actions ought to be taking us.

*Pause to consider: Who is leading me,
and to what future am I headed?*

—CMW

Out of Temptation

"God is faithful. He will keep the temptation from
becoming so strong that you can't stand up against it.
When you are tempted, he will show you a way out so
that you will not give in to it."

1 CORINTHIANS 10:13

I stared at my checkbook and wondered what to do. Car repairs
and lowered income had left us with three unpaid bills for the
month—and a depleted account. Payday? Another two weeks.
However, as director of a local writing organization, I held the
organization's checking account. . . .

You guessed it. I was tempted to "borrow"—just to keep our
insurance intact, our water flowing, and a few groceries in the
refrigerator. I cried and prayed for strength, pleading for a way
out of our financial mess.

That afternoon, the mail came with an envelope from
the headquarters of the very organization I was directing. And
inside the envelope—a Visa gift card! The note said, "Thanks
for all you do!"

It seems each director received this card, but I wonder,
could any of them say theirs was a true way out of temptation,
an answer direct from God?

When temptation imprisons you, remember:
God engineers surprising escapes.

—KATHRYN LAY

Transition

"Turn to me and have mercy on me,
for I am alone and in deep distress."
PSALM 25:16

What a tough transition! I'd been cruising the fast lane as a marketing professional constantly interacting with people, projects, and problems. My days were hectic and stressful. Now I was starting a new venture . . . working by myself at home.

After a couple of weeks of silent aloneness, I was ready to jump back into the hustle and bustle of office life, even with all its stress. Hey, I just wanted somebody to talk to.

However, it took me a while to admit my deep distress. We all have a tendency to deny loneliness. Once we face it, though, it can work something quite wonderful: It pushes us to reach out.

For me, that meant volunteering for several agencies and getting involved in local government in my spare time. Now my alone times feel less like loneliness and more like creative solitude.

*We can let our need for others move
us closer to potential friends.*

—CMW

Outrun the Light?

"Your word is a lamp for my feet
and a light for my path."
PSALMS 119:105

"Don't outrun your headlights," a seasoned motorcyclist told me shortly after I learned to ride. I didn't know what he meant until one pitch-black night as I rode alone.

When I finally escaped the lights of town, clouds covered the moon and stars. I strained to see ahead; the headlight didn't seem to illuminate what I needed to see as the curves rushed toward me. So I slowed down and let the light do its work. Within seconds, I could see the bends and turns more clearly, and travel safely.

My growth in the spiritual life seems like and unlike that dark-night experience. God's Word lights the path I'm on and guides my steps. But it doesn't show me what's just beyond the next curve or behind the bushes. It shows me where I am, it shows me the destination, it shows me the kind of heart I ought to have when I arrive.

Today, move ahead with the eyes of faith.

—CLAUDEAN BOATMAN

Keep Truckin'

"Come to me with your ears wide open.
Listen, for the life of your soul is at stake."
ISAIAH 55:3

"Truck," announces my little daughter cheerfully every morning as I enter her room. Sometimes she's gesturing to a delivery truck idling outside her bedroom window. Sometimes she's observing the school bus making steady progress down our street. Sometimes, there is no truck. Nevertheless, she greets me every morning with "truck."

Her persistence in greeting every dawn with the confidence that—with time and patience—her call of "truck" will indeed be answered, reminds me of the persistence of God in my life. Every day He calls me by name to come into His presence.

Some days I come quickly like the school bus and then depart filled with what is perceived as a "full load of God" for the day. Other days I linger like the delivery truck and slowly replenish my stores. Even when I do not come at all, still He calls.

Every day, God calls us into relationship with Him.

—ANGIE MURCHISON TALLY

The Real Thing

"You alone are the LORD. You made the skies and the heavens and all the stars. You made the earth and the seas and everything in them. You preserve and give life to everything, and all the angels of heaven worship you."

NEHEMIAH 9:6

My grandson hardly waited for me to put my suitcase down before grabbing my hand and rushing me to his bedroom. "You've got to see this, Grandma!" He talked excitedly while closing the door. "Sit down right here."

I sat cross-legged where he instructed—facing the wall. He made sure the curtains were drawn and the door tightly closed. Then he turned off the lights and came to sit in my lap. As he pointed out the different glow-in-the-dark stars that decorated his room, I asked him questions and matched his enthusiasm, star for star.

Not wanting to miss a teachable moment, I whispered, "Isaac, do you know who made the stars?"

Isaac froze. Slowly he turned to me. "Grandma," he said, his tone suggesting the reluctant delivery of sad news, "these aren't *real* stars." I half expected him to pat my hand in consolation. "But . . . God made the real ones."

Remember what is real, what is not, and who made it all.

—CLAUDEAN BOATMAN

He's Really There

"He breathed on them, and saith unto them,
Receive ye the Holy Ghost."
JOHN 20:22 (KJV)

"When something breathes beside you in the darkness," said C. S. Lewis, ". . . it is always shocking to meet life when we thought we were alone. 'Look out!' we cry, 'it's alive.'"

I often had that "yikes!" feeling after working the late-night shift at AM 1000 WCFL radio in Chicago. Done with my on-air shift at 2:00 in the morning, I had to leave the studio by a back entrance—and walk through a field in pitch darkness. Strangely, that field was full of rabbit holes! When I opened the back door, and the light hit scores of early-morning feeders, they all ran for cover.

It was kind of creepy to hear the sudden, rustling sounds of life in that dark stillness. It makes me think of the real, living Holy Ghost who lives inside me. When I turn on the light of my heart to "see" Him there . . . it's almost shocking.

The Spirit is alive and active within us.

—CMW

It Takes Practice

"The LORD gives his people strength.
The LORD blesses them with peace."
PSALM 29:11

One day while in the mountains, I stood looking up at an enormous spruce tree. Its tip reached up to the sky like a church steeple pointing up to God. Birds and squirrels had made their nests in its wide-reaching branches.

For many years it has grown there, unmoved by summer's heat or winter's storm. With its roots pushed deep into the heart of the mountain, it seemed to say, "Here I stand."

"Lord, I want to be like this tree," I prayed, "a strong shelter in the middle of life's storms, unshaken and giving praise to You. How can I be like this tree?"

That's when I noticed something lying on the ground. Someone had dropped a lapel pin. Written on it were only two words: "Practice Peace."

Strength and peace come from abiding in Christ.

—RENEE BOLKEMA

A Look of Love

"Look, there he is behind the wall! Now he is
looking into the window, gazing into the room."
SONG OF SOLOMON 2:9

Yells and screams, slammed doors, and lonely sobs were a common occurrence during my early years. I had to find a way to protect myself. Outwardly, I began to fight back against my parents' tirades; inwardly, I began building a wall around my heart. It was built with bricks I personally chose. One brick was unforgiveness. Others could be labeled "self-pity," "rebellion," and "rejection."

I carried these bricks into my adult life, and the wall around my heart grew thick and strong. I hoped it would protect me; instead it held my heart prisoner.

Then one day as I was praying for help, I realized that the wall would collapse if I surrendered it to God—brick by brick. I had blocked Him out; now He was gazing through, looking at me with love in His eyes.

Let every heart surrender and prepare Him room.

—GINNY CAROLEO

Just Turn Your Thoughts

"The LORD is close to all who call on him,
yes, to all who call on him sincerely."
PSALM 145:18

When we packed up to go away to college as newly married teenagers, I was moving far away from my home. I'd been born and raised in the same little house in small-town Florida, living there until I got married. Then my husband and I soon moved to downtown Chicago.

So many firsts for me there—first time seeing snow, first time riding a subway train, first time walking down an urban street, looking straight ahead . . . and *not* smiling at anybody walking toward me. Everything seemed different: the culture, the weather, the faces. And so many times I cried out to God, feeling like an alien from another planet.

How precious it was to be reminded: My Heavenly Father is right here in my heart. He remains—*dwells* there—forever, no matter where my travels may take me next.

*You are as close, dear Father, as my
decision to turn my thoughts to You.*

—CMW

Crushed Under Her Own Plans

"Humble yourselves under the mighty power of God,
and in his good time he will honor you."
1 PETER 5:6

The headline read, "130lb Woman Crushed Under 10,000lb Plans." Apparently, this poor woman's plans sat in a huge stack of paperwork. When she tried to retrieve them, the entire 10,000-pound stack fell over and killed her.

Today's Scripture calls us to bow our lives and our plans to the Lord. That is humility. Care to guess what the opposite of humility is? You got it, pride. When we try to lift ourselves with our self-made plans, we're heading into a danger zone. When we pursue personal satisfaction at the expense of others, we may be crushed by our own selfishness.

Next time you make yourself crazy with planning how to get into or out of a situation, try this: Picture yourself bowing under an enormous hand, and wait for that hand to lift you up before you do anything else by yourself.

God invites us into honorable planning for the Kingdom.

—ADREIENNE BICKERS

Looking for God

> "'Go out and stand before me on the
> mountain,' the LORD told him. And . . .
> there was the sound of a gentle whisper."
> 1 KINGS 19:11–12

Suppose you came to visit me at my house. I invited you in. As we talked, I kept moving from window to window, peering through the glass with a telescope. You asked me, "What are you doing?" I answered, "I'm looking for my home, but I just can't seem to find it." Wouldn't you find that rather peculiar?

Many people claim to be searching far and wide for God. They say, "I just can't seem to find Him." All the while, we are standing in His hands. All that He has created is trying to tell us that He is right here, that His presence surrounds us every day, whether we realize it or not.

We don't need a telescope to see Him, or even a cell phone to reach Him. We simply need to find a quiet space and . . . listen.

He's only a prayer away.

—RENEE BOLKEMA

Infinite in Both Directions

"He is the God who made the world and everything in it. . . . He himself gives life and breath to everything, and he satisfies every need there is. . . . His purpose in all of this was that the nations should seek after God and perhaps feel their way toward him and find him—though he is not far from any one of us."

ACTS 17:24–25, 27

I grew up near the space coast in Florida and saw virtually each new launching during the 1960s and 1970s. These days, back in Florida after being away for decades, I still enjoy watching the space shuttles hurtling on their way into and out of Earth's atmosphere.

I do have a great love for astronomy and telescopes—and all things space. It all tells me that my Lord is . . . *big*! Maybe that's why we usually look up to praise the Lord.

Tonight, that moon and those stars are so far away, making me think God dwells at some great distance as well. His sparkling creations astound me—the space and the height! Yet His essence is as close as my breath.

> *God is truly awesome on both sides of the scale—infinitely large, intimately small.*

—CMW

Accountable

"Be a good worker, one who
does not need to be ashamed and who
correctly explains the word of truth."
2 TIMOTHY 2:15

Nine-year-old Ben held up his hand after my husband and I finished our Vacation Bible School lesson. "Is that *really* in the Bible?" he asked. I read the Scripture aloud, but he still doubted. "Let me see," he said. I handed him the Bible to read the rather obscure story for himself.

Ben wasn't the only one who wanted to see the printed word. One of the teachers, a Bible-college graduate, leaned over Ben's shoulder to read. "I don't remember ever hearing that story," she said.

What a responsibility we have! The Scripture above admonishes us to know, and correctly explain, the Word of truth. For we never know when a child—or anyone else seeking spiritual things—may say, "Prove it to me!"

Let's be ready to explain what we believe—and why.

—LEANN CAMPBELL

Staying Present in the Plans

"I know the plans I have for you," says the LORD.
"They are plans for good and not for disaster,
to give you a future and a hope."
JEREMIAH 29:11

I have struggled all my life with worrying about the future rather than living in the present. Yet in speaking with a friend about my new writing and speaking ministry, I noticed another outlook forming within me. I told her that I felt I was in the "right" place in my life. And I was treasuring each day.

"What makes you say that?" she asked.

"Because for the first time I believe I'm fulfilling God's purpose for me. I am having a great time, too."

All of us want to identify the reason we were placed in this world. Rest assured, though, that God assigned you a purpose before you were born. Ultimately, that purpose is the same for us all: *to glorify Him in all we do.* The details—God's plans for you—well, together you will enjoy working them out!

In this moment the plan is simple—
be open to the Spirit's leading.

—CATHERINE M. SCHAFFER

My Side of the Story

"We are confident of all this because of
our great trust in God through Christ."
2 CORINTHIANS 3:4

After hearing my husband speak of his bout with stress-related depression, a woman turned to me and asked, "What was it like for *you*?"

I have to think for a moment. I was there with Bill through it all. I watched him experience deep anxiety, saw him deal with anger, and listened as he sorted out his life. So I answer, "My survival rests on a firm belief in Bill's inner strength and the ultimate strength of God in Bill. He'll come through a stronger person."

The apostle Paul had a similar confidence in the Corinthian believers. He could believe the best would occur in them because he trusted, ultimately, in the power of God to do the work of strengthening their faith. We can confidently believe in people when we know their confidence rests in the Lord.

God gives us Himself, and He is enough for any situation.

—ANN L. COKER

Can You Think a Little Higher?

"Just as the heavens are higher than the earth,
so are my ways higher than your ways and
my thoughts higher than your thoughts."
ISAIAH 55:9

I love radio. I don't completely understand how it works, though. It came into being at the end of the nineteenth century, so before that, all we had were letters, lights, telegraph, flags, birds, and smoke to communicate across the distances. (You can probably think of other ways.)

Then came radio, with the sound of the human voice wafting through the air. The rest is history.

My point is, who could have imagined such a thing just a generation earlier? And who of us can even imagine the new inventions to come just a generation from now?

Our imaginations are pitifully limited. So it's important, when it comes to our relationship with God, that we not let our thoughts limit His true ability for us. Let us pray, hope, and think high thoughts worthy of our Heavenly Father.

*Our most depressing problems are nothing
compared to God's awesome power.*

—CMW

Attitude of Gratitude

"Let the peace that comes from Christ rule in
your hearts. For as members of one body you are all
called to live in peace. And always be thankful."
COLOSSIANS 3:15

My husband's grandmother rarely completed a conversation
without the comment, "Lord, I'm so thankful."

It defied logic that 1951 would find Erma, a young widow
with five children, so grateful. True, her husband Louis had provided a home for his family; however, to make ends meet, she
had to clean houses for others. In later years, even physical pain
failed to diminish her gratitude to her Creator for the health
she described as "better than that of some my age."

Her birthday offered an annual excuse for the gathering of
her children, fourteen grandchildren, and almost as many great-
grandchildren. They returned to the porch that most of them
had scampered across as toddlers. Beaming at her family, Erma's
eyes would mist in acknowledgment of blessings received.

Five years after her passing, I continue to miss her gentle
presence, especially when I find myself moved to whisper, "Lord,
I'm so thankful."

Can you find cause for gratitude today?

—PHILLIS HARRIS-BROOKS

Point of View

"We have all benefited from the rich blessings he
brought to us—one gracious blessing after another."
JOHN 1:16

I thought about this verse of Scripture for a long time. And
the more I thought, the more I marveled at the great promise it contained. I began to realize, ever increasingly, that the
circumstances in my life are not what define me, but rather,
my point of view is. It's like the "glass-half-full/glass-half-empty"
principle.

Not only is it for me to see that my whole life is surrounded
by God's blessings, but it is also for me to be like Jesus and offer
blessings to all those I meet. That's how this verse stays true
generation after generation.

And that's why I've decided to keep my point of view
focused on Jesus and His ways—complete with all the promises
of joy, peace, love, and hope His loving words profess.

The gracious blessings of God benefit us all!

—SARA DAVENPORT

Hear Those Stars?

"The heavens tell of the glory of God.
The skies display his marvelous craftsmanship.
Day after day they continue to speak;
night after night they make him known."
PSALM 19:1–2

The sky "speaks"? Yes! I read about it in a news article recently (not to mention the message of the verse above). It seems that scientists who had been searching for outer-space signals came across an unexpected discovery: Lightning produces radio waves.

The researchers had been picking up strange transmissions that they couldn't identify—until they finally tied them to the flashes of lightning that interrupted their work around the world.

The sky—and all of Creation—does indeed speak, telling a revealing story. What is created proclaims an intelligent Creator of marvelous craftsmanship. And when this Creator Himself descended from the skies, the world received not only of His intelligence, but of His vast love as well. Thanks be to God!

*The night sky is beautiful—and full
of heavenly communication.*

—CMW

Feeling the Heat

"I will bring that group through the fire and make them pure, just as gold and silver are refined and purified by fire. They will call on my name, and I will answer them. I will say, 'These are my people,' and they will say, 'The LORD is our God.'"

ZECHARIAH 13:9

A refiner had a special way of purifying his silver. Using a large pot, he placed ore inside. He would build a huge, blazing fire underneath and carefully wait and watch as the contents started to melt. First, he skimmed large amounts of sediment from the top with a wooden spoon. Knowing the silver was not pure, he made the fire hotter by adding more wood to the already bright flames. Eventually, he'd be able to tell whether the silver was ready: He'd see a clear reflection of himself.

Our life's trials can grow intensely hot. But they come with a pretty cool blessing: They allow God to remove the sediment from our character that we may reflect His image in the world.

How do you handle the hot spots of your life?

—RHONDA DEYOUNG

Beyond What's Cozy

"I command you—be strong and courageous!
Do not be afraid or discouraged. For the LORD
your God is with you wherever you go."
JOSHUA 1:9

Peanuts character Charlie Brown said, "I'm only going to dread one day at a time." To what extent is fear robbing you of joy, day by day? Thankfully, we can decide what to do with our fears, and our choice will make all the difference.

I think of all the things some people do, things I'd surely be too afraid to try. Skydiving, for instance, or underwater cave exploring, or demolition-derby driving.

Yet here's the challenge: God is with us, but He's often in another "zone," unto which He beckons us to join Him. That is, He calls us beyond our comfort zone, one small step at a time. But those can be scary steps, and we need to take the words from Joshua deeply into our own hearts: "Be strong and courageous. . . . the Lord your God is with you wherever you go." He's there, even beyond what's cozy.

*Will you allow God to move you out of your
comfort zone today—and closer to Him?*

—CMW

Things Worth Remembering

"To all who believed him and accepted him,
he gave the right to become children of God."
JOHN 1:12

Everything changed for me on March 7, 1999, when I suffered a ruptured brain aneurysm and lost my short-term memory. I can't remember what I ate for dinner last night, but I do remember that I *did* eat and that I didn't go to bed hungry like too many others in this world of ours.

Some of my best memories are forever lost—like the cruise we took to the Bahamas just two weeks prior to my brain surgery. But I do recall our camping trip to the wilderness during my recovery period. I remember the look in my husband's eyes when I smiled by the campfire and marveled at the birds building their nests. I hold that particular memory close to my heart, as it was the week that I gave my heart to Jesus. Some things are *so* worth remembering!

Jesus never forgets us, no matter what our state of mind.

—MICHELE STARKEY

AUGUST

INTENSIVE CARING

"When others are happy, be happy with them.
If they are sad, share their sorrow."

ROMANS 12:15

*S*EVEN WEEKS MAY NOT SEEM LIKE A LONG TIME, but when it's spent in a hospital waiting room, it can seem like an eternity. I discovered this when my father needed heart surgery. The odyssey began when he developed chronic, severe shortness of breath. He stubbornly refused to seek treatment, but my mother and I persuaded him to go for diagnostic testing.

While the technician performed an echo sonogram on his heart, she told him, "Sir, if you were my father, I'd insist you go to the emergency room right now." That finally convinced him he was in serious trouble. The next day, after a five-hour, six-vessel bypass procedure, the surgeon announced, "It's a good thing he had this done now. I really didn't even expect him to make it off the operating table."

But he did, and we spent a fitful night in the ICU waiting room. Other families waited with us—scared and exhausted. At first we kept to ourselves, but after taking turns answering the waiting room phone, we learned each other's names.

Then came the quick trips to the vending machines and, once in a while, even the cafeteria. We always asked each other if we could run an errand, get a cup of coffee, or take messages for a family so they could have a break.

This went on for several days while each of our beloved high-risk patients lingered in the ICU. Dad seemed to be doing very well, and before long he moved to the regular medical floor. We said our good-byes to our friends and cheerfully accompanied him to the lower-risk floor.

But then Dad started to hallucinate. First he thought he saw a coffee urn floating in the corner of the room. Then he spoke to people who weren't there. Apparently, Dad had acquired a serious staph infection. So it was back to the ICU.

We discovered with a mixture of relief and disappointment that our friends in the waiting room were still there waiting for their loved ones to recover. One family in particular became our ICU buddies. The mother was the wife of another patient who had also been in for heart surgery. Like my dad, he wasn't doing well, and like my dad, she was a diabetic, so I encouraged her to eat regularly.

Several times during the ordeal we would visit Dad for a few minutes at a time, only to return and collapse on the waiting room sofa, sobbing. Others waiting—people we didn't even know—came up and hugged us, offering us tissues, water, and understanding.

It was "touch and go" for several weeks, but finally Dad improved. He returned to the medical floor, where he slowly recovered. Mom and I finally relaxed (but only a little), and when we did, I realized there were others on the floor above who weren't as fortunate.

On my return visit to the waiting room upstairs, I found them in their same place on the ICU sofa. The mother wept softly, and while I didn't want to intrude, I felt God wanted me to speak to her. So I knelt at her side, took her hand in mine, and asked quietly, "May I pray with you?" She nodded, and I began to ask God to be with her husband, her daughters, and most especially, with her. I felt a communion with her and with God, our Healer.

When we finished, she looked into my eyes and whispered, "Thank you." Then she began to explain that her husband had taken a turn for the worse, and she didn't understand all the medical issues involved. Because I'd been through many years of medical problems with Dad, I could explain things and offer her some clarity and compassion.

As I stood to go, I asked whether she needed anything and promised to visit again. She squeezed my hand and said, "You'll never know how much you've helped me." But as I returned to Dad's floor, I felt like the one being helped.

When I shared this woman's pain and offered her comfort, I forgot my own worries. And in doing so, I discovered an important secret. We can overcome life's tough times when we reach out in love and mercy to those around us.

—LISA M. KONZEN

The Purpose of Worship

"God is Spirit, so those who worship him
must worship in spirit and in truth."
JOHN 4:24

"Why is Jesus special, Aidan?" his church-school teacher asked. The little boy responded, "It's 'cause His body is made out of crackers and wine!"

Aidan is thinking about the *form* of Communion, missing its *spirit*. Of course, he is just a child, but I find I often respond somewhat similarly. I have actually complained in my heart about the Communion wafer, wishing someone would buy a tastier brand!

I focus too easily on the type of music, the competency of the worship team, the spelling errors in the bulletin, the colors, or the lights, or . . .

When I do this, I'm missing the purpose of worship: to honor and adore the living God. As my minister said recently, "The various worship forms do not *enable* worship; they only *enhance* it." To truly worship, I need to see past the form, and get into the Spirit.

Real worship is all about God, not about us.

—ELSI DODGE

Taking and Giving

"Remember the words of the Lord Jesus:
'It is more blessed to give than to receive.'"
ACTS 20:35

As one of the classic rock DJs in Chicago radio, I met lots of interesting people—Scottie Pippen, Walter Payton, Buster Douglas, just to name a few.

But, really, the most interesting people were the fellow "personalities" I worked with every day. Interesting and . . . *unusual.*

I recall one conversation at work in which I shared a particularly distressing personal problem. In response, the DJ running the studio looked away from the microphone and sincerely offered me his best advice: "Why don't you just take some drugs?"

Since then, I've learned to ask myself another shocking question: "Why don't you just try focusing on somebody else?" That usually leads me to some form of giving. And yes, I enjoy the blessing that comes as a result of following the Lord's good advice!

Know the joy of this privilege:
to sacrifice your time and your energy.

—CMW

Kindness Springs Forth

". . . As people sinned more and more,
God's wonderful kindness became more abundant."
ROMANS 5:20

"Look at this, Gramice!" my grandson blurted as he shoved his drawing in front of my face. My eyes blurred as I tried to focus on it. Abruptly, I pushed it aside; he had interrupted my progress through my busy day. How rude of him! Or was it?

God had graciously put a stop sign in my life. I needed to come to a full stop, look both ways, and proceed very cautiously. As I took my grandson on my lap, I apologized for my brusqueness and asked him to tell me about his picture. Several precious moments of closeness ensued.

Isn't it amazing how and where God's kindness springs forth? God is not the author of sin; it is our free choice. But He can redeem it with His grace, and He does that miracle every day of my life.

God's kindness blossoms even in rocky soil.

—MERCEDES EVANS

What's on Your Mind?

"Fix your thoughts on what is true and
honorable and right. Think about things that
are pure and lovely and admirable. Think about
things that are excellent and worthy of praise."
PHILIPPIANS 4:8

Two words: "reality TV." I want to say no but I often say yes. Especially after a long day, when all I really want to do is sit in front of the tube and veg out.

Can you relate? Some of those shows actually seem pretty harmless, like the one about exchanging places to fix up a neighbor's family room. Others, though, are just plain pathetic.

Computer programmers say, "Garbage in, garbage out." But doesn't that little rule apply to the human mind, as well? If so, we must constantly ask ourselves the following question: Do the things I think about help me grow spiritually and make me a more joyful person?

Lately, I've been trying to switch channels more often. Ah! There's the History Channel, beckoning me to learn more about the Roman Empire. There's some worthiness in that, right?

To be educated, choose the things that are enlightening.

—CMW

Care for That Friend!

"Neither shalt thou covet thy neighbor's house."
DEUTERONOMY 5:21

I received an e-mail from a high school friend now living in Florida. She reported that Hurricane Charley had ripped off a portion of her roof and dumped it into her pool. Remembering our humble beginnings as youths, I could only wonder, *Bev has a pool?*

When she reported that she and her family were safe, I said a brief prayer of thanksgiving to God. But I couldn't keep my mind off the picture of a teenage Bev now transported to a life of tropical luxury.

Today's paper reports that 3 million people are without electricity in Florida—after another hurricane. I suppose Bev is in that group. I don't amuse myself now by picturing her in a luxurious home. Instead, I consider why that pool once seemed so important to me.

Be thankful when friends do well, caring when they suffer.

—NITA WALKER FRAZIER

Spring Ahead

"I strain to reach the end of the race and
receive the prize for which God, through
Christ Jesus, is calling us up to heaven."
PHILIPPIANS 3:14

I hate change. I seem to want to hold on to what I have. I don't want to press onward. I even hate the change of seasons. I am nicely settled into *this* season, comfortable and satisfied. Leave it alone! (It's a difficult attitude to maintain when you're the wife of a farmer, depending on the cycles of the year.)

Rearing children and watching them go off and make lives of their own? Stop the music; let them stay here! I feel like an actor who walked out on the wrong stage, a stage where the props are always changing. I want my scenery unmovable, well anchored, predictable.

Can I live joyfully in Christ like this? No. He calls me to forget what is behind and strain onward to what is ahead. It is a special challenge for one like me. On the other hand, springtime is coming. . . . *Imagine the harvest . . .*

Look ahead with joy to your heavenly future.

—CAROL GUTHMILLER

Heavenly Hugs

"Then the one who looked like a man touched
me again, and I felt my strength returning."
DANIEL 10:18

Some people are huggers; some aren't. Me? I'm always ready
with open arms. Maybe it's because I'm so often on the go, go,
go. When day is done, or whenever there's a little break in the
action . . . *let's have a hug.*

I'm amazed and thankful that the Lord understands our
human need for touch, for warm contact with other people and
even from Him. No, we can't physically enjoy God's touch, but
He does have a way of reaching into our hearts. The prophet
Daniel needed that touch, and when he received it, he gained
renewed strength.

Do you need a touch from God at the moment? The wonderful thing is that God has empowered His people—all those
living in His kingdom—to administer that healing contact to
each other. So step closer . . . here . . . God bless you!

*We can joyfully celebrate God's love by
reaching out a warm, caring hand.*

—CMW

A Life Verse

"You are my servant. You have been chosen
to know me, believe in me, and understand
that I alone am God. There is no other God;
there never has been and never will be."

ISAIAH 43:10

About fifty years ago I sat on a lonely stretch of beach near Santa Monica, California, with my Bible open in front of me. I prayerfully set some goals for my life and, in the process, chose a life verse: Isaiah 43:10. This verse has anchored me all these years.

Have you chosen a life verse? I heartily recommend that you do. My life verse reminds me that I am God's witness and His servant. It also reminds me that He wants me to get to know Him.

As I pursue knowledge of Him, I find Him searching into my heart to help me know myself better. Sometimes I feel like a sardine can with the lid pulled back so He can expose my inmost thoughts. Yet how else would I prefer to be in the presence of the one true God—other than open, completely open to His goodness?

Let the Bible be the star to steer your ship by.

—FRANA HAMILTON

Big Little Difference

"Let the children come to me. Don't stop them!"
MARK 10:14

I have several nieces and nephews who are still just little tykes. I love seeing them at family gatherings, delighting in their zest for life and their innocent joy at play.

But it's easy to ignore the kids at those times, too, because we adults want to catch up on all the family "news." So throughout the day, I'll often hear phrases like this directed at the little ones:

"Not right now."
"Later."
"Hey, I'm talking here."
"Quiet now!"
"Just go out and play."
"See what's on TV."

I feel I have a special ministry in these situations. I *choose* to pay lots of attention to the kids. I remember what it's like to want to spend time with any adult who's truly interested in me. So I become that person, just for them, just for a while. I think it makes a big difference.

*Be alert to a child who needs
your undivided attention today.*

—CMW

Lights, Action!

"Though your hearts were once full of darkness,
now you are full of light from the Lord,
and your behavior should show it!"
EPHESIANS 5:8

My two-mile walk took me out of my residential area into
open space. Early one Sunday morning, the Colorado National
Monument glowed like embers as the rising sun shone on red
rock formations. Then, as I hiked up the last rise, a hot-air balloon rose between the pinnacles. As the yellow-, blue-, and
red-striped bulb ascended slowly and silently into the sky, the
sienna rocks accentuated its colors. The scene still vibrates in
my mind.

Light turns dull into exciting. Light shows us the way along
the path. Light helps us see things we would miss otherwise.

Jesus is the Light of the World. He loves, saves, and sustains us. His light gives our dull lives purpose. And full of Jesus'
light, we can reflect His love to others.

Ask Jesus to light up your life.

—JANE HEITMAN

Certainty

> "What is faith? It is the confident assurance
> that what we hope for is going to happen. It is
> the evidence of things we cannot yet see."
> HEBREWS 11:1

"If we begin with certainties, we shall end in doubts," said Francis Bacon, the seventeenth-century originator of the scientific method. "But if we begin with doubts, and are patient in them, we shall end in certainties."

Isn't that how it is with faith? We may not be sure, at first. But the more we live with God, the more we find His promises standing firm. And, ultimately, when we see the Lord face-to-face, all our doubts will be turned to eternal certainties.

One of my most precious faith-assurances is belief in the Resurrection. So many of my friends and family have died in my lifetime: mother, father, son. But somehow I manage to let them go. How is it possible? I know they will be raised . . . and I know I will follow.

Faith in God is never disappointed.

—CMW

Where Is God?

> "What is faith? It is the confident assurance
> that what we hope for is going to happen. It is
> the evidence of things we cannot yet see."
> HEBREWS 11:1

Where is God in all of this? I wondered after finding out I had colon cancer. Yet I realized I could have faith . . . or live amidst worry and doubt.

Envisioning the best outcome can't hurt. Then there's the work that goes with it. So many prayers blessed me that I learned it's vital to faithfully pray for our loved ones in crisis. Sharing cheerful greeting cards and flowers, consoling each other, and cultivating family rituals are other ways to demonstrate a caring faith.

Where is God in all of this? I want to see Him in all the corners of my life. Thankfully, the cancer was in its early stages, and I have recovered, at least for the present. And so faith, for me, is not only a deeply felt comfort in the face of death; it is helping me find a meaningful life.

God is always with you.

—BETTY JANE HEWITT

Cut List

"You are all children of God
through faith in Christ Jesus."
GALATIANS 3:26

I was a little "full bodied" in my school days, but I still wanted to be a cheerleader. I was coordinated, energetic, and filled with school spirit—so why not?

Okay, there was one reason: I just couldn't do those required cartwheels during the tryouts. Consequently, my name appeared on the cut list.

Oh, well. I could jump, cheer, holler. But cartwheels? Nope.

Thankfully, in the Kingdom of God there's a level playing field. Equal access. We are all equal members of God's family, having received forgiveness through Christ's work on the cross for us. And we have differing abilities and gifts to use in God's service.

Yes, others can outperform me in preaching or teaching, in giving or showing mercy, in evangelizing or administrating. But God only asks me to do what He's *equipped* me to do. I like that; I'll never show up on the celestial cut list.

*The Hand that points the way is the
same Hand that supplies the means.*

—CMW

Resignation

"'There is hope for your future,' says the LORD."
JEREMIAH 31:17

I recently wrote a resignation letter:

Dear Past,
I have endured the burden of working with you for the past thirty-five years. In that time I have not thrived under your constant scolding. I feel that with the lack of promotion I have experienced, I need change; therefore, I tender my resignation. I have been offered a position with an organization that offers forgiveness and change: The Future. Consequently, I am not open to the consideration of a counteroffer of either guilt or condemnation.

Thank you for the opportunity to sow sorrow and reap tears during the last few years. But I have absolutely no intention of completing the rest of my shift in this environment full of self-loathing.
Sincerely,
Rhonda

Is there anything in your past to
which you need to say good-bye?

—RHONDA DEYOUNG

Feelings Follow

"We will be confident when we stand before the Lord,
even if our hearts condemn us. For God is greater
than our hearts, and he knows everything."
1 JOHN 3:19–20

I'd been raised in a "free church," where worship was informal and impromptu. Then, some years after marriage, we began attending a liturgical church where worship was preplanned and perfectly purposeful. Now here's how this relates to our verse above: I had to work on my confidence in literally standing before the Lord.

In my old church, during communion, I'd be served with a little cup of juice as I sat quietly in the pew. In my new church, I had to stand, walk up to the altar rail, and kneel down.

Do I dare come? For a long time, I was afraid to take that walk—such a bold statement that God loved me and welcomed me at His family table.

I *did* believe! I believed in my forgiveness and my complete acceptance in Christ. Yet a sense of unworthiness condemned me.

My feelings needed to follow my footsteps. Eventually, they did.

*Keep believing and acting upon your convictions;
the feelings will follow.*

—CMW

The Dance Teacher

"David danced before the LORD with all his might."
2 Samuel 6:14

"Mom, Kara wants to come over sometime," said Bess, ". . . so you can show her how to dance." Nearly choking on my tea, I replied, "You can't be serious, honey. Why should she ask me, of all people?"

"Because of that song you wrote—the 'I Will Dance' one. She sings it all the time and wants to dance like the words say. But she doesn't know how."

Tears welled in my eyes. Imagine me teaching someone to dance! Me, the scared little girl (many years ago) who bombed ballet class, couldn't skip, and never made the team. Yet at home in my leisure and in my worship, the Lord had taught me to dance. My second left foot had disappeared as I sought the Lord and grew in His freedom.

Wiping a tear, I smiled at my daughter. "Ask Kara if she's free tomorrow."

As we spend time with the Lord, freedom grows.

—Betty Ray Hunter

What a Beauty!

"Don't be concerned about the outward beauty that depends on fancy hairstyles, expensive jewelry, or beautiful clothes. You should be known for the beauty that comes from within, the unfading beauty of a gentle and quiet spirit, which is so precious to God."

1 PETER 3:3–4

I took this Scripture's beauty advice to heart at a young age and dressed casually for school and even for church. Outward appearances weren't supposed to matter.

Then, as a young adult, I received a free makeover. It was impressive! Was that beauty in the mirror really . . . me?

Yes, it was nice. It was also temporary. That is, I just couldn't believe the work it would require, every morning, to get myself in makeover style each day. Hours and hours a week getting hair and face just right . . . and for what?

Here's how I see it: Highlight your best features, be clean and as attractive as you can be, and . . . get on with your life! According to the Scriptures, you'll be perfectly beautiful depending upon how the Lord has been grooming your inner spirit.

The beauty of a gentle spirit will shine through any face.

—CMW

He Cares

"Your heavenly Father already knows all your needs, and he will give you all you need from day to day if you live for him and make the Kingdom of God your primary concern."

MATTHEW 6:32–33

"Once upon a time, in a land far away . . ." That's how most fairy tales begin. As children, we read stories like *Beauty and the Beast* or *Snow White*, where ordinary women suddenly enter a crisis . . . get the handsome prince . . . and live happily ever after. *Sigh.*

In real life, many of us single women are still wondering, "Where is *my* Prince Charming?" I know women who put their lives on hold—or at least wait to buy good furniture—until they get married.

One of my favorite authors, Michelle McKinney-Hammond, writes, "Men are not your problem or your answer. What you need is a heavenly prince." I heartily agree. That prince is Jesus Christ, the One who wakes us up to the truth: The Heavenly Father is enough; look to Him first, and He will provide everything else.

God cares for all things, even your love life.

—JACKIE M. JOHNSON

The Purrrfect Solution

"Not even a sparrow, worth only half a penny, can
fall to the ground without your Father knowing it."
MATTHEW 10:29

Kayla, our seven-year-old granddaughter, told me how much she
still misses Leo, the family cat who died a year ago. Pets aren't
allowed by the new rental agreement Kayla's mother signed, but
I could keep a pet for her at our house. I prayed, "Lord, help me
find a cat for Kayla."

Yesterday when Kayla was visiting us, she said, "Grandma,
come see! This cat looks just like Leo." My husband recognized
the orange-and-white kitten taking a nap on our porch. Our
neighbor Mary had been feeding it—until moving recently.
She'd been concerned about what would happen to the strays
she left behind.

Now, whose prayer was answered—Mary's, Kayla's, or
mine? Perhaps all three. The orange kitten brought her salmon-
colored brother and their calico mother with her to our house
to feast on tuna. Three stray kitties got a new home.

God cares about the details of our lives.

—JEAN DAVIS

Walk Before Running

"You have been faithful in handling this small amount,
so now I will give you many more responsibilities."
MATTHEW 25:21

My toddler squares his tiny shoulders and steps out. His arms flap wildly. He manages one momentous step . . . and then another. But then he tries to walk faster and faster and, in spite of my warnings, breaks into a run—ending up flat on his face in the grass.

"Sweetheart, you must learn to walk before you can run," I say, smiling. But he won't listen. Little as he is, he scorns mere walking; he wants to race with the wind. He grabs hard at the nearest support—me!—pulls himself up, and he's off again.

I can almost hear a hint of laughter in my Heavenly Father's voice as He speaks to my heart: "My Daughter, you are like that little one. You, too, want to run before learning to walk; you, too, expect to accomplish great things overnight instead of faithfully carrying out the small tasks I entrust to you."

*Faithfulness in little things prepares
us to handle the big things.*

—TANYA FERDINANDUSZ

Spare Pegs, Rounded Wholes

"I will drive [my servant] like a peg into a firm place."
ISAIAH 22:23 (NIV)

Scarred with use, our vintage dresser holds orphaned gloves and hats, both trendy and passé. My great-grandfather planed its oak planks and fashioned each drawer without a single nail. Instead, he carved bull's-eye dovetails. To bore holes, then peg together hand-cut boards, takes time and skill. The cabinetmakers even carve extra pegs, in case one snaps. These days, such craftsmanship is rare.

Chisel, drill, sandpaper, hammer—the needed tools remind me how precisely God fits together the events of our lives, building character, making us stronger.

Yet there's a price for beauty. We may feel like one of those extra pieces that may never be needed. Or like my dresser, we're stuffed with memories nobody wants.

We may seem like square pegs in round holes, but in God's hands, we are sturdy, cherished, still serviceable: spare pegs becoming well-rounded wholes.

Jesus, the Master Carpenter, hones our inner natures.

—LAURIE KLEIN

Leaving the Nitty-Gritty

"My dear Martha, you are so upset
over all these details! There is really only one thing
worth being concerned about. Mary has
discovered it—and I won't take it away from her."
LUKE 10:41–42

My aunt was a neat, clean person, always well groomed. Her house was generally clutter-free, and I never once saw dishes left in the sink. But one chore she absolutely refused to do. "Why bother dusting?" she would say to anyone nervy enough to comment on the delicate layer gracing her coffee table. "It just comes back. Besides, there are more important things to do!"

I have to admit that Auntie knew what she was talking about. In her younger days, she'd been a world traveler, even visiting Cambodia during the middle of the Vietnam War. As she grew older, and her health declined, she focused her energies on giving to charities and sharing her wisdom with nieces and nephews. Her house was never dirty, but dusting was one nitty-gritty detail that just didn't matter.

*Slow down and focus on what's
really important in your life.*

—LISA M. KONZEN

Career of Peace

"God blesses those who work for peace,
for they will be called the children of God."
MATTHEW 5:9

When Katie and Kayla squabble among themselves, their mother, Eleanor, reminds them, "God blesses those who work for peace." Her words of caution always make me smile. Between sisters, peace rarely seems attainable.

At times we wonder whether peace is a reachable goal within the family of God, as well. One day, hearing Eleanor's familiar correction, the word "work" stood out to me. Instantly, I knew that tiny word is crucial.

In this world of quick fixes and instant potatoes, we like things to come easily for us. But peace takes work. If we can learn to smile through painful accusations, listen to differences of opinions, sincerely consider another's suggested plan, then peace will come to pass.

I want to work for peace. I want to be known as Pam, blessed child of God.

Make peace your career choice;
it yields a large salary of blessings.

—PAMELA J. KUHN

Worth the Move

> "Honor your father and mother.
> Then you will live a long, full life in the
> land the LORD your God will give you."
> EXODUS 20:12

Like any child, I had my times of being disrespectful to parents. I once responded to Mom's "No" with an obstinate, "No means yes, and yes means no!" That earned me some swift correction.

In my midlife years, I found this verse in Exodus coming to the forefront of my life. We lived in a beautiful mountainous area in Colorado . . . but Daddy was sick and hurting in Florida. Would we move down to help him through his last few years? Give up our good jobs, load everything up, and determine to serve him? *Honor* him?

Yes, we called the moving company. And it was a tough transition. But how glad I am that I was able to bless Daddy with my time and energy when he needed it most. For me, it was a once-in-a-lifetime opportunity.

Honoring our parents means sacrificing
for them in our middle age.

—CMW

Ruth

"She asked me this morning if she
could gather grain behind the harvesters.
She has been hard at work ever since, except
for a few minutes' rest over there in the shelter."
RUTH 2:7

Telephone calls and the list on my day planner seemed to scream for my attention as I halfheartedly sat down for devotions. But then I found myself immersed in the story of Ruth. Widowed, a poverty-stricken immigrant, Ruth adapted to the customs of a foreign culture and went to glean the leftover grain in a stranger's field.

My thoughts raced ahead of the story, and I wondered if she'd quickly glean the grain so she could retreat to Naomi's home—or would she work slowly, reliving each disappointment that had brought her there. No, Ruth's style was persistence. In fact, her performance was noteworthy, for the employed harvesters mentioned it to their boss.

Discouragement can attack any of us feeling stressed and overworked. But Ruth provides a wonderful way through: She did what she could, and trusted God with the rest.

Take one step at a time.

—CAROL ANN LANDIS

Food and a Roof

"You prepare a feast for me in the presence
of my enemies. You welcome me as a guest,
anointing my head with oil. My cup
overflows with blessings."
PSALM 23:5

It had begun innocently enough. My friends had charged a few things they couldn't afford "right at that moment," hoping next month would be better. Instead of better, it got worse. A premature baby and medical bills. A car accident and repair bills. A temporary layoff and . . . the bills kept coming. Eventually, they had to declare bankruptcy.

One thing they had going for them was the assurance that loyal relatives would help keep food on the table and a roof over their heads. Without that promise, they wouldn't have had the strength to keep trying, day after day, to pay off their debt.

We have a greater assurance. Christ prepares a place in Heaven for us. A place of beauty and grace. A place free from trouble. A place to forget that we ever even had troubles at all.

When daily living drags you down,
look to God's promises.

—SUSAN LYTTEK

Just in Time

"There is . . . a time to embrace."
ECCLESIASTES 3:1, 5

Carolyn's friend, Linda, had battled cancer for nine years. Now it was evident she was losing her fight and had only days to live.

When Carolyn went for a visit, Linda's daughter, Beth, was there. Carolyn asked Beth how she was coping. The question released a torrent of tears. Carolyn went to her and gave Beth a big hug.

At the funeral, Beth told Carolyn how much she had appreciated that hug. It came at a time when she needed encouragement. It was such a simple act, but it meant much to a young woman who sat by her mother's side as death drew near.

Most of us have been blessed through the kind, loving touch of others. Now it is time to pass along that love. We never know when we might give a hug, just in time, to someone struggling with a grievous burden.

There is someone near you who needs
a kind word or a touch of love.

—NORMA C. MEZOE

Rejoice!

"Even though the fig trees have no blossoms, and there are no grapes on the vine; even though the olive crop fails, and the fields lie empty and barren; even though the flocks die in the fields, and the cattle barns are empty, yet I will rejoice in the LORD! I will be joyful in the God of my salvation."

HABAKKUK 3:17–18

For the prophet Habakkuk, it was about poor crops and dwindling flocks. For me, it was about poor transportation. I'm talking about my car—an aging 1991 Hyundai Excel. I was on my way to an important meeting. And even though the oil is leaking and the seats have no softness and the windshield is cracked and the paint is rusting and the bumper is bashed and the mirror is broken . . .

. . . Yet . . . I will arrive.

It's true of all of us believers. Our lives here on Earth will, as Jesus said, swirl with trials and tribulations. That's a promise. But because our Savior has risen and arrived in Heaven—and is seated at the right hand of the Father—we too will arrive, safe and sound. Therefore, rejoice.

Let us be joyful, not in the circumstances,
but in the One who reigns over them.

—CMW

Before You Call

"I will answer them before they even call to me.
While they are still talking to me about their needs,
I will go ahead and answer their prayers!"
ISAIAH 65:24

There we were, standing on the ship's decks like a thousand penguins in orange vests. The ship's rules demanded that all passengers attend a safety drill.

After learning how to strap on my life jacket, I noticed a little whistle attached to the side. Blowing it would alert rescuers to my position among the waves.

As I stood through the rest of the demonstration, I thought about how God prepares us to be rescued from drowning in life's troubled waters. In many verses, He tells us to simply call. Here, He says He'll answer even sooner—*before* we call.

My prayers, then, are like the little whistle on my life jacket. With one big difference: My soul's rescuer already knows where I am, already knows my every need.

Have you talked with God today?

—DOROTHY MINEA

Big Bad Bear

"The LORD who saved me from the claws
of the lion and the bear will save me. . . ."
1 SAMUEL 17:37

As we were playing outside before school, some of the older boys ran out of the nearby woods hollering, "There's a huge bear coming!" We first-grade girls ran screaming into our classroom. We stood on tiptoe, peering out the windows, waiting for the terrible monster to appear.

I turned to the others and said, "Don't worry. My mama is coming to school this morning. She'll take care of us."

Of course, no bear materialized. Boys will be boys.

But even when I thought the threat was real, I was able to stand unafraid because I knew Mom was coming—the tiny woman who barely topped a hundred pounds.

Today, as an adult, I long to have a childlike trust in the all-powerful Father. To know that He will take care of me, regardless of the beastly dangers galloping my way.

God's presence can turn terror into trust.

—CORA LEE PLESS

Messy Solitude

"He never grows faint or weary. . . .
He gives power to those who are tired and
worn out; he offers strength to the weak."
ISAIAH 40:28–29

I plodded wearily to the annoying buzzer on my washing machine, jammed for the second time in half an hour. I had been up most of the night with a sick baby, so I was already exhausted. But my day was just beginning.

As I yanked open the lid to the soggy mess, I heard a distinct *plop*—my toddler trying to fill our toilet with her tubby toys, again. With a groan I left my twisted laundry and hurried to the next room to rescue the plumbing.

Ever feel alone in the mess? We want someone to understand when we're so tired we could cry, when our washer jams and our toddler makes a statement in our not-too-clean bathroom.

It helps to turn to God at those times. It helps to remember: We're known and understood by the One who sees our day *before* it begins.

In the exhausting chaos of your moments,
God sees and cares. You are not alone.

—MABELLE REAMER

SEPTEMBER

9/11 HOPE

"We have this hope as an anchor
for the soul, firm and secure."
HEBREWS 6:19 (NIV)

*J*WAS EIGHT MONTHS PREGNANT AND HEAVY WITH the weight of my unborn daughter when a routine ultrasound showed that the umbilical cord was wrapped around her neck. Not to worry, the doctor had said. It was quite common and not life threatening as far as he could tell.

The news however, was devastating to me as my mind drifted back to the hospital where I had gone to pray over the little body of my friend's infant son who had died in the womb two weeks before delivery. The autopsy had shown that he had been choked by the cord around his neck.

Their grief was still fresh in my heart, and I could not contain my tears. That very morning before my appointment, I had opened to Hebrews 6:19 and clung to those words—and to the Lord as my hope—though I wept anxious tears as I pleaded for divine intervention. "Please show me how to keep hope in you as my anchor," I prayed. That weekend, as I routinely timed the baby's movements, I was alarmed to find that there were no movements. Twenty minutes later, I tried again but still could feel no movements.

My husband rushed me to the hospital. After a lengthy checkup, the doctor assured me that the baby was fine and not to worry. But still I was uneasy. Then, a few days later, a friend called and said she had an image of a baby with a noose around its neck. She immediately discerned that I was in need of prayer and after praying for quite a while, she felt peace and heard in her mind the words, "Her name is Hosanna."

I recognized the word. *Hosanna* means "O Save!" or "God saves" in Hebrew. It was the cry of the Israeli people for a Savior in the Bible as they welcomed Jesus into Jerusalem, just days before he died to save them. Three days later, He rose from the dead to show that He had come not to assert a political kingdom but to save the people from the power of death. The name gave me a tremendous sense of peace. The following week, to my relief, the ultrasound test showed that the umbilical cord had slipped off of her neck. The doctor was baffled, as such an occurrence was highly unlikely that late in the term.

Four weeks later, on the 11th of September, my labor pains began. Bent over double, I watched in horror and disbelief as smoke poured out of what remained of the World Trade Center. The birth pains grew sharper and seemed to be connected with the pain and devastation I was seeing on the TV. Between contractions I prayed for myself, and the life within me, and for the people who had lost their loved ones.

I decided to ease my pain with a bath. We had planned to have a home birth with a midwife but figured that it would be a while before she needed to come—my first baby had taken thirty-nine hours to come into the world. Five hours later, however, my water broke. Before

283

the midwife could even get there, my daughter came into the world and into my husband's unprepared arms.

The cord was around her neck, and she was *not* crying.

Frantically, I slipped my finger under the grayish mass and gently lifted the cord over her head. To my intense relief, she promptly let out a lusty cry. Tears of joy filled my eyes as I witnessed the miracle of the birth of my healthy seven-pound baby girl.

That day, as we knelt to give thanks for her safe delivery, we were reminded of her name, "Hosanna—God Saves." We realized that her name was given not only to encourage us to have hope in the midst of our own private trial but as an encouragement to find hope in the midst of a much greater crisis that was now rending the heart of our nation. "Let this be a hope as an anchor for your soul," God seemed to say, "that I am the Savior."

Even now, though I have experienced plenty of crises since that time, I take heart in retelling this story. It reminds me to look for the hope and to let it continually be an anchor for my soul. Even in the midst of despair, there is always hope.

—COLLEEN YANG

Discipline

"As you endure this divine discipline, remember
that God is treating you as his own children.
Whoever heard of a child who was never disciplined?"
HEBREWS 12:7

Even as a teenager, I liked maintaining certain "daily disciplines": doing homework right after school, putting skin cream on my face every night, reading my Bible before falling asleep. God calls us to certain habits that will nurture our spiritual growth, and we can choose the ones that work best for us. But another kind of "discipline" God brings to us is His loving correction when we get off track.

Here's where the two disciplines meet: When I'm filling my life with the right habitual practices, I'm less likely to need the divine habitual corrections.

Yes, God will use our difficulties to bring growth into our lives: Otherwise we'd never develop patience, perseverance, or a compassionate heart. But why not forgo His painful correction by planning in advance to live a disciplined life?

*When life is perplexing, cling to the truth that God always
desires your highest welfare—even as He corrects you.*

—CMW

Scraps

"Yes, he humbled you by letting you go hungry and then feeding you with manna. . . . He did it to teach you that people need more than bread for their life; real life comes by feeding on every word of the LORD."

DEUTERONOMY 8:3

"Mom! Jezebel's begging again!" yelled my daughter, Meghan. Without shame, our dog set her plaintive eyes right on Meghan's sandwich.

"Is there any dog food in her dish?" I asked.

"I just filled it."

"Let me guess," I said. "She sniffed at it, then turned up her nose." Meghan agreed, shaking her head.

That's our dog. She ignores the food that's good for her to seek half-eaten tidbits from the table. Only when she realizes that her repeated pleading won't glean a single morsel will she eat what we set out for her.

It struck me that Jezebel's habit sometimes parallels my Christian walk. Instead of feasting on God's Word, I let other things consume my quiet time. Usually, though, it doesn't take long for me to recognize that real life doesn't come in the scraps scrounged from the world's table.

> *When it comes to knowing God,*
> *don't live a dog's life anymore.*

—LORI Z. SCOTT

Take Your Best Shot!

"The Lord is my helper, so I will not be afraid.
What can mere mortals do to me?"
HEBREWS 13:6

The most dangerous person in any negotiation is the one with nothing to lose. You can't persuade her or threaten her. You can't do anything to hurt her, so . . . she's not afraid, and she's in control. . . . Kinda like a wonder woman, armed with super-human power!

However, our Scripture today applies the concept in a wonderful way that I can claim when life plays rough. If the King of the Universe is on our side, how could we ever lose? Ultimately, every battle is won, every pain overcome, every tear wiped away.

Yes, there's suffering while we await the coming deliverance. But it will come. In the meantime, be dangerous for the Kingdom. Be fearless for the good.

With God as our helper, we can say to our tough
times, "Go ahead, take your best shot!"

—CMW

Captive to the Finite

"They will come to their senses and escape
from the Devil's trap. For they have been held
captive by him to do whatever he wants."
2 TIMOTHY 2:26

Seated upon the riding mower, I maneuvered between the trees when, suddenly, I realized I was being propelled up and not out. The chain of one of the swings had caught on the nose of the mower, and its front end was rising up as the mower balanced on its back wheels. I was riding a bucking bronco!

It's amazing how quickly unforeseen dangers can snare us, even in our spiritual growth. Each of us seems to have a special vulnerability, so take a moment to consider: What is it, for me, that most quickly entices my affections?

A deep-down longing resides in us all. It may attach to anything that seems to offer solace and satisfaction. Beware! Inordinate affection for what is only finite can draw a heart away from the Source of infinite bliss.

What is bedeviling you to turn away from Jesus today?

—PENNY SMITH

Credit

"To the man who does not work but trusts
God who justifies the wicked, his faith is
credited as righteousness."
ROMANS 4:5 (NIV)

When I was a child my parents bought me "magic sketch pads."
The magic was that each page had drawn on it an invisible
picture. An artist had already done all the work. I simply scrib-
bled with a pencil, and the original drawing became visible. I
couldn't take credit for the art, but I could enjoy the benefits of
it just the same.

We did not witness the miracles Jesus performed. We did
not see Him crucified. We were not with John when he found
the empty tomb. In accepting the gift of Jesus' perfect righteousness as our own, it is simply credited to our account.

Then, our lives change! We love others with Christ's love.
We live in the power of the same Holy Spirit who raised Jesus
from the dead. In believing (or scribbling), the invisible is made
visible in our lives.

*How good of God to freely credit
righteousness to our lifetime accounts!*

—RACHEL M. TAMILIO

SEPTEMBER 6

Just Passing Through

"We are citizens of heaven, where the
Lord Jesus Christ lives. And we are eagerly
waiting for him to return as our Savior."
PHILIPPIANS 3:20

Have you ever experienced homesickness? Oh, the heartache, the tears, the drama!

But what about "heavenly homesickness"—the feeling that there must be a better place than good ole Planet Earth? Bob Hartman of the rock band Petra says it right when he says we are "pilgrims in a strange land . . . so far from our homeland" ("Not of this World." 1983).

No wonder the Christian worldview seems alien at times. Today's Scripture reminds us of our special hope that keeps this mortal life in proper perspective. We're on a journey, just passin' through. And as citizens of heaven, we're a long way from home.

*Do not become overly attached to all the things
of your life; another existence awaits you.*

—CMW

Run to Daddy

"The LORD is like a father to his children,
tender and compassionate to those who fear him."
PSALM 103:13

When our daughter was a toddler, she was quite unsteady and yet quite daring as well. She loved to run, climb, crawl into little spaces, corner the dog, and try new things. Many times her adventurous spirit resulted in falls, scrapes, bruises, frights, and frustrations.

Yet whenever she cried out to her father, he was there to comfort and hold her, to encourage her to try again—or try something a better way. I loved watching my husband's interaction with her, the compassion he showed her in times of fear and disappointment.

God is the ultimate compassionate Father. He listens to my fears, gives me hope when I fall and fail, forgives my mistakes, and heals my bruised heart.

The best of all fathers, God wants the best for us. We know it's true, because it's exactly how we feel about our own kids.

The Father hurts when we hurt and rejoices in our joy.

—KATHRYN LAY

291

Two Questions

"A word aptly spoken is like apples
of gold in settings of silver."
Proverbs 25:11

The woman boarded the plane and stood beside my seat. I smiled and stood so she could get past me and sit down. She barely muttered a quiet thank-you. During the preflight instructions, the woman stared into space, her face grim, hands clasped tightly. A few minutes into the flight, I turned to her. "Where are you headed today?" I asked.

Soon I learned her father was critically ill. She'd made several trips to see him but now his condition had suddenly worsened. She was weary and exhausted. Would she make it one more time before he died?

When the flight ended, we walked together down the concourse. And I felt compelled to ask one more question, "May I pray with you?"

Place these words of wisdom in your conversational repertoire: "May I pray with you?"

—Claudean Boatman

A Fragrant Provision

"They are a sweet-smelling sacrifice
that is acceptable to God and pleases him."
PHILIPPIANS 4:18

Gail wrote us from Papua, New Guinea, far away from family
and friends. She'd received our missionary box, which included
one of her favorite foods: macaroni and cheese. As it cooked,
she thought of Paul when he thanked others for the gifts he
received: "I am amply supplied, now that I have received from
Epaphroditus the gifts you sent. They are a fragrant offering, an
acceptable sacrifice, pleasing to God."

The treats were fragrant, a touch of home. She had been
on the mission field for over a year and something as simple as
macaroni and cheese brought her close once again.

We have all been at a place in our lives where we just
needed that extra touch or smile . . . maybe something as simple as macaroni and cheese. Has God prompted you to offer
that kind of sacrifice for someone today?

It pleases God when we provide for His servants.

—FRANCINE DUCKWORTH

Always Wear the Love

"The most important piece of clothing you
must wear is love. Love is what binds us all
together in perfect harmony."
COLOSSIANS 3:14

When I was a young associate pastor in a small church, my husband and I would sometimes attend neighborhood picnics and special outings in clown outfits. We loved it when kids would come up and let us paint their faces or listen to the stories our puppets were telling.

We always stored our "clown clothes" somewhere in our cluttered attic, usually packed away in a plastic garbage bag. The bag would contain two of everything—wigs of blue hair and orange hair, red-and-white-striped overalls, and monstrously large green shoes. Fun!

And yet those clown clothes would have been nothing without the most important thing we could wear to any of those community events: our love for the children and our concern for their spiritual lives. Our silly clothes would often bring a chuckle. But our warm smiles—beaming right into their eyes—would spark something infinitely more wonderful.

Clothe yourself in the love of God every morning.

—CMW

Limited Perception?

"Whatever measure you use in judging others,
it will be used to measure how you are judged."
MATTHEW 7:2

Standing in the church corridor, I noticed a woman walk by in a revealing, sheer white dress. While pretending not to see her overexposed, shapely form, I thought, *Flaunting it, huh? And in church, no less!*

Later, I stopped in the restroom before entering the sanctuary. Panic gripped me while adjusting my clothes; I discovered I'd forgotten to wear my slip. I went to the mirror and saw the outline of my white undergarments.

Another case of flaunting! I felt trapped. I felt silly. I cracked open the door for a peek before venturing out. Wall-to-wall people.

With my Bible and notebook pressed in strategic places, I crossed the foyer and slid into a pew against the back wall. Then, a few minutes before the pastor dismissed the congregation, I dashed out. Scurrying to my car, I could almost hear God chuckling at my new understanding of humility.

*Acknowledge your limited perception and ask
God to forgive any judgmental attitudes.*

—CAROLE SUZANNE JACKSON

SEPTEMBER 12

Get out of the Way

"The LORD himself will fight for you.
You won't have to lift a finger in your defense!"
EXODUS 14:14

No sound in fourth grade held such terror for me as the St. Bernard Elementary dismissal bell. While classmates hustled to depart, my feet moved as though weighted by cinder blocks.

Bullies usually waited for me and my brother Sam. Jeering, they'd form a ring around us and then the fists would fly. Although my girlish defense amounted to ineffectual swings, Sam took manful swipes for us both.

My brother's prebell instructions never varied: "Take off running, and don't stop." Once he engaged our antagonists, he'd give me a shove. I pumped my skinny legs, skirt flying, as though my life depended on their stride.

Several decades later I recognize a marked difference between panicked defensive movements and the quiet anticipation of God's intercession on my behalf. Like it or not, some situations will exceed my span of control. Time to step back and let God be my Defender.

Sometimes being still is more difficult than doing battle.

—PHILLIS HARRIS-BROOKS

My Stars!

"Look at the lilies and how they grow. . . .
Solomon in all his glory was not dressed
as beautifully as they are."
MATTHEW 6:28–29

God must really like the five-pointed star shape. Consider the many places it appears in nature. Myriad flowers of every color and size have five-point blossoms. There's the periwinkle, morning glory, star jasmine, star magnolia, verbena, penstemon, blue phlox . . . and this only begins the list.

Look in the middle of an apple cut crossways at the core. A perfect star shape. Examine closely the stem end of a blueberry—another star. Investigate on your own, and you'll find many more examples in unexpected places.

Looking at the world around us we can easily see God appreciates variety and diversity, too. And what joy that brings to us. We are all created alike, yet different, the Lord of the Universe being the perfect designer.

Why do I fret, then, over how I am made—stick-straight hair, bumpy nose, pear-shaped figure?

God loves His creation, our human
bodies, in all their variety.

—BEVERLY MONEY LUKE

Roots

"Let your roots grow down into him and draw up nourishment from him, so you will grow in faith, strong and vigorous in the truth you were taught. Let your lives overflow with thanksgiving for all he has done."

COLOSSIANS 2:7

We were stunned by the four hurricanes that hit our Florida town in quick succession. Not only did we face fear before each storm hit. We also dealt with uncomfortable power outages afterward: sleeping in 90-degree nighttimes with no air-conditioning, eating peanut-butter sandwiches with warm water, lighting candles each evening—and *not* checking important e-mails.

Things could have been worse. Our house was saved, and our family members all survived without injury.

But not the trees! So many seemingly immovable oak trees lay on the grass all around town, tipped over by the wind as if they were light as paper. Some of them had lived for centuries, but apparently their roots were more shallow than anyone knew.

It can happen to us. But growing our roots strong in the nourishment of God's truth will keep us standing through the strongest storms. How is your root system these days?

Be thankful: God's truth is free and available to make you strong.

—CMW

A Tough Job

"Forgive us our debts, as we also
have forgiven our debtors."
MATTHEW 6:12

When I took on the job of stripping and waxing the church's nursery-room floors, I was excited, visualizing how beautiful those scuffed floors would soon look. The stripping solution did its work, and I dug into mopping up the sludge. *What have I gotten myself into?* The floor was a mess!

It reminded me of another tough job. When I set out to forgive the man who raped me, I naively thought it would be a quick fix to feeling better. Instead, I uncovered yucky goop.

I had to remove layers of false forgiveness. I mopped up forgetting it happened. I poured down the drain pretending rape wasn't a big deal. And then I had to dump the idea that I was too nice to get angry.

With all the junk cleared away, all that remained was my naked heart—only able to forgive because God asked me to do it.

When the offense is horrible and forgiveness is hard,
hang in there; it will be worth the hard work.

—TANYA T. WARRINGTON

Be Who You Are

"You made all the delicate, inner parts of my body
and knit me together in my mother's womb."
PSALM 139:13

When I first became a Christian, I thought I'd have to quit doing some things I loved to do, like wearing blue jeans and riding my motorcycle. But since then, I've learned that God certainly wants to cut sin out of my life . . . but as for everything else? I think he takes pleasure in my joy. After all, this is how he put me together—to love what I love.

As a matter of fact, He has even used my passion for motorcycling to impact others for Him. When a "chance encounter" reconnected me with my longtime friend Debi, I learned she had a motorcycle. "Can we ride together?" she asked.

"Hal and I are riding to church Sunday. Would you like to meet us?" I said.

"Yes!" she said. She has since joined a church and is growing in her new faith.

God doesn't want to change who you are; He created you.

—DIANNE E. BUTTS

The Blessing of Busyness

"She rises also while it is still night . . . gives food to her household . . . considers a field . . . grasps the spindle . . . makes coverings for herself . . . supplies belts to tradesmen . . . she smiles at the future."

PROVERBS 31

Many women look to the Proverbs 31 woman for inspiration. This biblical role model did it all—managing real estate, cooking, tailoring—and she dressed well while she was at it! She was smart, good-looking, and happy (she smiled at the future). She was also one thing above all others: She was *busy*.

I often hear speakers talk about busyness as if it were an incurable disease, when the truth is busyness is a natural outcome of health and prosperity. Most people in the world would be delighted to drive my minivan around all day with its air-conditioning, books on CD, even my choice of music at the touch of a button. Not exactly torture, but, yes, I agree I feel too busy.

I'm simply saying that even busyness can be a blessing. The key is: What am I busy *about*?

Give thanks for the chance to be busy doing good.

—KARLA DOYLE

Ageless

"We know that when this earthly tent we live in is taken down—when we die and leave these bodies—we will have a home in heaven, an eternal body made for us by God himself and not by human hands."

2 CORINTHIANS 5:1

It was hard to watch Dad's suffering as he approached death. His body had changed so much, ravaged by a stroke, by cancer, and now by congestive heart failure.

I saw his utter frailty, yes. But there were also times when I glimpsed something else in him. At certain moments, in the way he moved or talked or looked at me, I saw the young man once again, the one I'd seen in the old black-and-white pictures in the family albums.

I'm thankful for those glimpses. For I know that Dad—and all of us who believe—will inherit an ever-living body. The wrinkles on the skin we know now will eventually turn to dust. But in our life to come, through the ages, we are ageless.

Your home in Heaven awaits you.

—CMW

Life-Saving Comfort

"LORD, you know the hopes of the helpless.
Surely you will listen to their cries and comfort them."
PSALM 10:17

A friend once confessed that she frequently considered ending her life. What could I say that would not sound trite? I am not a counselor, and I didn't feel qualified to help.

"She needs more of You, Father," I prayed. "Is there anything I can say to this hurting woman?"

Remembering how God has helped me, I timidly began, "I don't know if this will help you, but when I felt worthless, God really comforted me with Psalm 139." I reached for my Bible and read the passage to her over the phone, and then we talked. . . . That is, I *listened.*

About fifteen years later, I was at a Christian women's retreat with this same friend. I overheard her share with another woman, "If I were going to read only one Bible passage every day, it would be Psalm 139. It comforts me each time I read it."

*We don't need to be counselors to
share God's lifesaving words.*

—TANYA T. WARRINGTON

Fit for Trouble

"Today's trouble is enough for today."
MATTHEW 6:34

Visiting the house of an old friend from high school, I saw a picture hanging above her washer and dryer. It was a nicely framed and neatly hung old cross-stitch showing a line of clean laundry hanging on a clothesline. The little poem at the bottom said, "If all of our troubles were hung on a line, you would take yours and I would take mine."

It summed up all I'd been thinking about life's trials. While I was glad not to have two children in diapers and one in kindergarten, my friend was glad not to be thinking of driver's education and the sight of a teenaged son with a power tool in his hand.

The little poem and today's Scripture help me remember two important things about life: My troubles are a pretty good fit for me—and I need deal with only a day's worth at a time.

Let your unique troubles mold you into the beautifully unique person you are to become.

—KARLA DOYLE

Toddling

> "I know the LORD is always with me.
> I will not be shaken, for he is right beside me."
> PSALM 16:8

"He's walking!" My daughter-in-law's excitement was contagious, even over the phone line. For weeks, she and our son had offered little Levi a hand to help him progress into official "toddlerdom." But day after day he'd refused and simply crawled away.

"What did the trick?" I asked.

"Well, he found an inflated balloon. Thinking it was tethered to something he could trust he held it high, left the table, and took his first little walk."

I'm so like my grandson. Instead of trusting the firm hand of the Lord, I often wait until I discover something I can see, feel, or touch—and grab hold. A friendship. A bank account. A bit of status. But why should I settle for unstable things and just toddle through life?

Why grasp for air when you can grasp
the outstretched hand of God?

—SANDRA THIESSEN

I Am

"In the beginning the Word already existed.
He was with God, and he was God. He was in
the beginning with God. He created everything
there is. Nothing exists that he didn't make."

JOHN 1:1–3

One of the most amazing things about Jesus is His awesome genealogy. In these initial verses from John's Gospel, I'm faced with a claim of His eternal existence. Will I dare to believe it? Or will I settle for calling Jesus merely a great teacher (which is the popular approach of our society today)?

One of my favorite things to think about, as a person who loves studying ancient history, is, "How did everything come to be?" The simple truth is that God thought, then *spoke.* There is something about that initial vibration; it set everything else into motion and into being.

But not Jesus. He always was. He always will be. Will You call Him Lord of all?

> *Jesus is a great teacher . . . but much more:*
> *your ever-living Lord.*

—CMW

More Than Max

"The LORD is like a father to his children, tender and
compassionate to those who fear him. For he understands
how weak we are; he knows we are only dust."
PSALM 103:13–14

One day Lori and Dean found a nest of wild baby ducks on the
large estate where they worked as caretakers. The mother lay
dead by the nest, and efforts to save the tiny creatures failed,
until only one little one remained.

They took Baby with them in the evening and placed him
in their fountain that flowed like a stream. "He can swim here,
and the wooden fence will keep him in the yard," Dean said.
Their yellow Labrador, Max, seemed to say, "Oh, what a sweet
little thing." He stood guard, and when Baby decided to take a
walk in the grass, Max gently nosed him back to the water.

Everyone loves Max. He's gentle and tender with his family
and any helpless little creatures around him.

But isn't it comforting to know that Jesus is a supremely
more tender and compassionate friend, even than Max?

*Welcome God's tenderness into
your life this very moment.*

—AUDREY HEBBERT

A Good Night's Sleep

"He giveth his beloved sleep."
PSALM 127:2 (KJV)

That little bald-headed, blue-eyed infant was my delight. Except for one thing. He was codependent on his pacifier. Wouldn't sleep without one in each hand and one in his mouth, and would drop them from his crib with frustrating consistency. So every night for six months, I would hear a scream, stumble into the little guy's room, dive under the crib, and retrieve the lost treasure.

"God, you know how much sleep I need!" I prayed with all the accusation of a woman scorned. Like an echo from the mountains, the answer came, "God, you know how much sleep I need!"

Yes, God really *does* know! He knows what I spent my time on yesterday, and what will be required of me tomorrow. If I am not sleeping at this moment, God will either let me catch extra minutes in the morning or give me less to do during the day. Thank God!

God measures our strength
according to our responsibilities.

—KARLA DOYLE

Tea, Anyone?

"You are united with the one who
was raised from the dead."
Romans 7:4

Jenny, the dining aide at the retirement home, knows Ava's routine. Ava takes her place at table number two, and Jenny brings her special china cup with a tea bag and silver spoon.

"Papaya Peppermint, my favorite. Pour the water onto the tea for better flavor; never dunk the bag in the water." Jenny always smiles at the oft-repeated words. Together the two wait for the tea to steep, and then Ava takes one spoonful of sugar and carefully stirs it in.

"Just right," she says after a first sip. "I love my tea."

One day I watched Ava's routine from table number three, and thought of our relationship with Jesus. Once Ava stirs that sugar, it becomes part of the tea, and no one can remove it. In similar fashion, Jesus becomes one with us when we accept His wonderful plan of salvation.

He permeates our lives as sugar permeates tea.

—Audrey Hebbert

Unconventional Beachcomber

"The LORD looks down from heaven
and sees the whole human race."
PSALM 33:13

My husband and I ambled along an Oregon beach at low tide. As we strolled, our eyes scanned the wet sand and flattening breakers, looking for unbroken shells and sand dollars.

It occurred to me that God isn't the ordinary beachcomber. His search is far different than mine. I'm intent on a flawless, unbroken shell. He seeks the flawed and broken—you and me.

For who of us can traverse a life span without being swept about in the tides of disappointment or despair? Being caught in an undertow of uncertainty and fear? Enduring the raging storms of pain and suffering?

Yet He searches. And, thankfully, He finds! Cupping us tenderly in His hands, God carries us home.

God rescues and repairs our broken hearts.

—MARLENE DEPLER

Where Is God?

"From the time the world was created, people have seen the earth and sky and all that God made. They can clearly see his invisible qualities—his eternal power and divine nature. . . ."

ROMANS 1:20

It is a family joke that my mother is constantly losing her keys. When I was a little girl, we'd all regularly turn the house upside down hunting for those keys. And they'd turn up in the most unexpected places. On one occasion, we found them freezing in the fridge. Another time, they had been neatly packed inside a picnic lunch. And quite often the keys would be "found" in my mother's pocket! Then we'd have a good laugh at Mum!

People sometimes say they are "searching" for God, as if He were lost or playing hide-and-seek. But God is not hiding; He is everywhere, revealing Himself in all of creation, in Jesus, in human beings who have been created in His image and likeness. We don't have to look very far to find Him. Just as far as our own hearts.

God is ever-present, as close as our next breath.

—TANYA FERDINANDUSZ

Limited

"[Christ] made himself nothing; he took the humble position of a slave and appeared in human form."
PHILIPPIANS 2:7

Our great Lord didn't remain outside His creation; He chose to *inhabit* it. But He had to limit Himself to do it. In fact, one Bible translation says that Christ "emptied himself" to come to earth. That is, He chose not to manifest all His heavenly glory among us. We wouldn't be able to take it!

It's like us reading a story and really *getting into* it. But we have to limit our thinking to the boundaries of the setting. If the story comes from centuries past, and from a different culture, then we must keep our minds in that framework. We empty out everything we know of our modern world to interact with characters who couldn't relate to computers and DVD players.

Similarly, Jesus humbly entered our existence. To relate to us. Someday we will relate to Him in all His fullness.

What a glorious future lies ahead!

—CMW

Gift from Granny

"Look here, you people who say, 'Today or tomorrow we are going to a certain town and will stay there a year.' What you ought to say is, 'If the Lord wants us to, we will live and do this or that.' Otherwise, you will be boasting about your own plans, and all such boasting is evil."

JAMES 4:13; 4:15–16

As a little girl, I would often go with Mom when she took my grandmother shopping. I began to notice that my initials, L. W., were always at the top of Granny's shopping list. I was certain this code was her reminder to buy a surprise for me. Each time we took Granny back to her house, I'd linger so she could give me my surprise.

When the surprise gift didn't appear after several shopping trips, I could stand the suspense no more. "Granny," I asked, "why do you always write L. W. at the top of your shopping list?"

"Well, dear," she replied, "that stands for 'Lord willing.' Before my day begins, I give my plans to the Lord." I was crestfallen to hear her explanation. But, through the years, I came to appreciate this special surprise gift: a lesson in putting God first in my life.

All our plans need to go through God's office first.

—LINDA K. HEIMBURGER

Heavenly Lullaby

"The Lord your God . . . will exult over you
by singing a happy song."
ZEPHANIAH 3:17

"Sing song—'nother one," my two-year-old granddaughter says as we rock back and forth. She enjoys hearing the lullabies, and for me it is pure pleasure.

I treasured the moments of rocking and singing to my children when they were small. Now it's the same with my grandchildren. For a few moments, I pull them close to my heart and look into their precious little faces. I express my delight and love for them by singing a melody. The soothing tones usually bring comfort and calm. Often, before I'm through, they have fallen asleep.

Here's a wonderful thing: The mighty Creator of the Universe desires to calm our fears and sing to us. In a sense, we are infants in His arms, carried close to His heart. He longs to quiet our anxiety with His love.

God's joy over you spills out into song!

—MARLENE DEPLER

OCTOBER

COMFORT COMES IN BUNCHES

"Don't be afraid. Just trust me."

MARK 5:36

ONE MOMENT I WAS FINE, OR AT LEAST I THOUGHT I was, and the next moment, the slippery slope of my world shifted. All the years of secrets appeared to have taken their toll. Usually when facing a crisis, I'd coach myself, "Just get through this. When this is over, you can do anything you want. Even have a nervous breakdown."

Although that had worked in the past, this time my body refused to cooperate. Just trying to focus left me as whipped as if I'd completed a marathon. At one point I tried to blurt my thoughts to a friend while grocery shopping, "Janice, do you ever wonder what's the point in all of this? I mean, don't you ever think of finding a brick wall and just pressing your foot to the accelerator?"

Good Catholic girls don't have such thoughts. Even if they did, they'd certainly resist the temptation to turn the frozen foods aisle into a confessional and their best friend into a personal confessor. Before I could finish, Janice clamped both hands over her ears and said, "I'm so sorry, Phillis, but I'm not sure I want to hear this."

But my painful childhood story tumbled out. . . .

During my naval father's absence, our housekeeper, Maud, hired Ruby to escort me to and from kindergarten. After school on fall afternoons I sat outside admiring

Ruby's precision as she thundered by on roller skates. On my next birthday I was going to get skates like hers. Meantime, I'd whirl about the porch in anticipation. Pretty and popular, fifteen-year-old Ruby good-naturedly tolerated my presence.

That abruptly ended one afternoon. With tears blinding my stumbling flight up the stairs into the house, I hurried to my room. Within minutes, I'd coiled into a knot on the floor until Maud found me.

"Ruby let a boy hurt me," I sobbed in disbelief.

Uncertainty misted the episode as I grew older. Did it happen, or was it a nightmare? Neither Maud nor I ever mentioned Ruby again. As far as I know, she never shared the episode with my quick-tempered father, either.

The next day, I trembled behind Maud's ample backside as she curtly informed Ruby she'd take me to school herself. Afterward, she cut a warm sweet-potato pie into as many slices as I wanted to eat. I became Maud's shadow. Climbing the unlit hallway stairs to my room reduced me to inconsolable weeping. Even the threat of a spanking or the label "crybaby" failed to stanch the storm of tears.

Some forty years later, I reluctantly admitted to myself that I hadn't quite yet awakened from the fright-mare. Various mental snapshots—a garage door, green curtains, a boy's voice, a slap—flashed before me.

Acting as my own therapist, I forced myself to record everything I could recall in my journal. Things seemed better, but I eventually fell into a depression. To make matters worse, I fretted about our twelve-year-old son. How could I care for him when this mind game sapped my energy?

Desperate, I approached our parish priest, Father Jim. He encouraged me to continue to journal. "And pray," he challenged. "Even if you doubt God hears your prayers. Pray regardless of how you feel, because God is big enough to handle your anger. So go ahead and tell him *why* you're angry."

"I'm not angry," I insisted. "Of course you aren't," he said as I clenched and unclenched my fists. . . .

Prayer became sand in my mouth. But Jim remained relentless: "If you can't pray, then cry or scream if you feel like it." Defiant, I demanded, "Why does God need my prayers anyway?"

He smiled. "He doesn't. You do."

Eighteen months passed before I realized that any fearful memory always presents us with a choice. Either we can exist as its captive or we can live outside the painful cocoon we try to build around ourselves. I was surprised how much healing flowed into my heart, once I faced this squarely. And another surprise surfaced when I heard other women sharing similar stories of abuse. Sisterhood extends beyond biology; comfort comes in bunches.

When did I know I was healed? Over time, my perspective shifted dramatically. I found words of prayer for Ruby. And I could even forgive that nameless young man from years ago—and hope the best for him.

Finally, memory had lost its sting.

—PHILLIS HARRIS-BROOKS

Hearing from God

"The LORD who created you says:
'Do not be afraid, for I have ransomed you.
I have called you by name; you are mine.'"
ISAIAH 43:1

My friend had been experiencing crippling bouts of panic attacks. She was over eight hundred miles away, so I couldn't reach out and hug her. But I prayed for her every day.

She called one day, saying, "Yesterday afternoon, I was upstairs in the hallway, seized by another panic attack, when I heard someone say, 'You are mine, trust me, you are mine.'" She thought her husband had called her from their bedroom. She went to the room, and nobody was there. "Please don't think I'm weird, but I believe the Lord spoke to me," she said.

I thought about the prayer I'd recorded in my journal: "God, please be real to her so she'll know, unmistakably, that You are there with her."

"I don't think you're weird at all," I replied. "But I've never seen the Lord work so fast to answer prayer!"

The Lord calls us by name and releases
us from our anxieties.

—LINDA K. HEIMBURGER

319

Wisely Share

"Cheerfully share your home with those
who need a meal or a place to stay."
1 PETER 4:9

This Scripture has gotten me into trouble with my family a few times. They call me a natural "loving nurturer." And I am! So . . . I often invite people in to talk, to share of what I have— and sometimes to stay for a while, if they have no place to go. (Yes, we've taken in a few desperate folks and families for days on end.)

My husband and two boys are also quite charitable. They do care. But they like their privacy too. They've encouraged me to draw some legitimate boundaries around the family home. Not everyone can be allowed immediate live-in status.

I know it's true, and I'm working on it. But I'm also thankful God gave me such a sensitive heart. The principle holds true: Be willing to share your home. Wisely, and with a full understanding of each family member's needs . . . *share!*

*Blessings are best when they are
given naturally, cheerfully.*

—CMW

Light in the Lord

"Though your hearts were once full of darkness,
now you are full of light from the Lord,
and your behavior should show it!"
EPHESIANS 5:8

Tuning our thoughts to God brings a marvelous clarity of thought—light—to our troubled minds.

I'd been giving lots of time and energy to the Girl Scouts of America. But recently I received what I thought was a clear leading from God to resign from leadership duties in the organization. I fought it, because scouting is . . . *fun*. To quit or not to quit? My thoughts chased themselves in my head. I couldn't seem to hold a thought long enough to examine it.

Finally, I gave up and said, "God, I'll do it your way." Immediately, my tired mind was flooded with a brilliant clarity of thought. My body fell back into its regular sleeping pattern.

God, it turned out, wasn't telling me to resign, but to accept a new direction, to become the leader of an outreach troop of girls who would otherwise be deprived of the scouting experience.

In quietness, open your troubled thoughts to God.

—NITA WALKER FRAZIER

Applause

"Not to us, O LORD, but to you goes all the glory
for your unfailing love and faithfulness."
PSALM 115:1

I opened my mouth to sing and nothing came out. Not a word. Not a note. Everyone in the church was staring at me expectantly, but I was silent. I had practiced and practiced, dreamed of giving a beautiful, lyrical message about God. Everyone would be inspired by my song and tell me what a great job I had done.

My voice was gone. As I pleaded with Him, God showed me that this gift was not my own, but His. If I allowed Him to sing through me, then I would experience the unsurpassed joy that comes from glorifying God.

After six months of voice rest, I was able to sing again, but on God's terms. What does that mean? Simply that I sing for the joy of it, with a grateful heart, applause or not.

There's true joy in serving God with the gifts He gives.

—MERCEDES EVANS

Taking a Time-Out

"Now that you have found God (or should I say, now that God has found you), why do you want to go back again and become slaves once more to the weak and useless spiritual powers of this world?"

GALATIANS 4:9

How can these temper tantrums last so long? I was more determined than ever not to give in; on the contrary, I stepped over the purple-faced child without acknowledging his outburst.

Everyone in the cereal aisle was watching. "Maybe he will be an opera star when he grows up," offered one young lady. A mature woman by the cornflakes came back with, "Or possibly a criminal attorney who can sway any jury to his side." It seemed she had been there, done that with her own kids.

Everyone laughed, with my chuckle being the loudest. The guffaws drowned out the scream, causing my son to realize he'd lost our attention. Back to his original shade of white, with chocolate-framed lips, he jerked to his feet, walked over, and hugged my leg.

Does the Lord ever choose to
ignore us until our tantrums are over?

—RHONDA DEYOUNG

He Will Honor You

"Humble yourselves under the mighty power of God,
and in his good time he will honor you."
1 PETER 5:6

For years I worked at a company and had a clearly defined work identity as a leader. I enjoyed a private office, a staff, and lots of responsibility!

Then I left all that behind in order to work at home as a freelancer. I loved my new freedom but missed the executive status.

In my mind, I knew that all these outer trappings of success didn't impress God, and I didn't want them to mean so much to me, either. Now I wanted to serve God with a humble heart, no matter what assignment He might send. As time passed, I learned some painful lessons in humility.

Then an amazing thing happened. I received a crucial assignment to work on a project with an assistant to the president of the United States! And he honored me with a special letter of thanks from the White House when our project ended.

All I could do was thank God for such an opportunity. For it was in His time, and in His service that this honor came.

Leave your honor and status up to the Lord.

—CMW

Giving up Control

"Blessed are those who trust in the Lord and
have made the Lord their hope and confidence."
JEREMIAH 17:7

"Do you ever try to control people?" the voice on my car radio asked.

"No way, not me," I answered aloud. Then I recalled something that happened only days before. I had had several family commitments when a friend called to invite me to dinner.

"I'd love to, Anne," I said, "but I can't right now." I explained my situation.

"Oh . . . ," Anne replied, after a long moment of silence.

"Well . . . maybe . . . I'll try," I continued, aiming to please.

Now it hit me! Although my friend had tried to control me through her attitude, I was guilty also. Because "people pleasing" is a way of controlling others too—altering my behavior to gain approval.

I had to wonder: How else might I try to control circumstances or people through my words, facial expressions, or even by withdrawal of my love?

Let go of control, trust God, and be blessed.

—LARAINE E. CENTINEO

Quick Angels?

"He orders his angels to protect you wherever you go.
They will hold you with their hands. . . ."
PSALMS 91:11–12

"No, Ronnie, I can't swim that far."

"I'll help you," my boyfriend said. So we plunged into the river. But a deep current pushed us downstream and made even floating impossible.

"Ronnie, I'm exhausted. I can't make it to the other side."

"I can't either," he called. I was on my own. Wildly, I looked around for help. No boaters . . . no people!

"God, I can't make it. Help me!"

A strong hand grabbed mine. Shocked, I looked up to see two men in a small motorboat. One was pulling me in. I hadn't called out for help, because there had been no one there when I had just looked. He then pulled in Ronnie, and they took us back to our picnic site.

After grabbing our towels, we turned to wave good-bye, but the men were gone. How did they disappear so fast?

*God hears the cries of His children and
may answer with His messengers.*

—GENA BRADFORD

Hidden Fruit

"When Daniel learned that the law had been signed, he went home and knelt down as usual in his upstairs room, with its windows open toward Jerusalem. He prayed three times a day, just as he had always done, giving thanks to his God."

DANIEL 6:10

Mmm, mmm. Lush, sweet raspberries. Is there anything better? Those red jewels will bring a taste of summer in January when I'm trying to remember if there really ever was a warm day. I thought I'd picked the vines pretty thoroughly, but my four-year-old granddaughter kept pointing out berries I'd missed. I got down to her level, on my knees, and sure enough . . . from that position I saw many more.

Daniel knew the importance of getting on his knees. When we are on our knees and looking up, we can see fruit that we can't see from any other position. And what better place from which to offer thanks?

If we get on our knees and give thanks,
we'll find jewels to be thankful for.

—CHARLA F. BAUMAN

Watch Those Words

"May the words of my mouth and
the thoughts of my heart be pleasing to you,
O LORD, my rock and my redeemer."
PSALM 19:14

I'm not proud of it, but in high school, my best friend and I would enter the cafeteria and sit where we could watch each person coming in. We'd huddle together and . . . *comment*.

You might call our stealthy conversations "slice and dice" time. Each kid walking into the room received our dubious assessments—especially the girls. The hair . . . the dress . . . the shoes . . . the makeup. Each "item" was meticulously evaluated, usually to the detriment of our unsuspecting victims.

Eventually, though, because I was a Bible-reading teenager, it hit me: no gossiping allowed!

Has it hit you yet? The beautiful thing about friendship is that it can be based on pleasing and encouraging words rather than resting on put-downs of others. And that approach is ever so much more satisfying for all involved (including God).

*Are the words rattling around in
your brain pleasing to the Lord?*

—CMW

He Allows It

"We know that God causes everything to
work together for the good of those who love God
and are called according to his purpose for them."
ROMANS 8:28

I have a default setting on my computer e-mail program that causes all junk mail to bypass my inbox and go straight to a special folder. I never see it, so I don't open documents that might contain viruses and infect my hard drive.

In a sense, we have a spiritual default setting by which anything and everything that wants to come into our "inbox" must first go through a filter and be determined to be "not junk." This filter is at the Father's throne. Even Satan has to get permission to test us, as he did Job (and Peter in Luke 22:31).

Yes, all that concerns us is filtered through the Father's hands. In fact, I'm realizing these days that even the most painful hardships I've experienced in my life were filtered through the Father's hands to work for my good.

*We can give thanks amidst each circumstance,
trusting the Father has allowed it.*

—CHARLA F. BAUMAN

Pray for Me!

"As iron sharpens iron, a friend sharpens a friend."
PROVERBS 27:17

"I need somebody to pray for me," Hazel told our Wednesday-night Bible-study group. When my turn came, I prayed for Hazel. At the end of the hour, the group broke up, and she came and put her arms around me. With tears in her eyes, she said, "I've never heard anyone pray aloud for me before."

Hazel has many friends who would willingly do anything for her, if only she asked. That night, she spoke up and told us what she needed. Such a simple request—she just needed to know that somebody in that room would pray for her.

Friends are like two pieces of iron that sharpen and strengthen each other. We can do it by caring enough to encourage or to confront or even just to pray.

Sharpen a friend with your words and your prayers.

—LEANN CAMPBELL

Staying Within the Banks

"Be silent, and know that I am God!"
PSALM 46:10

A "crick" ran through the small Montana town where I grew up, and almost every spring there was flooding. We used to drive around and just look to see how many homes and barnyards were under water. Even downtown businesses couldn't escape the threat.

Finally, the county built a dam. What a relief it was to have the water channeled and under control!

Last summer, we visited the Grand Coulee Dam. I was amazed at the electric power harnessed there. The dam supplies electricity to 2 million homes. Other benefits to having water channeled include irrigation, flood control, and recreation.

The visit made me realize I'd been running all over the place, trying to do everything. I needed some flood control! For me, that means taking time, silent time, to seek God about what I'm supposed to be doing rather than just running wild, beyond all legitimate personal boundaries.

*Work hard—but keep your busyness
within the boundaries.*

—CHARLA F. BAUMAN

Seeing Isn't Believing

"We live by believing and not by seeing."
2 CORINTHIANS 5:7

Sometimes we just have to "act as if." This came home to me powerfully when I worked in radio. I couldn't actually *see* anybody out there listening. But I certainly had to *act as if* it were so. In fact, I regularly envisioned at least one person, ears glued to her radio, hanging on my every word. It helped me speak effectively one-on-one.

I want that same kind of energy in my relationship with God. I can't see Him with me right now, but I know He's here. I can't see my future, but I know He's there too. So, Dear God, help me *act as if*. Help me take the next steps into my day by faith—no matter what I see, or don't see, in front of me.

*Though the path ahead is unclear,
you can still trust God's leading.*

—CMW

The Joke's on Me

"A cheerful heart is good medicine,
but a broken spirit saps a person's strength."
PROVERBS 17:22

"How did you like my squash pie?" my mother asked the threshing crew at her dining table. "Good," the men answered. And several said, "I could eat another piece."

With a twinkle in her eyes, Mother held up an unopened jar of squash. "Guess what I forgot to put in the pie." She laughed heartily at what she'd done.

Mother could have kept quiet and not told the men, for the spices and sugar filling made the pie tasty. She could even have agonized for days about her mistake. But not Mother—she could never pass up the opportunity for a good laugh, even if it was on herself. And she retold the story often.

*Cultivate the habit of being cheerful
amidst all the irritations of daily life.*

—LEANN CAMPBELL

Flowery Blessing

"If God cares so wonderfully for flowers
that are here today and gone tomorrow,
won't he more surely care for you?"
MATTHEW 6:30

My ailing grandmother had the whitest hair you ever saw. When I was ten, I gently brushed it with a soft brush, and she smiled and said, "Thank you, honey."

One day, in a surge of love for her, I went out and cut all the morning glories bursting off their vine, brought them in, and scattered them everywhere over Grandma's bed as she lay beneath her tapestry quilt. "These are for you, Grandma. They'll cheer you up!"

Her crinkly pink smile deepened. "A garden of blessings. Like the blessings God scatters over us every day."

Now grown up, when I'm blue, I remember that garden of pink, fuchsia, deep purple, and sky blue petals covering an old lady's bed and warming her heart. And I count my blessings.

Blessings cover you whether or
not you are aware of each one.

—LUCY L. WOODWARD

Demolishing Regrets

"I am focusing all my energies
on this one thing: Forgetting the past and
looking forward to what lies ahead."
PHILIPPIANS 3:13

In less than twenty seconds, Pittsburgh's Three Rivers Stadium imploded and collapsed in a cloud of dust. It was early on a Sunday morning, and I stood in front of my television watching the destruction before heading off to church. To my surprise, the demolition of the thirty-year-old stadium brought me to tears. Why did I feel as though I had lost a best friend?

The stadium was connected to my childhood memories. Its demolition felt like the demolition of my childhood. Granted, it wasn't your typical reaction. And those twenty years of growing up had been full of mistakes and wrong turns.

Like most people, the apostle Paul had many regrets. But he chose to put those things behind him and push forward in service to Christ. I needed to demolish my regrets just as thoroughly as Three Rivers Stadium had come tumbling down.

Demolish your regrets before they demolish you.

—JOYANN DWIRE

335

Dignified

"That night Matthew invited Jesus and his disciples to be his dinner guests, along with his fellow tax collectors and many other notorious sinners. The Pharisees were indignant. 'Why does your teacher eat with such scum?' they asked his disciples."

MATTHEW 9:10–11

The great American writer and diplomat Washington Irving said, "There is a healthful hardiness about real dignity that never dreads contact and communion with others, however humble." That was the dignity of Jesus. He hung out with the lowliest sinners, and it made Him even greater.

But how would you answer the religious leaders' question? Why did Jesus do it? Actually, He had clearly stated His reasons numerous times: "I came not to call the righteous, but sinners to repentance."

It's a great paradox that sets the Christian faith apart from all other religions. The religions tell us to work at being good enough to reach Heaven, or Nirvana, or the Void; the requirements are many. But in Christianity, there is only one requirement to be saved: You have to be a sinner.

Nothing you do can make God love you any
less or any more than He already does.

—CMW

Under God's Wings

"I will hide beneath the shadow of your
wings until this violent storm is past."
PSALM 57:1

"They didn't pray." That was my first thought when my car refused to start. I was 300 miles from home in a car with over 200,000 miles on it. Before I left on my trip, I had asked my teen class to pray for me, and up to this point, I was certain they had done so. I'd driven over 1,000 miles with no problem.

And now my car wouldn't start.

During the next twelve hours, I realized it had been easy for me to forget God while the trip was "smooth sailing." When things got rough, however, I had a choice: I could either get angry at God, or I could take refuge under His wings.

What would you choose in a situation like that?

Are you staying under His wings today?

—JOYANN DWIRE

337

Shining Good Deeds

"Let your good deeds shine out for all to see,
so that everyone will praise your heavenly Father."
MATTHEW 5:16

I was not in the shopping mood. Getting out of my car to enter the bustle of shoppers in Wal-Mart, I saw a young Mexican couple ready to get into their car. I spoke Spanish with them and told them I loved their language and their music. Then they got into the car, and I walked toward the store.

Then I heard someone yelling and turned around to see they were calling to me. As I approached them, the man held out a tape of Mexican music for me and wanted me to accept it as a gift. That act warmed my heart, and I thanked them with deep gratefulness.

They did much more for me than they could have imagined. They touched my heart with the brotherhood of love and sparked joy in me. I walked through the mall praising the Lord.

Good deeds shine for all to see.

—JOYCE ROBERTS LOTT

Snap It!

"The grass withers, and the flowers fade,
but the word of our God stands forever."
ISAIAH 40:8

My mother-in-law lives right next door, just behind our house, and she's a marvelous gardener. Every spring I'm impressed by the colorful red bromeliads that bloom so beautifully between our yards. And each year I plan to take pictures of them so I can savor their loveliness at any time of the year.

And . . . each year I've missed the opportunity. These special plants blossom only for a short period of time. I need to be quicker with my camera!

As the Scripture reminds us, too, plant life is here today and gone tomorrow. Even our own life, according to the Bible, is merely a mist that comes and goes so quickly. But God's Word? It lasts, it never fades, it's there long after all our gardens are just memories.

May you keep your spirit open to the everlasting Truth.

—CMW

Audience of One

"The LORD your God has arrived to live among you. He is a mighty savior. He will rejoice over you with great gladness. With his love, he will calm all your fears. He will exult over you by singing a happy song."

ZEPHANIAH 3:17

I often sit in a velvet chair near my daughter while she practices the piano. I curl up as her music fills the book-lined walls with melody, harmony, and . . . discord. Because I love her, whether she plays the wrong notes or the right ones, I applaud her dedicated efforts. I am her audience of one. She is my beloved.

You and I live before an audience of One as well. As we blend our notes together, seek harmony, and try to right life's discords, we practice life's song. We long for harmony, so we strive to learn what Christ teaches. We want to understand his melodies, so we ask for His help. And when we play our life-notes, He applauds our efforts with gladness. Therefore . . . rejoice!

As we practice Christ's presence, our notes
fill the world with His passionate song.

—PAMELA DOWD

Work

"Make it your ambition to lead a quiet life
and attend to your own business and work with
your hands, just as we commanded you."

1 THESSALONIANS 4:11

Isn't it amazing that our God is a worker? First, He did the work of Creation in six days. Then He did the work of saving that Creation by coming to earth, preaching, teaching, and dying for us.

For six days, God says, it is perfectly good and appropriate to work. Then, at 6:00 each morning, I think, Is it really time to go to work again? Ugh!

Have you been there? How inconvenient, upsetting, tension producing, exciting, invigorating, awe inspiring! Work—it's everything all rolled into one.

So I take a moment to ask God to bless me as I try to sort it out and learn to enjoy it. Yes, bless the work of my hands, God: the ideas of my mind, the strength of my body, the passion of my heart.

They are all gifts, just like Friday's paycheck.

*May you enjoy this Monday
as much as you'll enjoy Sunday.*

—CMW

Push the Needle Through

> "I am sure that God, who began the good work within you, will continue his work until it is finally finished on that day when Christ Jesus comes back again."
>
> PHILIPPIANS 1:6

While expecting twins, I was confined to six weeks of bed rest. In order to pass the time, I took up cross-stitching. How I struggled to count and match the colorful pattern on the alphabet print I'd selected! I finished all but the Z before I went into labor. I framed it just that way.

It has been said that our lives resemble an elegant tapestry woven by God. From our viewpoint, staring at the underbelly of his creation, all we can see is colorful string and multiple knots. Most tapestries look less than orderly from beneath. Mistakes, do-overs, and first tries can be reworked by the creator into beauty.

When dedicated to God, the top sides of our canvas-lives produce beautiful patterns. As we offer Christ our mistakes, he uses even those to enrich the design.

God knows exactly what our life-in-progress will look like upon completion.

—PAMELA DOWD

What I Want to Be

"I don't understand myself at all,
for I really want to do what is right,
but I don't do it. Instead,
I do the very thing I hate."
ROMANS 7:15

Have you ever gotten up in the morning resolving that *today* is going to be different—that you're *not* going to get irritated with your husband, that you're *not* going to be impatient with your toddler, that you're *not* going to lose your cool when something goes wrong at work? But before an hour has gone by, you blow it! You turn on yourself in frustration: Why can't I be the calm, unruffled, patient person I really *want* to be?

Paul addresses this problem in today's Scripture. He recognized the tremendous power of our sinful nature, waging war within us. But Paul ends on a note of hope: "Thank God!" You see, he discovered the answer: Simply focus on all the good the Christ is doing within you . . . and then keep going.

We can't fight the darkness; we can only add more light.

—TANYA FERDINANDUSZ

OCTOBER 26

Delightful Difficulties

"That is why, for Christ's sake,
I delight in weaknesses, in insults,
in hardships, in persecutions, in difficulties.
For when I am weak, then I am strong."
2 CORINTHIANS 12:10

"I just wish God would take this away," I said to my husband as I struggled with the pain of my ongoing illness. And why doesn't He?

Yet later, I began to wonder, If this prayer were answered, what would be my next prayer? How about straightening my teeth a bit? Or healing my several mild neuroses? Or what about making me a few inches taller? I suppose there's no end to the requests we'd make to a vending-machine God who answered our every whim. But would we grow spiritually?

Whatever Paul's particular weakness, he affirms something important: After asking God for relief, if it does not seem to come, we can assume that His glory would be better served by a display of His power in the midst of our weaknesses. To be used by the Lord this way, Paul knew, is a great blessing.

Even when we feel like giving up,
God has not given up on us.

—CMW

Heaven Sent

"This same God who takes care of me
will supply all your needs from his glorious riches,
which have been given to us in Christ Jesus."
PHILIPPIANS 4:19

"Guess what?" Just yesterday, Betty had told me how her brand-new gift—a sports watch—had been stolen by a friend's daughter who stayed with her during the recent power failure. She looked ready to burst, so I waited. "Well, somebody I don't know went and gave me a couch!"

"That's great." I often ask God to take care of Betty.

She slapped a hand to her cheek. "It gets better." Her dark eyes grew mischievous. "I was sittin' on it last night, and I reached my hand down between the cushions and pulled out . . . a Timex!" She showed me the gold encircled face. "It still had the tag on it."

"God sure does love you, Betty."

Her smile could have restored a power failure.

God has all the resources to meet your needs today.

—PAMELA DOWD

OCTOBER 28

Quiet Refuge

"In quietness and confidence is your strength."
ISAIAH 30:15

For two days of winter, I put the world aside and went on a personal retreat. I checked into a beach-view motel room and took off my watch. No distractions, no interruptions. Then I walked to the chilly beach. I didn't see a single person. For the first time in my life, I knew I was completely alone with God.

The next morning, I awoke early, grabbed a blanket, and retreated to my front porch to watch the sun as it opened a new day. It was an awesome sight. The ball of fire rose behind a cloud, which formed the most beautiful cross I had ever seen.

I realized then why I had come to this place at this particular time. I needed to feel the presence of Jesus away from the noisy activity of my world. In that silent place, I took refuge in my Lord and Savior.

In quietness, be where you are; there is God.

—NANCY B. GIBBS

He'll Finish It

"You have been my partners in spreading the Good News about Christ from the time you first heard it until now."

PHILIPPIANS 1:5

Because our son-in-law's job took him to the country of Turkey, we made the long thirteen-hour flight to see our daughter, her husband, and our three beautiful grandsons. We were there primarily to see our family, so we didn't anticipate the great joy of visiting the ancient ruins in this part of the world.

We walked where Paul walked as he was spreading the Gospel, imagining what it was like for him to walk streets now so weathered with time.

In his letter to the Philippians, Paul thanks God every time he remembered those believers. He prayed for them with joy because of their partnership in the Gospel. That was a long, long time ago.

And still, I am his partner, this very moment.

We are partners in Kingdom work, until the King returns.

—CAROL GUTHMILLER

What Is Your Heart-Legacy?

> "I will give you a new heart with new and
> right desires, and I will put a new spirit in you.
> I will take out your stony heart of sin
> and give you a new, obedient heart."
> EZEKIEL 36:26

Swedish statesman and Nobel Prize winner Dag Hammarskjöld once said that the longest journey is the journey inward. It is a quest that drives us to search for knowledge of our selves. It also spurs us to find the ultimate meaning of our lives. Isn't this what it means to acquire a new heart and a new spirit? During our lifetimes, we journey in a spiritual quest, letting God grow within us a transformed self—that we might acquire a pure heart, a humble heart, and a heart of love.

Hammarskjöld became the secretary-general of the United Nations in 1953, serving the world well until his death in a plane crash in 1961. He was known as a quiet, tactful, and highly active diplomat with a strong faith in God.

How would you like to be known when your days are done?

Aspire to be known as a woman of gentle heart.

—CMW

Winter Blooms Like Spring

"Are any among you suffering?
They should keep on praying about it.
And those who have reason to be thankful
should continually sing praises to the Lord."
JAMES 5:13

My husband, Rodney, lost his job due to outsourcing. When he'd been unemployed for three months, he bought me a generous gift—geraniums for the front- and backyard flowerbeds. He helped plant them, something he'd never done before. On that spring day, the job market looked ripe with opportunity.

Fall came, and although the geraniums kept blooming, Rodney remained out of work. Winter's ice assault killed the geraniums in the front bed. I assumed the back flowerbed had faced defeat as well. But when I looked, all twelve geraniums were rich and lush! To me, it was a miracle. We thanked God for what we could and couldn't see. A new career path soon followed.

Even in cold, desolate times, God is near.

—PAMELA DOWD

NOVEMBER

A TOUCH OF LOVE

"Being confident of this, that he who
began a good work in you will carry it on to
completion until the day of Christ Jesus."

PHILIPPIANS 1:6

"**N**O THANKS, GRANDMA, MOMMY IS MAKING ME eggs," Josiah responded to my mother's offer of breakfast. "It's her famous eggs, you know," he reasoned.

My mother shrugged, handing me the skillet. She pointed to the eggs sitting on the counter, and readied to walk away. Ever sensitive to others' feelings, six-year-old Josiah wrapped his small arms around her ample waist.

"But, I like your cake better."

"Sure you do."

"Let's go watch cartoons until my food's ready," Josiah said, pulling her out of the kitchen. Her chuckles floated down the hall.

Josiah chattered on and on about her great food, effectively shutting the Pandora's box he unwittingly opened with the "famous eggs" remark. While Mom didn't appreciate the comment, my father, who died a year before Josiah was born, would have loved it.

I was about five when my parents separated. My seven siblings and I lived with my dad, seeing my mother on special weekends and holidays.

When I was fourteen, Pops could no longer take care of us. He was an alcoholic who desperately needed help. We moved in with my mother. I hardly saw Pops, which was hard. I missed him, his dry wit, and his fried-egg sand-wiches. I called them "famous eggs." One fried egg, with a dash of pepper, on buttered toast. No one could make eggs like Pops—no one.

Pops stopped drinking while I was still in high school. My parents remarried each other shortly after I graduated from college. One year later, I moved back home from being out of state.

I arrived home to New York City just in time for Thanksgiving Day. A new job started the following Mon-day, and on that morning, I woke to the smell of Pops' cooking. My life had come full circle.

I rushed downstairs, hugging him. "Please make me one of your famous eggs," I purred, kissing Pops' leathery cheek. I knew the ex-military cook in him could never resist a food-related compliment.

Tickled, Pops rushed to comply. I scrutinized his every move, making a mental list of each step. He heavily coated the pan with cooking spray. Cooking spray. Check. He cracked the egg on the side of the pan. Crack egg—gently. Check. He dropped the egg in the center. Crack egg, drop in center. Check. He broke the yolk with the side of the shell. "Aw, Pops, that's disgusting," I groaned.

"That's why you should never come into the kitchen of a master chef," Pops laughed, offering me the hot food. I debated whether to eat it. Tentatively, I bit into the sandwich. It was as perfect as any I'd ever tasted. My eyes misted over.

Much later, Pops became ill. I delighted in cook-ing for him. Somehow, though, I never got the fried egg sandwich exactly right. So, I switched to something I could do: *scrambled* eggs. Pops loved them.

One day, he could barely eat. "Girl, you sure put some love in these eggs today," he said before pushing the plate aside after only a spoonful of food. Understanding dawned. I finally realized that love was the secret ingredient to his egg sandwiches. Every batch of eggs Pops cooked was salted with his feelings for us.

Pops died not long after that. Eight years later, I still miss our morning rituals. When my son was old enough to eat solid food, I tried to replicate my father's cooking, to no avail. I wanted him to "taste" my love. Finally, I opted for scrambled eggs. Josiah loved them.

I coated the pan, added an egg, and stirred. As I did, I thought about Josiah's fascination with cooking. I thought about my dad's struggles as a single parent, and the ones I also wrestle with daily. I wondered what kind of parent Josiah would be, and if grandkids would get his version of famous eggs.

The sizzling pan broke my reverie. Calling my son, I gave him the breakfast.

"They're purr-fect," he said between bites, mimicking the mascot from one of his favorite cereals. Right then I decided to share my secret ingredient with my son. Josiah needed to know about the one thing that makes famous eggs—and all of life—much more appetizing. I leaned over and gently touched his arm. . . .

—LISA CRAYTON

Tattoo

"See, I have written your name on my hand."
ISAIAH 49:16

Our skin burned and oozed for days after my friend Sharon and I scratched boys' names into each other's backs with hairpins. We were two very sorry fourteen-year-old girls. The scars lasted quite a while.

Several summer tans revealed the name of "Guy" across my shoulders. I don't recall the name I gouged into Sharon's back. Maybe she's even forgotten. However, I do know neither of us married the boys whose names we wore for so long.

Have you heard about the Hollywood couple who had each other's names tattooed onto their bodies? Now they're divorced. And how about the guy who married Flo—with "Rosie" tattooed on his chest? Vows can be broken. Tattoos can be removed, and scars fade.

But God says we are engraved on the palms of His hands. Even though a teen may quickly forget her first love, God promises never to forget us.

We are engraved on our Creator's hands.

—SANDEE HARDWIG

Cat Got Your Work?

"Work with enthusiasm, as though you were
working for the Lord rather than for people."
EPHESIANS 6:7

Dolphin, our little cat, crouches on the dashboard, his head turning with the windshield wipers. As he learns the pattern, the tip of his tail begins to twitch in rhythm. Then he leaps, paws snatching futilely at the passing blades. Occasionally he rolls to his back, so he can attack with all four feet. He can do this for hours, tracking the wipers and bounding after them. The sun comes out, and he takes a nap or finds another game. When next it rains, he is back, in eager pursuit.

Dolphin delightedly chases the windshield wipers with his whole heart. There is little I do into which I pour that level of involvement and pleasure. Yet Paul calls us to be enthusiastic in everything we do. If I took his advice seriously, how would my life be different—in the rain and in the sunshine?

*Attack your work with pleasure this day,
for you are serving God.*

—ELSI DODGE

Promises

"If you stay joined to me and
my words remain in you,
you may ask any request you like,
and it will be granted!"
JOHN 15:7

I couldn't believe it! My coworker had promised to mail a package for me; I assured the client it would be delivered. Later, I heard, "Sorry, Carol, I forgot to mail it."

Ouch! A blow to my business reputation.

How many promises have you received in your lifetime—assurances that were eventually broken? Take a moment right now to recall some of the most painful disappointments these broken pledges have caused you.

Then turn your gaze to God's goodness over the years. Recall that the Author of all promises about the things that matter most—truth and fiction, past and future, life and death—has been so kind to you, always doing what He says. The key is to stay close to Him, so close that our wills virtually mesh together. That way, even during the toughest times, we can pray with confidence.

The Lord always answers: Yes, No . . . or Wait.

—CMW

Worth Noting

> "Write them on the doorposts of
> your house and on your gates."
> DEUTERONOMY 6:9

My four-year-old had drawn with great abandon on our hallway wall. Short arms stretched to their limit to create a masterpiece. As she washed the wall, in my heart I couldn't much blame her. I never saw a blank sheet of paper that I didn't wish to fill with color.

Growing up, I had adhered to a rule: We do *not* write in our books. Since then, I've learned to make some very rewarding exceptions.

When God reveals new understanding to us, what handier place to record those thoughts than in the margin by a Scripture verse? These milestones direct and remind, warn and comfort us. We can look back at our notes, recall God's presence, and be encouraged for the future.

> *Write on the walls of your home if you want . . .*
> *but write with abandon on the pages of the Word.*

—ROXIE LYLE

Perfection Not Required

"We work together as partners who belong to God."
1 CORINTHIANS 3:9

"Elp! Elp! Elp," chirps my twenty-month-old grandson. Like a persistent little bird, he keeps calling until he gets his mother's attention. He's not in need or in danger. He's not calling *for* help. He's telling his mommy he wants *to* help.

John Henry's mother allows him to "elp" her even though it creates more work for her. She lets him stand on a chair by the sink to wash dishes. Later she places them in the dishwasher and mops the floor. Because she loves him and values his companionship, my daughter lets her son think he's helping her. But he is learning how to work through observing her. Someday, the dishes he washes will actually be clean.

In the same way, our Father in heaven allows us to "elp" Him. Thankfully, as we observe Jesus, as we talk with Him in prayer, the quality of our work improves!

God welcomes our help, not because we are so competent,
but because we are His beloved children.

—JANE M. AULT

Wounded Woman

"Then Jesus said to the woman, 'Your sins are forgiven.' The men at the table said among themselves, 'Who does this man think he is, going around forgiving sins?' And Jesus said to the woman, 'Your faith has saved you; go in peace.'"

LUKE 7:48–50

I was forty-nine years old before I found the forgiveness I needed. On the outside, I was a woman who handled everything pragmatically and quickly, while on the inside I hid my feelings of deepest regret and anguish. I did not linger on sadness and would not allow regret or sorrow to permeate my life. At twenty-one I had an abortion—and never stopped to look back.

By the age of thirty-eight, I was divorced and had troubles with a teenage daughter who was seriously depressed, and a teenage son involved with drugs and alcohol. I was leading a life of independent, intellectual logic while putting my spiritual needs on the back burner.

Finally, I discovered the One who offers complete forgiveness and restoration. The balm that my soul needed so badly came through in a small community church that taught the compassion, love, and forgiveness of Jesus Christ.

Only through God do we have real life.

—CATHERINE M. SCHAFFER

Say What?

"Yes, Lord, your servant is listening."
1 SAMUEL 3:9

I will remember the perplexed woman with the fast tongue. As we passed on the street, she stopped me. "You know," she said, "I'm really good at finding my way and normally don't need help. However, I can't find which way I'm supposed to go. I'm competent, you know. I *can* figure it out on my own eventually. Just thought I'd ask."

Looking everywhere but at me, she seemed to be talking to someone else. Without taking a breath, she continued, "You're probably very nice but you're not much help."

As I stood there with my mouth half open, she walked off, muttering about which direction to try next, and about how hard it is to get good help.

Lord, I thought, *is that how we approach You?*

When God speaks, may we be listening.

—ROXIE LYLE

To Own, Give Away

"It is more blessed to give than to receive."
ACTS 20:35

I love visiting the old cemetery in North Carolina where so many of my distant relatives are buried. The clapboard Presbyterian church standing there goes back to the late 1700s, and many of the graves hold Revolutionary War veterans.

Reading the statements on those stones can be sad or inspiring, but in any case, they are often quite instructive. One epitaph reads like this:

> What I gave, I have;
> what I spent, I had;
> what I kept, I lost.

Isn't it true that the only things we really own are the things we've given away? What would it mean for you, then, to loosen your grip on a few favorite possessions? Would it be worth a try to find out if it is, indeed, more blessed to give than to receive?

The more we give, the greater our contentment.

—CMW

That's So Funny!

"God has brought me laughter!
All who hear about this will laugh with me."
GENESIS 21:6

My husband was talking to me late one evening on his cell phone while traveling home from teaching a night class. In the middle of his account of the evening's activities, I heard a burst of laughter. "I've been sitting here waiting for a flashing yellow light to change," he told me. "Just wait until the people at work hear this one!"

Only a small, funny minute, but RB was determined to share his amusement. And when biblical Sarah—well past childbearing age—gave Abraham a son, she laughed and wanted to share her laughter with others too.

How many amusing incidents do we pass up each day without letting someone in on them with us? When we share, suddenly tense shoulders drop, peace slides over intense facial muscles, and red-rimmed eyes sparkle. All because of a mini-vacation down Humor Lane.

*Be mindful of the humor that sneaks
into your day—and share it.*

—PAMELA J. KUHN

He Cares Where You're . . . Becoming

"Show me the path where I should walk, O LORD;
point out the right road for me to follow."
PSALM 25:4

With our house on the market, and my husband already work-ing in our new town, I felt more than ready to move. I just needed a buyer for our home. I'd been praying for an interested party, and my husband, Hal, had been praying the Lord would bring a buyer "this month." Then our realtor called at 9:30 P.M. on August 31. These prospective buyers seemed to answer all our prayers.

But . . . their financing fell through and . . . the house still hasn't sold.

Okay, I know in little things and big, God is at work answering our prayers. It never comes the way I think it will; He always surprises me. Is that because the most important thing on His mind isn't what I'm *doing* next—but what I'm *becoming* next?

But Lord, I sure would like this house to sell!

> *God is leading us to become
> like His Son, Jesus!*

—DIANNE E. BUTTS

Justice Will Come

"I will take vengeance; I will repay those who deserve it. In due time their feet will slip. Their day of disaster will arrive, and their destiny will overtake them."

DEUTERONOMY 32:35

I had just walked out of a business meeting with only tiny shreds of my dignity intact. I'd been held responsible, scolded for mistakes—things that were clearly someone else's fault. And that "someone else" sat there smugly, knowing she'd won this power play. At the door she smiled at me and turned away, ambling back to her comfortable cubicle.

Okay, I admit it; vengeance, at that moment, would have been sweet. But God says, "Leave justice to me."

However, we can take a certain comfort in knowing that God will not endure rivalry forever—and that He will deal with those who oppose His work in our lives, too.

We won't be delivered from all our persecutors in this life. But we can let go of feelings of victimhood and keep clinging to the great Judge of the Universe.

Our day of vindication will come.

—CMW

It's an Action Word

"Love is patient and kind.
Love is not jealous or boastful or proud or rude.
Love does not demand its own way.
Love is not irritable."
1 CORINTHIANS 13:4–5

People can be so exasperating! Sometimes we are selfish, sometimes we are rude, sometimes we are just hard to get along with. Sometimes we aren't so very lovable.

I have to remind myself that love isn't just a warm, fuzzy feeling. Rather, it's a commitment to *choose* certain attitudes and actions. Basically, love is an action word.

The true test of love isn't how I behave when I feel loving, but how I behave when I feel otherwise—how I behave toward those who are as selfish and irritating as I myself can be. This kind of love doesn't depend on how someone is treating me. It depends on my commitment to obey God's Word and let Him love through me.

God's love is winsome; we are drawn to
the person who is truly loving in His name.

—FRANA HAMILTON

Joy in the Presence

"The trees of the field will clap their hands!"
ISAIAH 55:12

It is an early July morning, and I'm sitting in my favorite over-stuffed chair in the living room. My two farmers, hubby and son, have just eaten their breakfast and have left the house for the morning.

Outside, the morning began with thunder rumblings and sprinkles of rain. From our bedroom window I could hear the birds happily singing their early-morning songs, perched in the nearby cottonwood grove.

Then the wind came up with an intensity. The cotton-woods are now dancing with the wind. The tall tree trunks are steady and firm, but their branches move with freedom as the wind does its dance with them. The wind and the leaves display an intricate dance, a delight to the eye.

O God, help me to flow with the winds of life as easily as those leaves adjust to the movement of each current.

Joyfully sway with the winds of your life!

—CAROL GUTHMILLER

The Father Knows Best

"Be sure that you select as king the
man the LORD your God chooses."
DEUTERONOMY 17:15

What kind of king would God allow for Israel? He was to be a
fellow citizen, not from a foreign nation. He was not to build
large stables full of horses ready for war. He must not take foreign wives nor accumulate lots of gold and silver—all of which
could make him vulnerable to ungodly manipulation.

A king was to read the Law every day and carefully follow
it as he led the people with genuine humility. Most importantly,
the people were to choose the man that God chose.

As a citizen of a free nation that elects a president every four
years, I wonder if any of our presidential candidates would be
eligible if we used God's criteria. Sadly, even ancient Israel did
not always get what it hoped for in Saul, David, or Solomon.

*God's rulership guidelines are
wise principles for any voter.*

—CMW

Be Where You Are

"Jesus spoke to them at once.
'It's all right,' he said. 'I am here!
Don't be afraid.'"
MATTHEW 14:27

Have you been experiencing sleepless nights? Illness? Financial troubles? Interpersonal problems? Fear and worry sap our strength during these times. They fill us with stress and interfere with our physical and mental health.

"'Do not be afraid' appears 365 times in the Bible," a pastor once said. *Wow*, I thought, *that's once for every day!* Of course, the literal truth of the statement depends on which Bible translation one uses. But the point remains: Jesus is always with us; we need never be afraid.

What if we *are* afraid, though? That's the beauty of it. We simply welcome His presence there, too, into a heart of fearfulness. He comes to every open heart, whatever emotion it holds.

God wants to be with us, so let's be where we really are.

—JANE HEITMAN

Look Ahead!

"You must not forget, dear friends,
that a day is like a thousand years to the Lord,
and a thousand years is like a day."
2 PETER 3:8

Think about what you were doing on one of your longest days. You don't have to be an Einstein to be convinced that time is relative. How quickly the clock moves when we are caught up in a thoroughly enjoyable activity! But how slowly the minutes tick away when we're bored or suffering through a painful ordeal.

For Christians, the days and years have gradually accumulated since Jesus ascended into Heaven with a promise to return. What are we to do in the meantime?

Apostle Peter's answer: Keep living holy lives while watching for that blessed day. For as our Scripture today plainly tells us, God's timing is not ours. And the longer the wait, the greater the testimony to God's enduring patience, His willingness that we have every last minute to respond to His awesome love—in gratitude and holy living.

*In your prayer time today, ask the Lord
for a renewed anticipation of His arrival.*

—CMW

What You Sow

"My job was to plant the seed in your hearts, and Apollos
watered it, but it was God, not we, who made it grow."
1 CORINTHIANS 3:6

I put off buying the large, expensive planter, so imagine my
delight at finding one in front of a rental house my brother-
in-law was renovating. It was heavy, but I got it home without
dumping its soil. I left it on our patio, intending to fill it with
fragrant petunias.

I never got back to that planter until spring—and things
were sprouting in it that I didn't recognize: colorful nasturtiums.

I loved this free gift of color that overflowed the container.
The person who left that planter behind had flowery expectations of spring but never saw them there.

Have you, like me, given your time and talents in Kingdom
work and never seen the results of your labor? If so, take heart
and be thankful. Someone is surely reaping on your behalf.

Others will enjoy the brilliant color, and inhale
the sweet fragrance, of our gifts of love.

—IMOGENE JOHNSON

Rich in Good Deeds

"[They] prove they have changed
by the good things they do."
ACTS 26:20

As Max, my five-year-old grandson, and I hurried into the mall, he ran ahead and held the heavy door open for me. Then he murmured a few words. "What, Max? What did you say?"

Behind me his mother laughed. "He said he's leaving a heart print. In preschool the children were told that by doing nice things for people, they leave a heart print. Now Max scrambles to say and do kind things."

When his friend, Jay, had a temper tantrum, and his mother struggled to calm him, Max said, "Just think happy thoughts, Jay."

Max sometimes forgets and reverts to selfish ways. So do I. It takes daily discipline and real effort to put the principle into practice, doesn't it?

*Kind deeds are nonerasable;
they leave indelible marks.*

—JEWELL JOHNSON

Pain for All

"All of you together are Christ's body,
and each one of you is a separate
and necessary part of it."
1 CORINTHIANS 12:27

My Medicare-aged body betrayed me. It couldn't keep up with my young mind as I chased a tennis ball. There was instant pain in my hip, but I kept playing in our doubles match to see if it would work itself out. It was not to be; I was "benched" for days as I got therapy for that hip.

One part of my body affected the rest of me. I needed to care for that part until my whole body could return to the court.

Paul tells us the church consists of differing units, but every part has a place in God's plan. And since Christ is the head of the body, when its members are hurt, He feels the pain. The challenge for me, then, is this: Will I, too, feel the hurt in the lives of my brothers and sisters? Will I reach out with help and healing?

Today, be alert to the hurt.

—V. LOUISE CUNNINGHAM

Fund-raising

"Paul lived and worked with them,
for they were tentmakers just as he was."
ACTS 18:3

Ever see a famous media preacher fly into town? Some of them arrive at huge auditoriums in limousines, they have numerous "handlers" and bodyguards, they wear silk suits and sparkling jewelry. Watch out if you get too close!

Have they lost touch with the common bond of ministry that comes through working side by side with someone like . . . me? In contrast, the apostle Paul gave us a wonderful and effective model of ministry. He *lived* with the people and *worked* with the people.

If you're in Christian ministry, why expect a lavish life-style? Neither must you choose expensive venues in which to witness. Just be yourself and tell what God has done in your life. Doing this, while earning an honest living, will provide a most satisfying lifestyle (and won't require a single handler).

Like the apostle, we can work and witness,
trusting God to sustain us.

—CMW

Part of a Comforting Hand

"He comforts us in all our troubles so that we can comfort others. When others are troubled, we will be able to give them the same comfort God has given us."

2 CORINTHIANS 1:3–4

Sucking my thumb seems to give him security. It doesn't happen until after my bedtime reading. Once I'm curled up in the dark, the kitten walks up my chest and nestles his furry body on my shoulder. I hold out a thumb, and he takes it in his mouth. Drooling slightly, he sucks quietly until he falls asleep. When I feel the suction lessen, I gently remove my thumb and nod off to sleep myself.

It is a wonderful thing to give and receive comfort among God's creatures. Amazing, as well, to think that I can be the comforting Lord's hands when I send an encouraging e-mail, stop to listen, or offer a hug to someone whose heart is broken. I can't meet my kitten's every need perfectly—nor another human's needs. But I can offer a helping hand . . . or at least part of one!

God's comfort is all around us,
both to give and to receive.

—ELSI DODGE

In the Same Boat

"He rebuked the wind and said to the waters,
'Quiet down!'"
MARK 4:39

It was my first pregnancy, and my contractions began in the seventh month. The doctor ordered me to bed, starting me on a course of injections to strengthen my baby's lungs in case of a premature birth. "Lungs are the last vital organs to develop," he explained. Cruel needles stabbed my flesh repeatedly during the next couple of weeks. *Ouch!* But because I trusted my doctor, I put up with the pain and discomfort; I knew those injections would help my unborn baby.

Jesus was asleep in the boat when a fierce storm broke, and He chose to still the waters. Sometimes, however, the Lord lets us endure the pain, knowing it will strengthen our endurance in the long run. Faith in God cannot prevent suffering, but faith assures us that God is with us in the midst of all our difficulties.

Jesus always rides in the same boat with us.

—TANYA FERDINANDUSZ

More Precious Than a List

"The world offers only the lust for physical pleasure,
the lust for everything we see,
and pride in our possessions.
These are not from the Father."
1 JOHN 2:16

My grandmother passed away last month, and yesterday my father asked me to make a list of the things I would like to have from her house. I thought for a while and made a short list. Later, as I tried to think of the things that most reminded me of her, the material things were quickly pushed aside in my mind by the memories of my precious times with Granny. The things I most wanted were to hear her voice, to see her eyes, and to hold her hand.

So often, possessions rule my life. I work to buy them, work to clean them, and work to keep them put away. In times like this, I am reminded how very little value such possessions possess. So little worth compared to the people I love.

Special people and memories are precious gifts from God.

—ANGIE MURCHISON TALLY

Security

"Search me, O God, and know my heart;
test me and know my thoughts."
PSALM 139:23

After moving to another state, I felt super-stressed. My emotions were on fire and far too near the surface. Time and again I walked myself through the 139th Psalm: "Test me and know my thoughts." In other words, *Lord, tell me what's the matter!*

One day as I returned home from the grocery store, I locked the garage door and fumbled for my keys to unlock the house. I thought, "My, how I hate to lock and unlock everything." It hit me: My problem was a fearful sense of insecurity. Then an incident brought the lesson home.

Our daughter would often come home late from work, after we'd gone to bed. One morning, I opened the front door to get the newspaper. There was her house key, still in the lock. I laughed aloud, realizing that the important thing wasn't that she remember to lock the door but that nothing happened—and nothing had. I said, "Thank you, Lord." It was a beginning.

God is working for our good, all the time.

—ANN L. COKER

The More Things Change . . .

> "History merely repeats itself.
> It has all been done before.
> Nothing under the sun is truly new."
> ECCLESIASTES 1:9

It seems like only a few years ago when my mother-in-law bought us our first microwave oven. She figured we needed to "finally move into the twentieth century." Now I've got a cell phone and a fax machine—and e-mails to answer every day.

What a fast-paced, constantly changing world we live in! Sometimes I wonder, Does anything ever stay the same?

And yet I know it does. When it comes to the inner life—the essential needs and longings, the motives and goals of us all—these things have always been the same, and will remain so.

It is a cause for greater contentment in our days. Within the next apparent crisis, we might pause to wonder, How will this make a difference a year from now? Will I even remember it at all?

The undercurrents of your spiritual life
flow deeper than the changing, wave-tossed surface.

—CMW

Just in Time

"My times are in thy hand."
PSALM 31:15

Margaret, the scrub nurse, was getting ready for surgery when she said, "Gail, listen to this! I was looking all over for the suture that we need for this case—2-0 silk on a small needle—and we didn't have it anywhere. I went to pray with the patient and the mom. When I came back to the OR, I noticed two large boxes. I opened one. Right inside were the 2-0 needles, exactly what we needed."

I discovered the box had arrived the day before. But the church in the States had mailed it six months before that! I don't even know how long the members had been collecting items to send to us before they mailed it. But this one thing I do know: It arrived at the exact time we needed it. Isn't God great?

God's timing for our times is . . . perfect.

—FRANCINE DUCKWORTH

Nathan Came Safely Home

"I also tell you this:
If two of you agree down here on earth
concerning anything you ask,
my Father in heaven will do it for you."
MATTHEW 18:19

Bev came in distraught. "Sit," I said, pouring tea. "What's wrong?"

"Sue, I had a terrible night, afraid, imagining blood, death. I couldn't sleep. I couldn't even pray."

"You haven't heard anything yet?"

"Not a word. Do you think Nathan is dead?" Her eyes were bloodshot. I would weep too, if my Joe were in harm's way like Nathan, volunteering to fight terrorists abroad.

"Let's ask God to help you." Her cold hand lay stiff in my grasp. "Lord, Bev doesn't know what's happening to Nathan. She can't help him. She's weak and afraid. Please comfort her."

Bev's hand relaxed. She murmured, "God, I trust You. So I'm giving Nathan to You. Whatever happens, You're in charge." Her eyes filled, but I heard new hope in her words. "It's nice having a Father take care of things, isn't it?"

I smiled. "Now that you've let go, God can take over."

Faith in God brings inner peace.

—LUCY L. WOODWARD

NOVEMBER 28

Forgive, and Keep Going

"You must make allowance for each other's faults
and forgive the person who offends you. Remember,
the Lord forgave you, so you must forgive others."
COLOSSIANS 3:13

As my brother Fred rode his Harley-Davidson home after a date,
a car pulled out in front of him. Minutes after the crash, he
bled to death.

The driver of that car had been drunk—and now my stomach churned as I saw him again months later in a courtroom.
To tell you the truth, I wished I could make him hurt the way
I hurt.

I felt that way for years, until I met Christ and purposely
chose forgiveness. Over time the stress and pain left, and
that's when I learned that Jesus' command to forgive isn't
merely for the benefit of the one who did wrong. I saw that my
anger never hurt that man; he never even knew about my rage
toward him. But it was eating me up inside. I needed to forgive
so I could . . . live.

To forgive is to enter back into life.

—DIANNE E. BUTTS

382

And Then . . .

"The unfailing love of the LORD never ends!
By his mercies we have been kept from complete
destruction. Great is his faithfulness;
his mercies begin afresh each day."
LAMENTATIONS 3:22–23

Ever have one of those days? or weeks? or life phases? Yeah, I know, me too. It all starts out looking so innocent, and then . . . *BAM!* Unexpected events put a crimp in your daily agenda. And some of the more intense experiences can change your life forever.

My father-in-law recently injured his right hand and now begins the long process of rehabilitation. As a family, we will all need to rethink some of our long-term plans.

And, I find that, in times like these, when I can't seem to just "buck up" or "keep a stiff upper lip," it's the assurances of God that carry me through. He runs to you, wraps His loving arms around you, and protects you from the storms of life. And the best news of all is that His love is never exhausted and is always renewed each morning!

God's love and mercy are everlasting!

—SARA DAVENPORT

Alone Time?

"[Jesus] went higher into the hills alone."
JOHN 6:15

I'm struck by how often Jesus chose to be alone. He willingly decided to refresh and renew—by being with Himself. That's hard for many of us to do, isn't it? Most of the time, we'd rather "refresh" by gathering a group of good friends and having a good time.

But if I gather a few minutes out of this day to be quiet, I will have chosen to live inside my own skin for a while. Will that be a welcome experience?

If I rush through my day, my hurried gorging seems natural. If I'm feeling brutalized by deadlines, my coarse bickering with the kids or coworkers appears justified. And if I've had "important" work to do all day, then my escape in front of the TV all evening may feel like a deserved retreat. Unless . . . unless I choose instead to be quiet, to be with myself.

It's important to have some quiet time,
to listen in on your own soul.

—CMW

DECEMBER

My Dad's Christmas

"Wise speech is rarer and more
valuable than gold and rubies."

PROVERBS 20:15

*M*OM SNAPPED A PHOTO ON CHRISTMAS morning many years ago, and it has become our family's all-time favorite. My dad is playing his violin, my oldest sister is seated at the piano, and my two other sisters and I are singing "Away in a Manger." We are gathered around my grandfather's old upright, the one we inherited along with his house when he died suddenly two years earlier.

My parents, busy with work and rearing their four daughters, had not yet made changes to the living room's décor, so the furnishings captured in the picture reflect the style of my grandparents' day. An oriental rug covers the hardwood floor with a colorful pattern of flora and fauna. Crocheted coverings protect the arms of the red velvet loveseat. Near the piano, to throw extra light on the sheet music, stands a floor lamp with a hexagonal shade, and above the piano hangs a framed canvas depicting a Victorian courting scene.

The painting fascinated me, even at five years of age. A young man, seated on a park bench, glances longingly at a demure young lady. He shares the bench, not with his beloved, but with her chaperoning parents. The mother is intent on engaging the young man in conversation, and the father is patiently sitting with his hands extended and wrapped with yarn as his daughter, seated across from him, winds the wool into a large ball.

The painting evokes a number of stories, featuring the love-struck fellow, the woman who shyly holds his attention, and the chatty mother. But the most striking message for me concerns the father. Sitting quietly, he's just there, unobtrusively watching out for the welfare of his daughter just as my dad would do for his four girls on that Christmas morning.

Like most children, I'd gone to bed the night before all pumped up with anticipation for Santa's visit and the wonderful gifts I hoped he would leave. When morning came, my sisters and I charged down the stairs to find a glistening tree with a number of intriguing packages waiting for us. We were "hopped up" and eager to explore and possess, but my dad called a halt to our rush.

"Let's keep everything in perspective," he said, glancing at the gifts before turning his attention back to us. "Christmas is about the birth of Jesus. Before we do anything else, let's sing a few carols."

Mom agreed and sent us upstairs to dress for church. Dad readied his violin bow with rosin and when we returned, Thyra took her seat on the piano bench. Dorothy, Marilyn, and I, now dressed in our Sunday best, stood and sang. In that moment, my mother snapped the treasured photo.

I cannot remember what marvelous items we found wrapped under the tree that morning. Whatever they were, I'm sure they were wonderful and made us happy. They have long since perished. One gift, however, has lasted—the memory of my dad keeping Christ in Christmas.

The longer I live, the more evidence I see that the riches of this world do not last. What counts most are the unseen riches of love, peace, harmony, a good name and reputation, the fellowship of faithful friends, and the ties of a loving family. And even greater than these, is the blessing God gives when He brings people into our lives who will point us to Christ and, with great wisdom, show us the way to peace.

—HELENE C. KUONI

Part of the Crowd

"Since we are surrounded by such a huge crowd of witnesses to the life of faith, let us strip off every weight that slows us down, especially the sin that so easily hinders our progress. And let us run with endurance the race that God has set before us."

HEBREWS 12:1

Althea was a treasured friend—a mother-mentor. We met while I was in college, and later I did my student teaching in her city so I could live with her and her husband. Ever so practical, she taught me the value of ministering without excessive fanfare. She prayed with me. She helped me take God seriously. As I grew up, married, and got busy with life, Althea continued to be that example of faith.

One morning I learned Althea had passed away, and I had missed the opportunity to say good-bye. For weeks, sadness dominated my life. I caught myself thinking in her voice, laughing at shared experiences, and crying when I should have been working.

When the pain subsided, I found rejoicing possible. I had always counted Althea among God's faithful; now she is with those the Bible describes as the "huge crowd of witnesses."

The witnesses encourage us, who are left behind,
to continue in faithfulness.

—CLAUDEAN BOATMAN

Availability

"Love never gives up,
never loses faith, is always hopeful,
and endures through every circumstance."
1 CORINTHIANS 13:7

"I can't forgive him," I cried. "I am simply unable." My pastor listened to my story of Dad's hurtful behaviors and how I had lost hope of ever trusting him again. After years of rejection and criticism due to his alcoholism, I'd vowed to never let him hurt me again.

Pastor Jake responded, "God doesn't want your ability, He wants your *avail*ability. Are you willing to forgive your dad? If you are, then God is able."

That afternoon, I asked the Lord to protect my heart. I called my father and told him I forgave him. I didn't know that for months, he'd been suffering guilt and sorrow for the pain he'd caused me. He showed up on my doorstep the next day with flowers. We reconciled, and not only did he accept me as his daughter, he accepted the Lord Jesus Christ as his Savior.

God delights when we obey the leading of His Spirit to forgive and reconcile with another.

—GENA BRADFORD

Faith, Our Servant

"'Even if you had faith as small as a mustard seed,' the Lord answered, 'you could say to this mulberry tree, "May God uproot you and throw you into the sea," and it would obey you!'"

LUKE 17:6

I had long been a slave of faith. You see, in any given situation I would look at my store of faith and wonder how much striving I'd need to go through to make sure I had *enough* faith for God to be able to work. How wide and high and deep did I have to push to come up with an amount of trust God would honor? My faith bank account never seemed big enough to fit the mustard-seed bill.

The disciples asked Jesus to increase their faith. But He proceeded to explain the relationship between a servant and his master, saying that the servant merely does what he's *supposed* to do.

Then I realized Jesus was talking about "faith" being *my* servant. When I came to Jesus, He gave forgiveness *and* provision for living a trusting life. Faith was part of my new nature, already in place.

We can relax in God's luxurious
provision—faith—as it performs its natural function.

—ROXIE LYLE

An Open Book

"Search me, O God, and know my heart;
test me and know my thoughts.
Point out anything in me that offends you,
and lead me along the path of everlasting life."
PSALM 139:23–24

Is your heart an open book before the Lord? Can you let Him see everything that's there without flinching? One thing that helps me is regular journaling. I write to the Lord about everything in my life. Often, it's a conflict situation in which I'm asking, "Is it me or is it the other guy, Lord?"

Amazing how often I'm led to see how I myself can change, how I can adjust my actions or attitudes to make things better in a relationship.

In school we had to do it all the time: take quizzes and exams. But we can examine our spiritual growth occasionally, too, during our times of solitude. In those quiet moments of contemplation, we can rummage back through our days to discover areas of our lives that still need heavenly repair work.

*In my prayers, I can have a completely open heart
with the One who loves me unconditionally.*

—CMW

Waiting for the Best

> "Abraham waited patiently, and he
> received what God had promised."
> HEBREWS 6:15

"I'm tired of waiting, Mommy," my daughter said. We'd been standing in a long, winding line for the Mine Train roller coaster at Six Flags for about thirty minutes. She fidgeted, having been excited all week about her first chance to ride the roller coaster.

"I don't want to wait anymore; let's leave," she said. I knew she'd regret it if we did, so I convinced her to wait it out. Then, after we'd screamed and laughed our way through the ride, she pointed to the line. "Let's go again!"

I'm not a patient waiter either. My husband and I waited through ten years of infertility and frustration before God placed this lovely daughter into our lives through adoption.

Yes, it's tough to wait. But when God's time arrives, and I'm on the ride of my life, I thank Him for the perfect moment of answered prayer and fulfilled dreams.

God's promises are worth the wait.

—KATHRYN LAY

It's All about Attitude

"Your attitude should be the same that
Christ Jesus had. Though he was God,
he did not demand and cling to his rights as God."
PHILIPPIANS 2:5–6

It is so much easier to want to be right than to put another's best interests at the top of our priority list. If we look long enough, we'll find this at the heart of almost every conflict.

No wonder Jesus' behavior is so incomprehensible to us! He didn't curse His accusers or open His mouth in His own defense. He didn't scold his disciples in their time of weakness or demand their loyalty. His decision to choose love left a footprint on history like no one else's ever will.

If only we could reflect such a selfless attitude. Our church members would live and worship in harmony, our relationships would thrive and go deep, our lives would become beacons of hope in a warring world.

Jesus is the perfect role model for the best attitude.

—RACHEL M. TAMILIO

Me, a Hypocrite?

> "Why worry about a speck in your friend's
> eye when you have a log in your own?"
> MATTHEW 7:3

When asked why they don't attend church, many people answer, "Because the church is full of hypocrites."

And yes, they are right. Just as in Jesus' day, it's still easier to judge people who don't follow our rules than it is to admit our own faults and shortcomings.

Have I ever been a hypocrite? Yes, I must have acted like a big fat one a time or two, but honestly, I don't remember.

You see, Jesus really knew what he was talking about. People don't want to see themselves the way others see them.

I don't want to pull that big log out of my own eye. That would hurt a lot, and I just want to forget about it.

And that's why I really need a Savior!

Dare to let Jesus give you 20/20 vision today.

—CMW

Neighbor

"Don't let evil get the best of you,
but conquer evil by doing good."
ROMANS 12:21

Colleen and her husband bought a double-wide prefabricated home, along with a lot to place it on. Colleen looked forward to moving in, but then two of the neighbors began stirring up trouble. A man circulated a petition encouraging those up to three blocks away to try to keep the "cheap" house from coming to their nice neighborhood.

The woman who would live next door told Colleen, "You're really not welcome here."

A year after Colleen and her husband moved in, the neighbor's husband died. Setting aside the unkind words of the past, Colleen extended sympathy to the grieving widow.

It was the best way Colleen could resist all the opposition. It was the way of Jesus: simple kindness, no matter what.

*God will help us be kind to those
who have caused us pain.*

—NORMA C. MEZOE

Watching for the Mailman

> ". . . My ways are far beyond anything
> you could imagine."
> ISAIAH 55:8

I knew how God could answer my prayer, and it would be so simple: just touch the heart of one of His wealthy servants, and that servant would obediently send me a sizable check in the mail. That easy!

Then I considered: How had God answered prayers in the Bible? Surely He could have grown food in the desert for Moses' wandering Israelites. Instead, God rained a heavenly cuisine from Heaven. And when Elijah was hiding from King Ahab, there could have been a nice garden growing by the brook. No, God sent Elijah his meals by airmail ravens. In New Testament days, God provided money for Peter's taxes . . . from the mouth of a fish.

God loves to surprise us with creative, unimaginable answers to our prayers. In fact, perhaps it's time for me to stop watching for the mailman.

> *When you pray, you can expect*
> *God to answer—creatively!*

—PAMELA J. KUHN

Equation of the Cross

"God forbid that I should boast about anything
except the cross of our Lord Jesus Christ."
GALATIANS 6:14

Remember the 1977 film *Oh, God?* The Almighty was played by octogenarian George Burns sporting big glasses and white hair.

Though some people may view God as a kindly old grandpa, I think few do. Actually, many women I've known carry around with them a sense that God is quite displeased with them. Perhaps for you, God is constantly frowning—never quite satisfied, though you may desperately need a rest from all your efforts at becoming a "better person."

That's when I take out a fine silver chain with its cross to wear at my neck. And I remember: If this cross were viewed as a giant plus sign, it would fit into this equation: Holiness + Love = Mercy. Surely that is why the person who once courageously befriended that cross can now call out to all of us without judgment: "Come unto me."

Through the cross, God smiles at you.

—CMW

You Can!

"No discipline is enjoyable while it is
happening—it is painful! But afterward
there will be a quiet harvest of right living
for those who are trained in this way."
HEBREWS 12:11

Jill discovered she was going to have to work both Saturday and
Sunday to get her software presentation ready for the incoming
VIPs from Saigon. This meeting would be the culmination of
a year's work.

Though thrilled at the opportunity, the personal cost
weighed heavily on Jill's conscience. Saturday was her son Lannie's last Indian Guide meeting. She had missed so many. As
a single parent, she wanted more time with her family, but she
felt helpless to change her situation.

Late Friday night, as Jill got out of her car, she stepped on
Lannie's aluminum bat and fell. She heard rather than felt the
bone in her arm snap. Later, back home and still reeling from
the ER's powerful painkiller, she awkwardly dialed her boss's
home phone number. She felt strange.

Then she recognized the feeling. She was happy. She was
going to an Indian Guide meeting.

Even in our pain, we can slow down and look up.

—MARILYN KREYER

DECEMBER 12

Not for a Second

"Be sure of this: I am with you always,
even to the end of the age."
JEREMIAH 29:11

The house was quiet as I waited anxiously for my husband to return. Hours earlier, he had sat across the table from me, something clearly troubling him. Then he spoke: "I have to leave; I have thinking to do." The next morning, he returned with a shocking announcement: He was leaving me for a younger woman.

After twenty-seven years of marriage and three children, suddenly my world, as I knew it, was disintegrating. I had to make a new beginning, and with the guidance of God and the encouragement of family and friends, I did.

In the intervening twenty-two years, I have encountered many problems, but I have never trudged through them alone. Always I have known the Lord was walking beside me. No matter what heartache or frustration we may face, we can know this: Not for one precious second are we alone.

What a blessing to know Jesus walks by our side.

—NORMA C. MEZOE

Just Ask

"She came and worshiped him and
pleaded again, 'Lord, help me!'"
MATTHEW 15:25

I was no stranger to pain; heartache had been my companion for years. With each rebuff and each failure, my self-esteem shriveled—and I edged closer and closer to self-destruction.

Yes, I had made some bad choices, but finally God said, "Enough." One Sunday morning, while randomly channel surfing the television, I once again heard the familiar Gospel message. This time, it was as though Jesus Himself were standing before me, the presence of the message was so strong. My old self crumbled and, reaching out, I surrendered. "I do not understand, but I do believe You, Lord. If You will have me, I am Yours."

That was over twenty years ago, and just like the woman of Canaan, I am still fed by the Lord. I do not dine on crumbs, though, but on the riches of His love. I only wish I'd asked sooner.

Time and again, Jesus has told us, you only have to ask.

—MARILYN KREYER

Wide Open Message

"Because I preach this Good News,
I am suffering and have been chained like a criminal.
But the word of God cannot be chained."
2 TIMOTHY 2:9

Our little Yorkie dog is limited by a large screened porch at the back of our house. He can play, but his ability to roam is quite limited. But the screens sure don't stop his barking at everything that moves!

In much the same way, Paul tells Timothy that the authorities may lock him up for preaching the Gospel of Jesus Christ, but God's Word is hardly screened off! Paul's message had already reached far beyond his jail in Rome, spread by believers until it reached the known world.

Even death could not silence the message. Timothy, and others yet to come, would take up the task and carry on. That's how Paul could endure suffering for the cause of the Gospel. Physical limitations are no match for unconditional love.

Proclaim the Good News to all, with no limits.

—CMW

Wider Awake to the Awesome

"Morning by morning he wakens me and
opens my understanding to his will."
ISAIAH 50:4

Sometimes I think awe is like a muscle, atrophied by fast-lane living. Honest awe requires focused attention, which takes time. Amid the relentless bustle of work, leisure, and church activities, we can always alight, however briefly. Even the Psalms use the word *selah*, thought to mean "a holy pause."

No spare moments? Well, we have to eat. We could start by paying closer attention at mealtimes today, remembering this loaf, or leaf, or berry that we're chewing was growing once, alive with light, water, sap. It was nurtured by someone. When we swallow it, an extended chain of life becomes part of us, nourishing our minds and bodies. That's worth a smile, a quietly breathed prayer.

And may we remember that whatever time we have, it's always possible to savor God's gifts, cherish the moments, and still accomplish all God desires.

*May God's presence awaken our senses to all
that is sacred in common surroundings.*

—LAURIE KLEIN

Forward Together

"God has given me the responsibility of serving his
church by proclaiming his message in all its fullness. . . ."
COLOSSIANS 1:25

As my friend Ann prepares to speak at a women's gathering, I
listen to her enthusiasm and hear the excitement in her voice.
"Do you think I should promote this to friends and relatives?"

We plan to collaborate on a flier that she can send out as a
personal invitation. "Stop by my office early next week. I have
a flier on my computer."

It is with joy that we serve one another. No one person
can do everything alone. With the help of newsletters, bulle-
tins, PowerPoint presentations, and announcements, we spread
the word about events.

With the giving attitude of cooks, servers, setup and
cleanup crews, decorations people, and speakers, we can effectively communicate the Gospel message by creating an environment conducive to fellowship.

Serving together as the body of Christ,
we move forward in one spirit.

—LAROSE KARR

Comfort for Sorrow

"He comforts us in all our troubles."
2 CORINTHIANS 1:4

When a friend's five-year-old son was murdered, I could hardly eat or sleep for weeks. My prayer life ceased. I cried easily and experienced a searing grief I'd never felt before.

One evening, I dropped to my knees beside the bed and began to sing hymns and worship songs. I quoted every Bible verse I'd ever memorized. Then I fell asleep.

The next morning, I felt a measure of peace returning to my spirit. It was as though the gaping wound inside me was being gently pushed together by healing hands.

Jesus uses a variety of ways to comfort our grieving spirits: a friend's embrace, a song, a poem, a piece of prose, a verse of Scripture. It will take much time for deep wounds to mend, and some scars never fade. We let the pain become a part of us as we move forward by God's grace.

God's provision for your sorrow is
His Comforter, the Holy Spirit.

—JEWELL JOHNSON

My King and My God!

"Listen to my cry for help, my King and
my God, for I will never pray to anyone but you."
PSALM 5:2

We needed help. I'd befriended a beautiful family from France, a mother and three daughters whose father had died tragically after moving them to the United States. They were running out of money as eviction notices gathered on their apartment's front door.

I came to them not only as a friend, but also as a Christian who believes in prayer. At this moment, our prayer was specific: "Help us pay the rent—just one more month." We all kneeled down in the living room, some of us saying words, others just weeping.

And the money came. All of it, week after week, one way or another.

That was four years ago. I am so happy to report that the family is thriving. The girls now have a wonderful American stepfather with a beautiful home. And each of them is excelling in school, sports, and music. What power in crying out to the King for help!

*Kneeling is a most excellent way
of approaching your King.*

—CMW

Good News from Afar

"Good news from far away is like
cold water to the thirsty."
PROVERBS 25:25

"Hey, girl! How are you doing?"

My friend Don always has an uplifting attitude. He is an old high school classmate and occasionally we talk by phone. Almost thirty years after our school years ended, our friendship has resumed. When we get in touch, we first discuss our families and then always move on to our hometown.

Since I live a thousand miles from my hometown, and did not have much contact with my classmates for many years, news from home is welcome—like a well-worn and favorite book read once again.

Once, Don said to me, "I will never call you when I'm having a bad day."

Not all friends are that considerate. Of course, I don't mind bearing burdens, but here is one person I know will always greet me with uplifting conversation.

The Lord gives us special people
to travel with us on life's road.

—LaRose Karr

Sustaining Strength

"... When you go through rivers of difficulty,
you will not drown! When you walk through
the fire of oppression, you will not be burned up;
the flames will not consume you."
ISAIAH 43:2

For several years I had been reading my Bible and praying each day. Had these disciplines made a difference in my life? I didn't see any clear evidence of it until a "fire and flood" experience left our seventeen-year-old grandson paralyzed after a fall.

During his rehabilitation, I helped care for him. I learned to suction his tracheotomy, position him to prevent pressure sores, and exercise his limbs. Wonder of wonders, I had strength for the tasks. I have no doubt that through daily meditation and prayer, I'd been storing up patience and courage for such a time.

God doesn't plan for you to faint or fail in difficult situations. He knows the future and helps you prepare for it. Consistent reading and applying words from the Bible play a part in your preparation for life's fires and floods.

Trust God to carry you through without harm.

—JEWELL JOHNSON

Never Alone

"No, I will not abandon you as
orphans—I will come to you."
JOHN 14:18

My husband lay near death in a special hospital ward that did not allow me to see him. Once or twice a day I phoned the hospital, where medical personnel told me about his condition and treatment.

Following one call, I cried aloud to God, not in words but in sobs. Then I remembered how God's own son, Jesus, died on the cross so that we could have forgiveness and eternal life. He knew my pain, and I was not alone.

Jesus promised He'd never abandon us, and He keeps His promises. That day, He gave me peace and rest—and kept giving through the dark days that loomed ahead. I'm comforted to know what the Lord knows: my deepest, darkest fears and sorrows, like no one else.

As a member of God's family, I'll never be an orphan.

—JANE HEITMAN

DECEMBER 22

Suffering Will End

"How long, O LORD, must I call for help?
But you do not listen!"
HABAKKUK 1:2

I've got a tooth that just won't stop being sore. Ouch! Time to see the dentist.

Whenever pain cuts into our lives, we want to find out exactly why. That was the prophet Habakkuk's initial goal when he began questioning the Lord: "Why are wicked, foreign nations allowed to devastate God's people?" And, for a long time, God was silent on the issue.

But the question of suffering goes deeper: Why does it exist at all, especially in a world God loves? The biblical prophet wrangled with the Almighty about this, too, and received a straightforward answer about the divine plan to set things right—eventually. Habakkuk also learned much about heavenly wisdom, a lesson more valuable than anything else.

We know that pain is a bad thing, but it can have some good effects. It can grow our own souls, and even call onlookers to grow in compassion.

*At the end of time, by God's power, complete
justice will prevail, and suffering will end.*

—CMW

Who's Talking?

"I will delight in your principles
and not neglect your Word."
PSALM 119:16

Often when I pray, I'm doing all the talking and expecting God to do all the listening. When I read the Bible too, it becomes more of a two-way conversation. God is speaking to me through His Word, and I am responding in prayer. Surely God's words to me are as important as my words to Him!

Prayer by itself, apart from Scripture, can easily become "me-centered." But when I open my Bible, it's no longer all about me. It's about God and His plans and purposes. He invites me to be a part of His life and work.

One of the benefits of memorizing Scripture is that no matter where I am, the Holy Spirit can bring His Word to my mind and speak to my heart. That way, I can always count on having a two-way conversation with my Heavenly Father.

Be sure to let God get a word in edgewise.

—FRANA HAMILTON

Perfect in Weakness

"My gracious favor is all you need.
My power works best in your weakness."
2 CORINTHIANS 12:9

"I can't do this! I *cannot* do this!" The words rang in my mind loudly, blocking out anything else. My hands visibly shook as I picked up my notes, rehearsing again what I would say for my presentation at work that morning.

But in the midst of my terror, I couldn't deny that God created me as I am. God gave me this job, knowing this moment would come.

I stepped forward in my weakness . . . and God met me there! He was there with my shaking hands, my pounding heart, and my trembling voice. Afterward, my coworkers were shocked to hear I'd been nervous at all.

It made me think: Suppose I had tried to deny my weakness? Would that have denied me God's power as well?

Even the most paralyzing fear can't overpower
His mercy and His strength.

—ANNE GOLDSMITH

Open All of Those Gifts!

"How we praise God, the Father of our
Lord Jesus Christ, who has blessed us
with every spiritual blessing in the heavenly
realms because we belong to Christ."
EPHESIANS 1:3

After ripping opening his first Christmas present—a shiny toy truck—the one-year-old boy wasn't interested in opening any more. As he scooted away, his mother reached out and grabbed the top of his pants to pull him back. It happened again and again, until all the gifts were opened. The child then played with his first gift, that little red truck.

We may be so engrossed with our forgiveness (the very first gift packaged with salvation) that we overlook what else He has planned for us: every spiritual blessing.

At times, I believe, God pulls us back amidst some sudden crisis or painful decision. This is a time when He can get our attention. He says, in effect, "Look, unopened boxes. They're for *you!*" Truly, it can be Christmas any time of the year.

Discover all the good things God has for you.

—V. LOUISE CUNNINGHAM

Throwing in the Towel

"Elijah was afraid and fled for his life."
1 KINGS 19:3

One question I face today: How will I handle the pressure? What will I confront in this day that will require me boldly to meet my obligations, or will tempt me to run in the opposite direction?

A bold prophet named Elijah, just after a smashing success in a showdown with foreign gods, got scared and took off running. Perhaps he was afraid he'd now have to maintain his miracle-working reputation forever.

A story like that means a lot to me because I, too, get scared by the demand to keep producing at ever more spectacular levels. But, at any moment, I can turn to help from above. Though tempted to throw in the towel (right now?), no doubt today, or tomorrow, or next week, I'll feel some sparks of heavenly boldness reigniting my courage.

God gives uncommon boldness to
meet our pressure-filled days.

—CMW

Rich

"You are already rich!"
1 CORINTHIANS 4:8

I am truly rich. Oh, I often struggle with bills and I don't possess much of what my neighbors have. When I see recreation vehicles pulled over at roadside parks, sometimes I think how nice it would be to own one. When I cross the bridge that takes me to my new home, I spy numerous boats and jet skis on the water. I don't have those things.

I may not be wealthy, but my abundance doesn't depend on money. I grew up with two parents who cared about me. I had a brother who loved me most of the time. I had the opportunity to go to school to gain the knowledge I needed to live a good life.

Years later, I married a wonderful man and gave birth to three beautiful children. I'm now the proud grandmother of three little girls. All of these blessings make me rich indeed.

*Being rich is not having everything I want,
but wanting the things I have.*

—NANCY B. GIBBS

DECEMBER 28

Barking Dogs

"But among the Israelites it will be so
peaceful that not even a dog will bark."
EXODUS 11:7

Nutmeg emitted a deep-throated purr of a growl rather than the expected bark.

"What's up with your dog?" I asked my friend Vickie.

"I taught her not to bark."

Apparently Vicky's lessons took hold, as Nutmeg never barked during my stay. In the silence of that Charleston afternoon, I considered my own behavior. Didn't my tendency to demand attention constitute a form of barking?

Earlier, despite initial reservations, I had applied for a promotion. Oh, I did take a minute to pray as I typed my resume, "Lord, I really want this job." The subsequent interview highlighted how ill-equipped I was for the additional responsibility. Hardly a surprise, given how I'd barked my demands to God, then without thought to any divine plans, pursued my own inclinations. What I'd barked for was a far cry from what I needed.

In your prayers, be thoughtful.

—PHILLIS HARRIS-BROOKS

The Direct Approach for Any Woman

"This High Priest of ours understands our weaknesses, for he faced all of the same temptations we do, yet he did not sin. So let us come boldly to the throne of our gracious God. There we will receive his mercy, and we will find grace to help us when we need it."

HEBREWS 4:14–15

Since the earliest of times, priests have functioned as "go-betweens," bringing a reconnection where the lines of communication and fellowship have been broken. And, as the author of Hebrews points out, Jesus is the great High Priest because He is perfectly suited to bring us before His Father.

When I'm reluctant to approach this Priest, I consider: He is able to "feel my pain," He has experienced the kinds of trials and temptations I'm experiencing, He is ready to offer me mercy and grace in my time of need—right now.

Martin Luther, the priest who launched a church reformation movement centuries ago, began a new chapter with Hebrews 4:14 in his translation of the New Testament, saying, "After pouring wine into our wound, the writer now pours in oil." Enjoy this soothing salve of a direct and comforting approach to God—through your great High Priest.

At any time or place, any woman may
lift her requests to God's throne.

—CMW

Just Play

> "Forgetting the past and looking forward to what lies
> ahead, I strain to reach the end of the race."
> PHILIPPIANS 3:13–14

"I messed up again!" wailed my nine-year-old daughter. I winced as she crashed her hands down on the piano keyboard, the discordant notes jarring my senses. I knew what was coming next: a blow-by-blow description of exactly what she had done wrong. This pattern—mistake, wail, rehash—was one she repeated nearly every practice session.

One day, I sat down on the piano bench beside her and looked her in the eye. "Look," I said gently. "It's okay to make a mistake. That's how you learn. Now stop talking about it, and just play."

When I mess up in my own life, how often do I fall into the same pattern as my daughter? How God must long for me to take my eyes off myself and look instead to Him, to hear Him say, "That's okay! That's why I sent my Son. Now stop talking about it, and just play!"

God wants us to confess our sin,
accept His forgiveness, then move on.

—BECKY FULCHER

A Closing Prayer for You

". . . May your roots go down deep into the soil of God's marvelous love. And may you have the power to understand, as all God's people should, how wide, how long, how high, and how deep his love really is. May you experience the love of Christ, though it is so great you will never fully understand it. Then you will be filled with the fullness of life and power that comes from God."

EPHESIANS 3:17–19

The apostle Paul was constantly praying for the people he had ministered to and had grown to love. In the book of Ephesians, several of these prayers come through, each glowing with a warm and heartfelt sincerity.

I'm struck by how doctrinal these prayers are. Paul was no mere sentimentalist. He knew that his feelings of love for the church members rested upon the truth of an objective unity that bound them together: the fellowship of the indwelling Holy Spirit. Therefore, since he knew that the deepest relationships were founded in the truths of the Scriptures, he also filled His prayers with theological truth.

So here is the most profound truth he could leave with the Ephesians, the truth with which I'd like to close this book: *God's love for you is infinite—and completely available*. Right now.

May you, indeed, experience all the fullness
of life and power that comes from God!

—CMW

Contributors

Ruthanne N. Arrington's writing credits include *Marriage Partnership, The Upper Room,* and *Christian Home & School.* She writes from Spartanburg, South Carolina.

Jane M. Ault is a poet, counselor, and teacher. She shares her spiritual journey in her book, *Heart Connections: Finding Joy through Openness with God.*

Charla F. Bauman, a missionary and ministry leader living in Spokane, Washington, loves to communicate God's truth-nuggets through writing and speaking.

Adreienne Bickers is a stay-at-home mother of two living in Philadelphia. Through writing, she aspires to show women their potential in the Lord.

Claudean Boatman is a writer and teacher who delights in seeing God's handiwork in everyday life.

Renee Bolkema, wife and mother of three, writes from her home on a Colorado ranch.

Gena Bradford is an educator, writer, and grandmother from Washington State. Sharing about God's love and faithfulness is her passion.

Dianne E. Butts wrote her book *Dear America* to share her faith after the terrorist attacks on 9/11. She also writes for numerous Christian periodicals.

LeAnn Campbell, of Lamar, Missouri, is a retired special education teacher. She has published over a thousand articles since she began writing fifteen years ago.

Ginny Caroleo and her husband have been married for sixteen years. She's the mother of two homeschoolers living in Blue Point, New York.

Laraine E. Centineo is a freelance writer and artist living in Manasquan, New Jersey. She enjoys taking morning walks down by the ocean.

Amy Fogelstrom Chai is a physician, wife, and mother. She enjoys writing and encouraging the Body of Christ.

Gwen Rice Clark is a writer with a seasonal change of address. She and her husband divide their year between West Carrollton, Ohio, and LaBelle, Florida.

Ann L. Coker is married to her favorite pastor, whose sermons get better each Sunday. She is a crisis pregnancy center director in Terre Haute, Indiana.

Joy Cooley was born and raised in Lansing, Michigan, with five brothers and sisters. She taught for three years in India at a mission high school.

Lisa A. Crayton is publisher of spirit-ledwriter.com. An award-winning freelancer, she teaches at conferences and mentors aspiring scribes.

V. Louise Cunningham writes curriculum for a women's Sunday school class in Renton, Washington. She has published three books.

Sara Davenport, living in Lakewood, Colorado, is a speaker and personal consultant on a variety of motivational topics.

Jean Davis writes from Clarksville, Delaware, where she lives with her husband.

Wendy Lynn Decker is a wife and mother of two from Jackson, New Jersey. She has been published in *Cross-Times*, *The JBC Chronicle*, and *Sisters in the Lord*.

Marlene Depler is a freelance writer, speaker, and teacher. She enjoys spending time with her family and friends, as well as gardening, reading, and hiking.

CONTRIBUTORS

Rhonda DeYoung, of Littleton, Colorado, has written articles for *Clubhouse, MomSense, The Gem, Devotions,* and *Devozine* magazines as well as several e-zines.

Elsi Dodge is a divorced, single, retired teacher. She travels in an RV with her dog and cat and delights in God's transforming power.

Bonnie J. Doran works as a part-time bookkeeper for her church. Besides writing, she enjoys reading, cooking, and scuba diving.

Pamela Dowd is the author of a holiday novella, *All Jingled Out.* She and her husband, Rodney, have three daughters and live in Marshall, Texas.

Karla Doyle has walked beside her husband in ministry and marriage for twenty years. She's planning a huge celebration of her fiftieth wedding anniversary in 2033.

Francine Duckworth. Missionary to Samoa 1977–1997. Pastor's wife, mother, grandmother, teacher.

Joyann Dwire is coauthor of *The Miracle of Dormel Farms*, the story of the Quecreek mine rescue. She lives in Rockwood, Pennsylvania.

Dee East retired from the Delaware Department of Transportation. Living in Camden, Delaware, she now shares in caregiving and ministry to other widows.

Mata Elliott resides in Pennsylvania with her husband and two cats. She is a writer and reviewer for soulpen.com.

Mercedes Evans is a full-time writer of children's picture books and devotionals for adults. She also spent three years as a storyteller at Newtown Bookshop in Newtown, Pennsylvania.

Elizabeth Fabiani, of Gibbstown, New Jersey, recently started a new job, which is a perfect fit. She loves to write, quilt, travel, and collect rocks.

Tanya Ferdinandusz is a freelance writer specializing in devotional and Sunday school materials. She and her family worship at St. Theresa's Church, Colombo, Sri Lanka.

CONTRIBUTORS

Nita Walker Frazier, of Plainview, Texas, is involved in Girl Scouts and recently began gardening. She has two adult children and one extremely spoiled shih tzu.

Becky Fulcher, mother of two, lives and writes in Monument, Colorado.

Nancy B. Gibbs, of Cordele, Georgia, has authored four books. She is a weekly columnist whose articles have also appeared in hundreds of periodicals.

Anne Goldsmith is the senior acquisitions editor for fiction at Tyndale House Publishers. Living in the Chicago area, she loves coffee, books, and Jesus.

Carol Guthmiller lives with her husband on a third-generation farm in Tripp, South Dakota. She has published two books, including *Prairie Ponderings*.

Frana Hamilton, of Modesto, California, is a writer with eleven grandchildren. She also teaches at an adult vocational school and loves it.

SanDee Hardwig resides in Brown Deer, Wisconsin. She writes devotional, educational, and public service materials and is active in prison ministry.

Phillis Harris-Brooks enjoys the aspens of Colorado with her husband and son.

Audrey Hebbert lives in Omaha, Nebraska, where she writes and serves as a volunteer Bible teacher and mentor for her church.

Linda K. Heimburger is a college librarian in South Carolina. Her poetry has appeared in *Voices from Within* (1992).

Jane Heitman is a frequently published freelance writer. A former teacher, she currently works as a library technician at Mesa State College.

Betty Jane Hewitt, of Newton Falls, Ohio, is a columnist who's also finishing up her book, *Brown Bag Blessings: Finding Contentment in Everyday Living.*

CONTRIBUTORS

Betty Ray Hunter is an occupational therapist who works with special children. She and her husband live in Milton, Delaware.

Carole Suzanne Jackson is a freelance writer, speaker, and entrepreneur currently living in central Florida, where she has taught at Valencia Community College.

Imogene Johnson writes from rural Lawrenceville, Virginia, where she is an adult Bible teacher and freelance writer. She enjoys retirement and travel with her husband, O. W.

Jackie M. Johnson is a marketing writer who has also written articles, poetry, and hundreds of devotionals for Focus on the Family's *Renewing the Heart* Web site.

Jewell Johnson is a mother of six children and grandmother of seven. She and her husband live in Arizona, where she enjoys reading, walking, and quilting.

LaRose Karr is a church secretary, freelance writer, and speaker. She enjoys ministering to women through the church.

Laurie Klein is an award-winning author of poetry and prose. Her forthcoming book of poems, winner of the 2004 Owl Creek Prize, is *Bodies of Water, Bodies of Flesh*.

Mimi Greenwood Knight lives in Folsom, Louisiana, with her husband, David; four kids; four cats; and four dogs. She enjoys the lost art of letter writing.

Lisa M. Konzen is an administrative assistant, parish education coordinator for her church, and a freelance writer. She enjoys cooking, reading, and baseball.

Marilyn Kreyer is a great-grandmother and Sunday school teacher—also a twenty-five-year veteran of Bible study . . . and still learning.

Pamela J. Kuhn is published in many periodicals, such as *Christian Parenting Today*. She has written sixteen books, including Rainbow Books' best-selling series Instant Bible Lessons.

Helene C. Kuoni's work is published in many magazines. She recently coauthored a book with her husband, John: *Her Pen for His Glory: The 1860s Verse of Isabella Stiles Mead.*

Carol Ann Landis is involved in lay ministry in her home congregation. She cherishes her family and friends, and most of all her relationship with her eternally faithful Heavenly Father.

Kathryn Lay is a children's author and writing instructor living in Arlington, Texas. She has published more than 1,000 articles and essays.

Joyce Roberts Lott, a native Kansan, taught French, English grammar and composition, and Spanish in Denver for fifteen years before becoming a translator in Greenville, South Carolina.

Debbie Lowe is a wife, mother, businesswoman, speaker, and writer living in Mystic, Connecticut.

Beverly Money Luke has published children's short stories and is currently working on a nonfiction book for women.

Roxie Lyle lives in Kansas City, Kansas, near most of her children and grandchildren. She is a supervisor in a health care facility.

Susan Lyttek writes from the suburbs of the nation's capital (whenever her two sons don't need the computer for their homeschooling projects).

Norma C. Mezoe's desire is that her writing will honor God and give encouragement to her readers.

Diane Rosier Miles is a wife, mom, and freelance writer who bakes the world's best chocolate chip cookies.

Dorothy Minea, a writer and speaker in Camarillo, California, is also a hospice worker. She has four children and four grandsons.

Paula Moldenhauer, mother of four, is published in periodicals and book compilations. She also has her own devotional Web site, *www.soulscents.us.*

CONTRIBUTORS

Maralee Parker is a former children's curriculum editor, currently working as marketing manager of an adult bachelor's degree program at Judson College, Elgin, Illinois.

Cora Lee Pless, a writer with two grown children, enjoys teaching Sunday school, leading Bible studies, gardening, and reading. She lives in Mooresville, North Carolina.

Mabelle Reamer, a preschool teacher for ten years in Sicklerville, New Jersey, recently graduated from Philadelphia Biblical University with a master's degree in counseling.

Catherine M. Schaffer, of Bridgeport, New York, is a writer and speaker who deals with Christian business ethics, the persecuted church, the wounded woman, and finding purpose.

Lori Z. Scott lives in Terre Haute, Indiana. She has learned much about the nature of God through interacting with her two children, and through the loving support of her husband.

Susan Kelly Skitt is a wife and mother of two boys, one teen and one toddler. Hiking, playing the piano, and teaching children about Jesus are her passions.

Penny Smith has authored *Gateways to Growth*, an inspirational treatment of the book of Esther. She has five grandchildren and a magnificent mutt named Maggie.

Michele Starkey is a brain aneurysm survivor who enjoys writing. She is living life to the fullest with her husband, Keith, in the Hudson Valley of New York.

Marcia Swearingen, of Hixson, Tennessee, is a former newspaper editor and columnist, now freelancing full time.

Angie Murchison Tally has worked as an elementary school teacher and school counselor and is currently a children's bookseller living in Whispering Pines, North Carolina.

Rachel M. Tamilio is a published freelance writer who attends BrookRidge Community Church in Bradford, Massachusetts.

Sandra Thiessen lives with her husband, Glen, in Centennial, Colorado. Sandra sings and speaks professionally and loves to focus on the goodness of the Lord.

Angelique C. Thomas writes about self-esteem issues for teens and single women. She works as an adolescent therapist and church youth leader in Blackwood, New Jersey.

Tanya T. Warrington writes from Fort Collins, Colorado, while raising a big family with her husband. She loves sharing with others about God's goodness.

Lucy L. Woodward writes poetry and plays about Jesus' disciples, showing how knowing Him changed them. She lives in Casper, Wyoming.

Elisa Yager-Villas is the intercessory prayer team leader for her church, located in western New Jersey. By day she is a human resources manager for a large manufacturer.

Colleen Yang was a missionary in Japan for nine years. She now specializes in writing and illustrating books for children, from Carol Stream, Illinois.

Mary J. Yerkes resides in Manassas, Virginia, with her husband, Paul. Her publishing credits include contributions to *People of the Bible Newsletter*, *Progressive Vision*, and *The Journal of Biblical Counseling*.

Subject Index

Scripture Index

SCRIPTURE INDEX

Scripture Index

The *Cup of Comfort* Series!

All titles are $9.95 unless otherwise noted.

A Cup of Comfort
1-58062-524-X

A Cup of Comfort Cookbook ($12.95)
1-58062-788-9

A Cup of Comfort for Christmas
1-58062-921-0

A Cup of Comfort Devotional ($12.95)
1-59337-090-3

A Cup of Comfort for Friends
1-58062-622-X

A Cup of Comfort for Inspiration
1-58062-914-8

A Cup of Comfort for Mothers and Daughters
1-58062-844-3

A Cup of Comfort for Mothers and Sons
1-59337-257-4

A Cup of Comfort for Sisters
1-59337-097-0

A Cup of Comfort for Teachers
1-59337-008-3

A Cup of Comfort for Women
1-58062-748-X

A Cup of Comfort for Women In Love
1-59337-362-7